BY PAUL HORGAN

TRACINGS

PAUL HORGAN

TRACINGS

A Book of

Partial Portraits

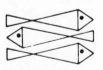

Farrar Straus Giroux

NEW YORK

Parts of this book have appeared earlier in the following publications: America; The American Poetry Review; The American Scholar; Art and Antiques; Encounters, edited by Kai Erikson; The New York Times Book Review; The New Yorker; Opera News; and The Yale Review; and in three of the author's books, all published by the Wesleyan University Press: Approaches to Writing, A Certain Climate, and Encounters with Stravinsky.
Designed by Cynthia Krupat

Library of Congress Cataloging-in-Publication Data
Horgan, Paul.
Tracings: a book of partial portraits / Paul Horgan.
p. cm.
1. Horgan, Paul. —Friends and associates. 2. Authors, American—20th century—Biography. 3. Journalists—United States—Biography. 4. Biography—20th century. I. Title
PS3515.06583Z473   1993   813'.52—dc20   93-12381 CIP

FOR

HENRIETTA

Contents

TRACINGS

1922

Vachel Lindsay and
The Book of the Dead

i

FOR ABOUT A YEAR, spanning most of 1921 and 1922, I was at
the age of eighteen the junior reporter on the *Albuquerque Morning
Journal*. My beat was eclectic. I covered the county courthouse, the
city hall, the municipal jail, and also the town's cultural events in
music, drama, art, and literature. During the early twentieth century,
the arts and the higher graces of society everywhere in the Southwest
were delegated to "the ladies." The masculine world was glad to be
left alone with its "real" preoccupations—making a living, raising
cattle, competing in business, going hunting, flogging politics, disturbing the peace in appropriate forms on Saturday night, keeping
a handgun for private use in personal irritation or insult, and otherwise in a general way working to preserve the public order. Let the
leddies *have* their ly-*ce*-ums, drawn-shade tea parties, book-study lectures, and like that—it don't do no harm and it might just keep them
happy. Under this principle a society managed its balance, and
under mine, I duly reported, and even wrote reckless criticisms of,
the lady-directed acts of culture.

Not that I was welcome to attend all the meetings of the Albuquerque Women's Club in Gold Avenue—these generally were
for women only. But when the announcement came that Vachel

Lindsay, eminent American poet of the day, was coming to give a reading of his work at the Women's Club, I knew I must attend on two counts—first was to cover the event for the *Journal;* and second, my private but inflated condition as a poet myself.

For I was writing poetry as well as short stories and newspaper pieces. I had been to Santa Fe, where I met real poets—Yvor Winters, Maurice Lesemann, Alice Corbin Henderson. I had been kindly received by painters—Josef Bakos, Willard Nash, Frank Applegate. Santa Fe and Taos were in their early ferment of the arts, with all the airs and releases of a libertarian style of life. I breathed it with an adolescent's sense of self-recognition. Overnight I was prepared to be a Modernist, and my text in all the arts was *The Dial,* the magazine in whose pages I encountered T. S. Eliot, Picasso, Segonzac, Stravinsky (in reports by Paul Rosenfeld), Thomas Mann, Ezra Pound, Brancusi, Yeats, Lachaise, Ortega y Gasset, and the rest. The mundane railroad-ranching-sanatorium fabric of life in my New Mexico town might be the backdrop of my daily life, but in no sense did it limit my sense of style and reference. In the swelling vitality of youth and the energetic turmoil of a dozen aesthetic drives, I studied and harshly judged my environment even as I was held in its conventions.

One day in the street near the *Journal* I encountered an elderly Pueblo Indian who was standing at a curbside. He wore a much-used red headband, a dark coarse work shirt, denim trousers, and tennis shoes. His face was lifted to the sky. His eyes were closed. His arms were crossed on his breast. He seemed hardly to breathe. I paused to regard him. Presently he felt this. He slowly turned and acknowledged me with a little lift of his chin—the native New Mexican greeting.

"Excuse me," I said.

He met this with civil silence. I had never addressed an Indian before. I had seen the Corn Dance at the pueblo of Santo Domingo —that great collective physical prayer for rain, growth, and harvest. It had moved me to an experimental poem directly influenced by Vachel Lindsay, with bold rhythmic poundings and marginal directions of vocal scoring. But I had yet to find the central image for the Pueblo people and their danced prayer. My poem was unfinished.

How did they behold themselves? After a long moment of our exchanged silences, I said to the Indian at the curb, "Do you hear
English?"

He nodded. I went on: "Pueblo people—how do they say who
they are? What name? I mean, I am an American; what are the
Pueblo people?"

"Ha-no-o-shatch," he said.

I repeated the words. He nodded.

"What does that mean?" I asked.

"Children of the sun. We are the children of the sun."

I must have lighted up with joy, for he leaned back slightly, let his
eyelids drop a trifle, and smiled, and then gravely went on his way
across the street.

But he left me with a wonderfully suggestive image of his people,
and that night after the paper went to bed I hurried home and
worked until daylight on revising my poem. It took the form of a solo
voice with choral interludes, drumbeats, and recurring invocations of
the sun, and I gave it the title *The Dance of Ha-no-o-shatch*. It ran for
five pages—the most ambitious literary work of my life so far; and
clearly, its ancestry included Vachel Lindsay's *The Congo*.

In those days Lindsay was accepted as one of the most important
exponents of "The New Poetry." I had encountered him in the
anthology of that name edited by Harriet Monroe and Alice Corbin
Henderson. His most powerful effects were obtained by use of words
of strong, direct beat, and patterns of percussive rhythms. He was
ideal for reading aloud by oneself. He was famous as a wandering
bard, an Apostle of Beauty. He held me more than his fellow stars
of the New Poetry did—Amy Lowell, Edna St. Vincent Millay, E. A.
Robinson, Robert Frost. He would soon be coming to Albuquerque
for his reading at the Albuquerque Women's Club. I laid my plans.

ii

As I arrived, the atmosphere was subdued by intense respect for
culture. If anyone spoke, it was in cleared throat and whispers. The
club public room held portable chairs for perhaps fifty people. All

were taken. It was a warm evening. The air was close. The draperies at the windows were drawn together against the vulgar world. In the bare floor area that served as a stage a vase of florist's flowers stood on a small, tapestry-covered table. A door to the left was closed. It closeted the room from which the poet would emerge, as we could tell by the low rumbling sound of a heavy voice warming up. Inside my jacket bulked the sheaf of my poem under which my heart went tumbling.

Suddenly, and with dramatic violence, the side door was flung open, and the poet came before us, treading a dance step. I had formed no image of him, but still his appearance was startling. Of medium height and stocky frame, he had a thatch of carrot-colored hair that quivered every which way with energy above his pallid, mole-studded face. His brow seemed swollen above his small deep-set eyes with their white lashes. His nose was wide and flat; the nostrils flared. His lips were thick and his chin resigned itself toward his active Adam's apple. If he seemed oddly out-of-focus, the effect was increased by how he held his gaze above all our heads and shifted it from side to side rapidly, a sideways blink, while we welcomed him with applause that rang flat in the confined clubroom.

He stood in silence, a moment of concentration, while we examined in amazement how he was dressed. I had supposed that in his character of wandering poet he might appear in something loosely unconventional—open collar, flowing scarf, velvet jacket; but here he posed in full formal evening dress. His black tailcoat gaped about his shoulders. His white stiff collar and tie stood away from his neck. His starched cuffs were too long and his white waistcoat did not quite meet his trousers. The boiled front of his shirt was already buckled by body heat. He reminded me of the comedy "Toby" character in the travelling tent shows that toured country towns—straw should have escaped from his collar. He was a hayseed, dressed in misplaced elegance conforming to the tradition that concerts and recitals required full evening dress.

A hayseed—but in a moment, a commanding hayseed; for in a bass voice of beaded heaviness he suddenly announced *The Congo*, and the painfully refined little clubroom throbbed to the impact of his barbaric lines:

Fat black bucks in a wine-barrel room,
Barrel-house kings, with feet unstable,
Sagged and reeled and pounded on the table,
Pounded on the table,
Beat an empty barrel with the handle of a broom,
Hard as they were able,
Boom, boom, BOOM,
With silk umbrella and the handle of a broom,
Boomlay, boomlay, boomlay, BOOM . . .

THEN I SAW THE CONGO, CREEPING THROUGH THE BLACK,
CUTTING THROUGH THE JUNGLE WITH A GOLDEN TRACK . . .

He made the room resonate. His whole body gave out the rhythms in convulsive strikes. He became a total instrument. The charge upon us was so direct and sudden that I felt an irrational impulse to laugh, and at the same moment, somehow, to join with him in full communion of voice and gesture. He choreographed his poem as much as declaimed it. To support his lyrics he made his fists into great drumsticks, beating the air. His face became a grotesque mask and then seemed to melt into blind ecstasy. He twisted his torso and sent his coattails flying. He pumped his thighs and beat the floor with full foot for his heavy accents. He leaped into space in a trance. He waved his hands in the air for religious glory. He spent himself wholly.

Transfixed, like the culture-hungry matrons all about, I was pulled into the poem more fully than I could have been by simply reading his lines upon the page.

Wild crap-shooters with a whoop and a call
Danced the juba in their gambling hall,
And laughed fit to kill, and shook the town,
And guyed the policemen and laughed them down,
With a boomlay, boomlay, boomlay, BOOM . . .

and on for nearly half an hour.

And they all repented, a thousand strong,
From their stupor and savagery and sin and wrong

And slammed with their hymn books till they shook the room,
With "Glory, glory, glory,"
And "Boom, boom, BOOM."
THEN I SAW THE CONGO, CREEPING THROUGH THE BLACK . . .

and at the end, the jungle powers are conquered—no longer

"Mumbo-Jumbo will hoo-doo you . . ."

This finale was delivered, according to the marginal direction, *Dying down into a penetrating, terrifying whisper.*

An exhausted silence overcame us in our metal chairs as the poet tripped away to his offstage room. He left us in his spell, and when he returned he was in another mode, balanced lightly on tiptoe, with his arms floating before him as if to describe and enfold some mysterious element of grace. He rose to it in strange delight. If you thought of what he really looked like, his delicacy was absurd; but in his self-tranced state, it was moving and exquisite. *The Chinese Nightingale: A Song in Chinese Tapestries,* he announced as he reached center-stage, and began:

"How, how," he said. "Friend Chang," I said,
"San Francisco sleeps as the dead—
Ended license, lust and play:
Why do you iron the night away?"

It was another long narrative, combining tourist Chinatown and passionate fairy tale. Firecrackers and joss sticks, faraway princess, "marvel and dream," Chinese nightingale, bird as prophet:

Do you remember,
Ages after,
Our palace of heart-red stone?
Do you remember
The little doll-faced children
With their lanterns full of moon-fire . . .
"Darling . . . darling . . . darling"
Said the Chinese nightingale.

The lines came in heightened song, now a whisper, now a long flute-like note. The poet strained upward on tiptoe, striving to levitate, arms like temple towers, hands fluttering like birds of desire, eyes shut away by visions far beyond the Women's Club of Albuquerque, New Mexico.

> I remember, I remember
> There were ghostly veils and laces . . .
> In the shadowy, bowery places . . .
> With lovers' ardent faces
> Bending to one another,
> Speaking each his part.
> They infinitely echo
> In the red cave of my heart.
> "Sweetheart, sweetheart, sweetheart!"
> "One thing I remember:
> Spring came on forever,
> Spring came on forever,"
> Said the Chinese nightingale.

Another dying fall. The poet retired. We stirred and sighed. Gone was Toby in his carrot wig and his rumpled dress suit. Even the sense of the lines—and there was not all that much sense—did not matter.

It was the abstract fabric of sound, the poet's passion of conviction, the dancing actor's gift of self, that enthralled us. Awash in floating images, we awaited his return.

When he came, it was in another mood. He was quiet, direct, lyrical, as he recited a group of shorter poems, including *"Abraham Lincoln Walks at Midnight (In Springfield, Illinois)."*

> It is portentous, and a thing of state
> That here at midnight, in our little town
> A mourning figure walks, and will not rest,
> Near the old court-house pacing up and down . . .

The concert was over. The president of the Women's Club went forward to thank and congratulate. She indicated that many ladies would like to do the same. Meantime the aroma of fresh coffee emerged from the side room; trays of miniature sandwiches appeared. Ardent listeners crowded about Vachel Lindsay. He smiled and nodded, smiled and nodded, consuming handfuls of the special delicacies and several cups of coffee. I remained in my seat. I had come to present myself and my poem, but I suddenly felt shy about accosting the poet.

It was not long until I was aware that Lindsay was eyeing me across matronly shoulders. He seemed to invite me forward, the only one in the room not reaching for him.

He received me with mute appraisal. His tangled white eyelashes, the silent stare of uncertainty, made me think for a moment of a white-faced calf. His face was coarsely porous. I held my poem in its large envelope. Finally he said,

"Is that a manuscript?"

"Yes," I said.

He took it and slapped it smartly against his breast, and said, now with a gentle smile,

"Yes, this is what happens, I am always glad to—so come and have breakfast with me tomorrow morning. I am staying at the Alvarado"—the railroad hotel in midtown—"and we shall discuss your work. Come at seven-thirty. My train for the West leaves at eight-fifteen. Lovely. Good night."

He was suddenly tired. With a hurried wave he made a blanket farewell to the members, snatched up his check from the madame president (seventy-five dollars, we heard), and was gone. Why, I wondered, apart from homage to poetry, did I feel something both pathetic and comic about the whole evening? I said to myself, "Poetry must be hard work."

iii

At half past seven next morning I found him in the dining room of the Alvarado Hotel. He saw me in the doorway and waved me to him. He was dressed now in ordinary day clothes, a shapeless tweed suit of rust color, a starched high collar with its exposed collar button above the necktie knot. He was in a jovial mood. As they used to say, he was making a good breakfast, with grapefruit, coffee, toast, preserves, eggs, pancakes, bacon, and fried potatoes deployed before him. He urged me to sit down and order breakfast for myself but I was too diffident to eat. All I wanted was to hear about my manuscript. But,

"See here," he said, indicating a large open book that he had set up against a sugar bowl. His words rang throughout the dining room. He had an irreducible bass voice—the kind that makes itself heard above anything else in any enclosed space. I was increasingly embarrassed to be a partner to it. "This is *The Egyptian Book of the Dead,* which always travels with me. It is a book of the ghostliest wisdom, out of the deep past, and with a tremendous message for the present we live in now."

He showed me the pages. They were divided into upper and lower halves. The upper carried reproductions of hieratic and hieroglyphic inscriptions; the lower, translations into English.

"Do you know what this book is about?"

"No."

"It is a brave and compassionate hymn against the evils that threaten the soul on its way to eternal life. Imagine the beauty and power of this idea!"

The text, it seems, consisted of inscriptions painted or drawn or incised on walls of tombs, pyramids, or coffin lids, and copied into papyrus rolls by scribes. The rolls were then buried with the dead person to protect against the spells of Set, the "arch-liar and god of evil." I do not recall exactly all the learned scraps that Vachel Lindsay poured out upon me that morning as he pursued pancakes and home fries and coffee; but to suggest the substance of his rapt recital I have consulted the 1920 monograph on *The Book of the Dead* by the British Museum's Professor E. A. Wallis Budge of the Department of Egyptian and Assyrian Antiquities. What I do remember is Lindsay's eloquence as he stifled my impatience to hear him talk not about funerary customs of four millennia past but about my poem.

Yes: it seems that Rā was the king of the sky, and Osiris was the king of the Dead-land, or Tat. Grand polarities! And think of the humble acts of judgment upon those passing from sky to Tat: the heart was actually weighed on scales to determine its state of virtue or vice. What a power in that image to evoke the eternal good:

"Here!" he said. "Look at this tiny, sweet picture of the heart on the scales!" I could not decipher it.

(The clock on the dining-room wall was ticking off minutes to train time—the tracks were just outside the hotel. Soon he must run for it, and where was my manuscript?)

"See this image"—he showed me the Holy Ape Gods singing to Rā at sunrise, with a great bird facing *left* toward the dawn; and then opposite, the Holy Jackal Gods singing to Rā at sundown, with the great bird facing *right* to the coming night. And every inflection came not from words but—this was it!—from pictures!

(His train would leave in eighteen minutes.)

He was still enjoying his breakfast, though without interrupting his echoing rhapsody of the dead in the Fred Harvey dining room, while people at other tables looked at each other in a certain way.

So: what was the immense, wonderful lesson in *The Book of the Dead* for us in our time? It was nothing less than its prediction, through its preservation and transfer of meaning, that all knowledge in the future would come through pictures? Did I understand? Pictures only!

(No, and I had the courage to point to the clock.)

Ignoring this, he made a mellow, pumpkin face to convey wonder at revelation, and he said,

"What it means is that the literature of words is done for! Everything will be told in pictures, and not so far off! Look: what art reaches more people now than any known before by man?" I was blank. "Why, what about the moving picture! Its inventor, Edison, is the new Gutenberg!" he cried. He had published, in 1915, one of the earliest critical books about the movies, *The Art of the Motion Picture*. It came out just after *The Birth of a Nation* had been released. At that time it was unusual for anyone to propose, as his book did, that films were worth careful consideration. "The moving picture needs no words—only movement, gestures, the darling eloquence of the human face! Mary Pickford, Douglas Fairbanks, Theda Bara, Mae Marsh, William Farnum, Mabel Tallaferro, John Bunny, Blanche Sweet—the conduits of genius! Think! when all is to be learned only from images!"

(At a nearby table the train conductor rose from his own breakfast and headed for the tracks. He knew his train time. I pointed.)

"Yes, yes, we might go now. Come with me."

Shutting his book and snatching up from under the table his battered, many-strapped Gladstone suitcase, he clutched my arm and we loped out to the tracks. At the last car he paused to speak to the conductor like one son of labor to another, confided that he was "for California," and leaped to the car step. I began to frame a bitter farewell, but he reached for my arm and pulled me on board. Foraging down the aisle of the car, he found two empty seats on the sunny side, settled in at the window, and drew me down next to him.

"I'd better say goodbye, Mr. Lindsay. The train is about to—"

"No, no, my lad, plenty of time. —Do you see it all? Rā the sun god will be duplicated in the ray of arc light needed to project the film, while we *watch* instead of *read* the story unfolding before us! In the darkened room we will be in the kingdom of Osiris! *The Book of the Dead* will teach us life anew through the moving picture!"

It must have been eight-fifteen, for the conductor outside gave his long cry, "All 'board!" and I stood up.

"Well, goodbye, Mr. Lindsay," I said. "May I have my poem back? I have to go now."

"Ah, it is in my Gladstone. I will write to you." The train began to move. He shook my hand. "Think of me as the disciple of the all-picture mind!"

"I really have to—"

"Then goodbye! goodbye! if you must!"

I ran the length of the car, out the rear door, and threw myself half-falling on to the brick-and-cinders platform of the trackside as Santa Fe train number 9 picked up speed for Belen, Gallup, Flagstaff, and the Coast.

iv

In my consuming disappointment over Vachel Lindsay's failure to talk about my poem and drown it with his praise, I wondered why he had instead given over my precious forty-five minutes with him to a monologue about *The Book of the Dead.* I had no answer then.

But almost a year later I received a letter from the poet. He enclosed my original typescript of *The Dance of Ha-no-o-shatch.* Its margins were filled with comments in large, scroll-like writing that leaned toward the backhand. He filled an added page with criticism. His verdict was negative. I cannot quote him—I kept my typescript and his letter for years until they disappeared when a flood destroyed files in my library at Roswell, New Mexico; but I do remember the main point of his response.

All that was wrong with my poem lay in the fact that it was not really *my* poem—it was a well-tried imitation of his own work, notably in *The Congo.* If my piece was meant as a compliment to him, it was not a compliment—it was an intrusion. In honesty, he could not accept as true poetry anything so unoriginal. He would wish more success for me in other works that would be forged from within my own experience and vision of form. Meantime, he recognized a certain facility in my handling of the language, which, when refined until it should sound like that of no one else, might exhibit a true literary style. It had been a pleasure to meet me, and he wished me as a fellow poet all fulfillment in the future . . .

I licked my wounds for a day or two until I began to admit the justice of his general thrust. He was, I granted, quite right. With that recognition out of the way, I was free to wonder all over again why he had devoted our brief time together to *The Book of the Dead* rather than to me, the living.

All I know is that he was enraptured as he spoke to me of his discoveries and theories. Perhaps the awesome mystery of the dynasties and the beauty of their hope of the afterlife obsessed his imagination to the exclusion of nearer concerns. Throughout wondering generations people have felt the brooding impact of the spirit preserved in papyrus and tomb, and have responded to it in a hundred different ways. Credulities about the occult have changed people's lives, sometimes with tragic effect.

Intermittently, Lindsay returned in mid-life, and finally for the rest of his last years, to the house in Springfield, Illinois, where he was born. It was a fine mid-American house, at 603 South Fifth Street— a flatly American address. (In mid-century it had been the scene of a farewell party for Abraham Lincoln as he set forth from Springfield for Washington and the presidency.)

In that South Fifth Street house, his first and last home, Vachel Lindsay, preoccupied for so long with his analyzed ancient system— a poetics of death—took his own life by swallowing Lysol on September 5, 1931. I do not suggest cause and effect; only complete the record. He was fifty-two years old when, under the solemnities of Osiris in *The Book of the Dead,* his heart would have been weighed on scales to determine its state of virtue. . . .

Living concerns with the powers of Tat, the Dead-land, have also changed human lives, even, of course, in our day, and sometimes have done so hilariously: I know of a civil service employee in a Washington office who circulated a form letter throughout his vast bureau that read:

> *To Whom It May Concern*
>
> From this day forward, the undersigned desires to be known as Aman Rā.
>
> (signed) Aman Rā.

1924

Chaliapin's Demon

i

IN THE SPRING OF 1924 the city was quickened by what was coming. The Metropolitan Opera Company would present two performances in the Eastman Theatre of Rochester, New York. One of these would be Gounod's *Faust,* on the evening of May 5. Of the two, it was this performance which kindled our expectations, for we were opera snobs, and only the greatest artists—in this case Feodor Chaliapin—excited our gossip and our lofty judgments. We—students of the Eastman School of Music—spent long moments lingering to read the huge block letters on tall yellow posters which we saw all over town. Some of us were members of the newly formed Rochester American Opera Company under the co-directors Vladimir Rosing and Rouben Mamoulian. Our sopranos, our tenors and baritones, saw themselves in the famous names on the great Metropolitan playbills:

Faust	EDWARD JOHNSON
Marguérite	FRANCES ALDA
Méphistophélès	FEODOR CHALIAPIN

—and all the others in the cast.

For many days the principal arias of *Faust* soared out from the vocal studios of the music school as our young artists prepared themselves to hear the coming performance. We were told by our directors what to listen for. They were particularly exciting as they spoke of Chaliapin, their illustrious countryman. He was not only the greatest singer in the world, they said, he was also the greatest actor. They had known him in Europe. A giant of a man, imperious, a law unto himself musically and dramatically, he was the terror of conductors, accompanists, and fellow singers. When he thought waywardly that something had gone wrong with the pianist, in concert, or the conductor, in opera, he furiously stepped out of the mood and began to beat time, often with his huge white kerchief. It was the more distressing because his sense of time was erratic.

He was a Don Giovanni with women. In Russia he was a national hero. Even as he enraptured multitudes, he offended many by his shocking interpretation of certain roles. In Boito's *Mephistopheles* he was half naked and given to obscene gestures. In Rossini's *Barber of Seville* he made Don Basilio, the abbé, a figure so revolting, with rotten teeth, drooling nose and lips, filthy *soutane* stained with food remnants and nose wipings, and a demeanor of nasty servility, that legions of Catholics were outraged by his libel upon holy orders. Sole inventor of his operatic characters, he obliged stage directors to conform to his business if they hoped to see the curtain go up at all.

It was all most promising.

ii

What New York could take for granted for eight months of the year Rochester, once a year, made into a great occasion. The grand department stores of Main Street dressed their windows with tableaux of operatic characters and displays of gala evening dress. Dinner parties before the opera and supper parties afterward were set in train. The limousines of Rochester would draw up in a long line to the gold-lighted canopy of the Eastman Theatre—surely the most beautiful theatre in America. Mr. George Eastman had given the conjoined theatre and School of Music (designed by McKim, Mead, and White) to the University of Rochester. For grand occasions, Mr. Eastman would arrive accompanied by the elegant, white-haired, pink-faced lady who acted as his hostess for his formal parties. Like him, a lover of music, she was the charming wife of the city's preeminent surgeon.

The evening of May 5 finally came. Once inside the theatre, I admired the spectacle of the audience members, glistening and weaving as they made their way to their seats: so many white ties, so many long white gloves, such a sense of neighborly pleasure as Rochester gathered for the festival. In their top balcony seats the music students from the school gave their excitement to the scene. The great volume of the auditorium was made intimate by the warm gray of the limestone walls and the gray velvet of the chairs. At the center of the gold-coffered ceiling the immense chandelier of crystals cast a golden light on the mural paintings of Barry Faulkner and Ezra Winter. The front curtain of the stage was heavy with bronze-and-gold brocade, already softly bathed upward by the footlights with their mixture of colored bulbs—red, blue, amber, and white. I knew about this detail and so much else of the theatre's fittings because in addition to my lessons in the music school I was busy with my job as scenic artist for our own young opera company.

In this post, I needed to have the run of the theatre, and so I possessed a master key which admitted me everywhere. It burned in my pocket like a magical talisman that would admit me to powerful secrets and private places. Translated, this meant that with my key I could find my way under the auditorium to the nether world of the theatre by a shortcut backstage where so much of my work was carried out. At twenty years of age I had responsibilities and demands beyond my ability; but energy and confidence, allied to inspired proddings by my directors—notably Rouben Mamoulian, with whom I worked most often—helped to hold me on my course.

At last, the footlights were slowly growing brighter, the chandelier was marvellously losing radiance. The orchestra players were at their lighted stands. Mist'Eastman (as he was always spoken of) and Mrs. Mulligan were calmly in place in their accustomed seats at front row center of the mezzanine. There was a small stir at one end of the orchestra pit. It was the conductor, Louis Hasselmans, making his way to his desk.

A hush—the most theatrical of events—then the downbeat.

iii

I thought Gounod's orchestral prelude to *Faust* one of the most foreboding and evocative spells in all theatre. Hearing it in the darkened house, we felt the menace of Satan in the opening chords in the winds; the longings of Faust in the strings; and the doomed goodness of Marguérite in the reeds. The woodwinds piping the heedless joy of youths and maidens were both saddening and delightful. We were going to hear about youth and the mortal cost exacted by life.

As the curtain slowly lifts its folds aside, we lean forward to see old Doctor Faust in his study at Wittenberg. He cries *"Rien!"*—he cries it several times, and we shiver at the silvery voice of Edward Johnson. His full white beard trembles over his despair at the futility of old age. He prepares a deathly draught in a great chalice and is about to drink it when youths and maidens carolling in the fair outdoors arrest him. They possess what is no longer his, and they are thanking God for it—the blessing of nature and the gift of receiving it. It causes his bitter cup to overflow. God? He rages at the God who will not give him back his youth, and faith, and love. *"A moi, Satan! A moi!"* he calls.

At one moment we see only the weary old Doctor of Nuremberg, and then out of nowhere a shape in the circular tumult of a storm cloud is there upon the stage, and we see a vast black cloak settle and fall to reveal an arm pointing upward from a huge figure, as though to command heaven itself. *"Me voici!"* it declares in a dropping octave. The tone is sardonic, as though with indulgent kindness addressing an idiot. It is the astounding materialisation of Méphistophélès and our first view of Feodor Chaliapin.

Everything at once takes on a new nerve. It is not only because the character in the story—the Devil—requires this. It is because the inhabitant of the role is who he is. Thereafter throughout the performance it is Chaliapin who seems to sap the vitality of all the other players and gather to himself the control of events. One reason that we cannot take our eyes off him is that he is never still. (In only one moment, to come later, is he ever still; and then it is to become more sinister than ever.) All his movements are greatly enlarged by his huge cloak, which he keeps in motion so that the initial effect of a black cloud is never lost. If he is to stay in one place, he moves in slow, insinuating waves from side to side, forward, backward. His whole body seems to express elegant contempt; and when larger action comes, his gestures are eruptive—the great cloak rises and flies in frightening arcs of energy. His flowing movement is like a tide of evil, ebbing and ripping about all life. He says with his entire presence that evil is never at rest, it is everywhere, it mocks, it storms, it woos; and its source is the dark embodiment that hypnotizes us. When he invokes the vision of Marguérite at her spinning wheel to ensnare Faust who is hungry for the world— *"A moi les plaisirs, les jeunes maîtresses, à moi leurs caresses, à moi leurs désirs!"*—Mephisto leans into Faust as though breathing intentions upon him with his whole body.

Now beyond her gauze scrim, lighted by amber gelatine sunshine, Madame Frances Alda in swelling blue satin, blond braids, and blue downcast eyelids, neatly works her treadle and spins her wheel, doing her matronly best to fulfill her contract at playing a virginal maiden in medieval Wittenberg. It doesn't matter. Nor does it matter that Edward Johnson, now a slim youth in gallant doublet, hose, pageboy wig, is enraptured on the instant, crying out, *"O merveille!"* at the vision that would lead Faust to his doom. The soprano and the tenor are seasoned professionals doing their excellent work, and we accept them for their vocal skills and their practiced gestures. What does matter is that we forget Chaliapin and see and hear only the Fiend Incarnate in his malign grace which chills and fascinates us.

iv

So it is that a lifetime later what I remember of the performance are moments only of Chaliapin, onstage and off, and not much else. He had the obliterating characteristic of genius, that wherever he was, in whatever circumstance, he dominated. In the church scene, for example, when Marguérite kneels outside the sanctuary, comes the Demon to torment the betrayed maiden who now carries Faust's child. She is afraid, unworthy, to join the sacred service beyond the rood screen. She prays in despair. Suddenly near her that black cloud looms: its mocking voice assures her that she is beyond redemption. Amid the roiling black panoply the predatory white hands and face glare forth. Madame Alda falters becomingly. The Prince of Darkness is triumphant again—but wait: from the vaults of the distant apse rise the strains of the choir praising God—the Divine Power shakes the air.

And now comes an act of theatrical genius that surpasses every other moment of the performance in dramatic power. Attacked by the prayer exalting Heaven, Méphistophélès falls away from the kneeling figure of Marguérite. He whips forth his long rapier. With its point he catches the hem of his cloak. Raising it in a swift upward spiral, he shrouds his face and figure with the cloak. He takes it high, higher, until a pillar of black is erect in stillness more terrible than all the ceaseless motion of evil in its earlier presence. We gasp.

Even as we are transfixed by the power of the symbol, we have to think of the mastery with which the artist managed his props in one long movement until the frozen pinnacle is achieved. How does he know just where to pick the edge of the cloak with his rapier so that in raising the heavy fabric it will not slip, come loose, and ruin the effect? How can he contrive to seem as tall as a church spire in his stark quiet? Scarcely a minute of time, this transformation, yet it seems an eternity.

And when at last the choir ceases and the Divine Good is away, the tip of the black tower trembles in little playful circles: it is like a mocking chuckle. The rapier within the cloak begins to dance and heft its way down to earth; the black folds fall apart and down, and the debonair monster slowly comes to sight in all his swaying elegance. He is abroad again in the vale of tears. When he roars his curse, *"Marguérite, sois maudite! à toi l'enfer!"* we sink back in our seats and exhale, echoing silently Madame Alda's scream of despair as the curtain rushes its halves together and the fringes settle gold in the footlights, and Mr. Hasselmans lays down his stick.

v

The scene left me with so much to think about that I was restless. I decided to use my master key to dash through the tunnels under the house, and entering the backstage elevator arrive at the stage floor to see what went on for the setting of the final act. This would be the prison where Marguérite, now mad and dreaming of happier days, would lie incarcerated.

Behind the proscenium at stage right was the stage manager's command center—a broad lectern bracketed to the wall. Above it was the call-board with its electric buttons numbered to correspond with the tiers of dressing rooms that rose offstage right with their metal decks and railings.

I came upon turmoil. Ben Connelly, our stage manager, who looked like an Irish bullfrog and had a voice to match, was at his desk. He was staring out at the half-lit stage with disgust. He was professionally affronted at what he saw. His ordinary speech could be called Primal Truck Driver, into which he often interjected an elaborate word which he had acquired under his program of self-improvement. I now heard him rumble, "The son of a bitch is purely loathsome." On the dim stage the visiting stagehands were setting up the scene, and there, lashing at them, was Chaliapin, ordering this to be put there, and that to be pulled here, shouting *"Idiots! Move! Faster! Faster!"*, his arms whirling, his voice cracking with rage.

"What?" I said.

"Them Russkies," snorted Ben, "they're all *non mentis*, if you ask me. He comes bowling out here when the curtain falls and he begins to yell that he has to catch the midnight train to New York, it is his only connection to get him to the ship tomorrow morning. So he is going to Yurrup, and we have to get this show over quick. —So he orders me to get out there and get the stage crew moving. So I tell him it ain't my job—the Met stage manager is in charge, or there will be union trouble. So he goes out on stage himself and you can see him there."

In fact, Chaliapin was everywhere among the stagehands, thrashing out directions. In his fearsome makeup and flailing costume he was an exotic sight at which the stagehands, ignoring his intrusion on union rules, laughed and joked—a response that infuriated him further. Actually, he was in the way, delaying the work he meant to speed up. At one point he was bumped into by a bale of straw being hauled to its place by two stagehands. He roared a curse at them, to which a stagehand replied with grainy Brooklyn profanity.

Soon enough, the scene was set. The lighting director went to work at the great switchboard behind us. Chaliapin came whipping off the stage. I retreated to shadows under the dressing room deck. He shouted to Ben,

"Now to bring everybody!"

"I don't have my cue yet."

"So *I* will!"

Chaliapin moved to reach the call-board.

"Oh no, you don't, there!" grunted Ben, and put up his arm to fend off his intruder.

A further incident was prevented when the Metropolitan Opera stage manager appeared and said to Ben, "Now, Mr. Connelly: please ring for places on stage."

With exaggerated elegance to accent his rightful control, Ben touched the dressing-room call buttons for Madame Alda, Mr. Johnson, and Mr. Hasselmans. The offstage choir was marshalled out of sight across the stage. We could hear the orchestra players moving from the tuning room below out into the pit. Mr. Johnson came uneventfully from his dressing room to wait for the moment when they would go onstage together on their way to Marguérite's dungeon cell. Chaliapin waved his imperious arm at the large clock above the call-board. Time was not waiting for him.

"Vhere is *she?*" he shouted. Marguérite had not appeared. "Ring her!" he commanded Ben.

"I already have rung the lady."

"So, *I* will!"

Chaliapin, now moving so fast that Ben could not prevent him, reached the call-board and with doubled fists beat upon all the buttons in a tattoo of fury. Mr. Johnson lifted his eyebrows at the spectacle. Chaliapin then gave up the call-board to Ben, whirled about, and stood looking up at the first dressing-room door on the metal deck above.

"Alda!" he shouted. *"Come down here!"*

There was a bated pause; and then languidly the dressing-room door was opened. Madame Alda, wearing a sky-blue flannel wrapper, emerged. She was holding a large powder puff. She came to the metal pipe railing and leaned amply over it. Her golden braids fell free. She was sucking a pastille, no doubt to keep her throat moist for the final ordeal of the evening. Levelling her huge blue eyelids at Chaliapin, she called down to him in a deadly, mild voice,

"Fa heaven's sake, what's eatin ya?"

At this, Chaliapin shook with rage. He pointed to the clock and made choked sounds in his throat. Madame Alda nodded as though to diagnose aberrant behavior. She lifted her powder puff. In a remarkable transfer of aggression to an unlikely weapon of offense, she powdered her face *at* him, and then in maddening composure returned to her dressing room and closed the door. Like a bull in danger, Chaliapin menaced everyone there with waving thrusts of his heavy head.

But soon enough Madame Alda appeared among us in the rags of her prison costume. She was ready. Serenely she said to Chaliapin as she passed him on her way to the stage,

"Come on, *dear*, what are you just standing there?"

vi

Suddenly it was time to begin the act, which I must see from the house. I hurried down to my subterranean passage and emerged to take my seat in the mezzanine just as the house lights went down. I was delighted to have a backstage scandal to report after the opera.

Despite Chaliapin's fury to get to the New York Central Station there was still a final act of the opera to perform, and I knew word for word and note for note what was coming.

Long ago I had read the pathetic synopsis of the prison scene in the *Victor Book of the Opera* and over and over I had heard the incomparable Victor Red Seal recording of it by Geraldine Farrar, Enrico Caruso, and Marcel Journet. Now it would all come again—the Fiend bringing Faust to the prison to bear Marguérite away, the awakened Marguérite on her pallet of straw, Faust's entreaties that she rise and flee with him, her torturing sweetness as, quite mad, she

instead relives the moments of her love with him, the sudden eruption of Mephisto in the prison with warnings that dawn is near, they
must fly at once, Marguérite's demented refusal at seeing him in the
shock that kills her, Mephisto's shout of victory at her unshriven
death— *"Jugée!"*— and as the heavenly choir offstage redeems her—
"Sauvée"—the terrible moment at the end as Mephisto enfolds Faust
with his evil cloak and leads him to the fires of hell as represented by
a flaring aurora of red light against an infinity of darkness upstage.
The whole short scene has a rising intensity of drama, and casts a
cumulative spell that must not be broken.

Chaliapin, now onstage with Madame Alda and Mr. Johnson,
begins to destroy all the illusion which the Metropolitan Opera
Company, its singers, players, designers, have worked to create. In
his rage at the *entr'acte* delay that might yet cause him to miss the New
York Central train, he begins to abuse the tempo, rushing everything. In vain the orchestra tries to hold him back properly. Mr.
Hasselmans has to race after him. In unseemly haste, the act runs to
its end. Madame Alda's high notes are like beams of pure light in the
trio that invokes the angels—but she is cut short *in alt.* All the more
terrible, then, her scream— *"Ahhh!"*—at the menace of the Fiend as
she falls lifeless on her prison straw. When the celestial music of the
chorale redeems Marguerite— *"Sauvée"*—we lean forward to see Mephisto carry Faust off to the inferno.

But Chaliapin, having uttered his last contractual note— *"Jugée!"*
—leaves Faust to his own fate, charges angrily down to the footlights
and with giant steps strides off in full sight.

As he goes, we see him tear away his mustaches and beard and
throw them into the orchestra pit. He pulls off his tight black skullcap
with its sinister feather and casts it into the footlights. He unbuckles
his rapier until it clatters along on the floor. He rips open his doublet
and unclasps his cloak and rolls it up into what might be a bundle
of laundry. Having destroyed the character of Méphistophélès and
the crowning illusion in full view of the dismayed audience, Chaliapin disappears into the wings on his escape to the railroad station.
Mr. Johnson, obedient to the final strains of the opera, can only
depart for *l'enfer* by himself. The curtains fall together to scattered,
bewildered applause.

After stretched moments of uncertainty, someone pokes the curtains from behind. Spotlights come on. Without Chaliapin, the destroyer, Frances Alda and Edward Johnson straggle out in subdued comradeship with high-clasped hands, to collect their dispirited curtain calls.

An evening begun in splendor has ended in a vague general air of disgrace.

vii

Our early seasons of the Rochester American Opera Company, under the auspices of the Eastman Theatre and School of Music, were largely training sessions. Our first public performances were given to one-act excerpts out of various great repertory operas— *Rigoletto, The Barber of Seville, Tannhäuser, Il Trovatore.* Our artists gained assurance as emerging opera singers. Tenors and baritones took to wearing spats, sopranos and mezzos went in for feathers, veils, and cloaks, and spoke of their professional resource as "the voice." Youth, beauty, and talent reigned together—nowhere with more excitement than in our preparations to perform the palace scenes out of Moussorgsky's *Boris Godunov.*

These scenes were Act II, in the imperial apartment in the Kremlin, where the Tsar Boris finds tender moments with his children the Tsarevitch and Xenia the sister—yet where a scheming visitor comes to remind Boris of his crime in murdering the child Dimitri, the rightful tsar, thus attaining the throne for himself; and Act IV, Scene ii, in the council room of the Granovitaya Palace in the Kremlin, where driven mad by guilt Boris in hallucination sees the murdered young tsar and in the presence of his council of state dies of terror and remorse. This production, like all of ours, was sung in English, as a condition required by George Eastman in subsidising the company: Mist' Eastman was both generous and firm in his philanthropies. The *Boris* excerpts, directed by Rouben Mamoulian, formed half of a double bill; the other half was given over to *I Pagliacci,* directed by Valdimir Rosing. (Sir) Eugene Goossens conducted the Rochester Philharmonic Orchestra in the pit. The decor was by Norman Edwards, the professional scenic artist who was engaged in the second season to take over and more ably fulfill my assignment as stage designer, while I was appointed general production assistant to Mr. Mamoulian.

In a costume rehearsal our *Boris* the bass-baritone was already living his role at all hours. Drawing the tsar's golden mantle about his tall figure, he strode to the light of the window and struck an attitude, right arm in the air as if to invoke the powers of an imperial heaven, left hand thrust forward with fingers spread in command to quell the peasantry to kneel and desist.

This was George Houston, my closest friend in the company. He was six or eight years older than I, closer in age to Mamoulian, who was magically conferring upon him in rehearsal the memory, the tragic nobility, of Holy Russia. George was learning to be an ideal singing-actor. His voice had a rich, dark sound with an urgent timbre; and as an American, and an athlete, he knew how to drive it with physical exuberance.

We all believed that he was meant for greatness on the stage. He seemed to bring a greater authority, a richer fabric of experience, to his acting and singing than we could. "There are a million degrees of losing," he would declare in a kingly way, "and only one of winning." He was, we knew, wonderfully "right" for Boris Godunov. During the days of rehearsal, he brooded loftily at lunch, as though tormented by great guilt, nobly suppressed. After lunch one day we shopped critically at Woolworth's for Boris's finger rings and other jewels. He thanked for small favors with imperial gravity. His gestures assumed a carved grandeur. The pitch of his voice in speech dropped half an octave. We looked to see if his dark glossy hair was touched with gray. His absorption in Boris set a powerful example for others in the cast, who infused their ordinary selves with their stage characters even away from rehearsal. Mamoulian regarded it all with barely concealed smiles, yet with satisfaction in the intensity of his creatures as they prepared to enact their incarnations.

And when our curtain rose at last on November 20, 1924, to reveal the imperial family—father, son, daughter, nurse—in their apartment in the Kremlin Palace we knew we were to be fulfilled as artists whether on stage or in the audience. We were all proud of the sorrow, the nobility, the rich color, and the bells of Holy Russia that we reinvented from Moussorgsky. With Mamoulian's direction, the conducting of Goossens, with Nicolas Slonimsky as chorus master, and above all George's performance, everything came together in grave beauty and serious impact.

One performance only—yet it remains powerfully alive in my memory. Rouben Mamoulian, who knew that there were no absolutes in art, and who never agreed that anything was ever perfect, was to be trusted in his sacred honesty. He let it be known that George's Boris was a genuinely important theatrical and musical achievement. If it did not attain, it could honestly be measured against, the highest standard—that created by Feodor Chaliapin in the role of Boris. The name had hovered over all our rehearsals; not that Mamoulian asked George for an impersonation of the Russian basso; the Rochester *Boris* was to be conceived freshly, in terms of the character and degree of experience we could show. Yet Chaliapin was in everybody's thought, in echoes of Mamoulian's attendance on Boris in Paris, Goossens's at Covent Garden, and the recordings and pictures that the rest of us had recourse to. What was more, Mamoulian knew him; had spoken with him in Europe; could show us certain gestures—not to copy but to admire. We must all aspire, but in our own ways.

What we all felt was that Moussorgsky's opera belonged to us, now, no matter what we had heard about Feodor Chaliapin and his world dominance of the role of Boris. Our excitement was all the greater, then, when in mid-spring of 1925 came the announcement from the Metropolitan Opera that in their forthcoming post-season tour they would present, among other works, *Boris Godunov* with Chaliapin. What would it be like?—eager as puppies.

"We'll see," said George calmly.

viii

I attended with George. We had orchestra seats well down front. To see Chaliapin emerging from the cathedral as the newly anointed tsar was a shock—he seemed so much larger than life or legend. I felt George stiffen next to me. As yet making no sound, Chaliapin made subjects of the audience, and we rejoiced with the jubilee of towers and bells. Now in that moment of sacred glory, he made us feel a pang of foreboding. In Russian, *"Skorbit dusha,"* he intoned with an inward voice, "My soul is sad," dwelling on his burden of guilt for his murder of the young Prince Dimitri, whose throne he attained through mortal crime. A figure monolithic in golden robes whose front was crusted with jewels, he loomed over the kneeling people. His head was noble in its beauty; his eyes were porched by deep and brooding brows; his cheeks were runnelled above his gray-flecked beard. He wore his crown-like cap of gold with the weight of its surmounting cross. As though to himself he uttered his remorse, his fear: "O saints long dead, O though my imperial Father, thou see'st in heaven thy faithful servant's tears!" He implored mercy for himself and Russia, and he would now go to pray at the tombs of Russia's tsars. A murderer—yet he begged for goodness, and he made us know how evil and nobility might terribly exist together.

And then his aspect grew lighter. He opened himself to the people with the blessing of his embrace, and, an imperial father and host, he bade them—and us—to feasting for his coronation. The bells tolled and beat their tumult of joy; voices rose; the light of day grew brighter. Canopied by bells and sunlight, he made his way past the crowds and by the manner of his walk he had us holding our breath as we saw the troubled man become one with the consecrated ikon of majesty. He ascended the stairs to his private apartments. The curtains fell together, ending the prologue. We sat back stunned by our encounter with depths of human character revealed in so few minutes with so few gestures. I thought it tactless to exchange a word or a look with George, but I could see in a side glance that he was replaying his own role along with Chaliapin's, and that he was suffering.

For it was to suffer, with an exalting sense of beauty, to feel with Chaliapin those universal and soul-shaking emotions of which that opera was crafted. He reached our hearts in the tenderness of his fatherhood. When at the end Tsar Boris was stricken upon his throne and thrown down to the level of earth itself at its foot, it was not so much a matter of a man dying in agony as of the Kremlin Palace itself falling apart like the stones of a corrupt kingdom. The long opera passed to its end in a spell.

ix

A long silence held the theatre after the last notes; but finally all Rochester let go with a tempest of applause the like of which no one, they said, could remember. It kept up until the riffling of the curtain from behind told that someone was there, they are coming out—the old magic of the curtain call. They came out and we greeted them —Xenia the nurse, the Tsarevitch, the little Tsarevna, the Princess Marina, the Prince Shuisky, Pimen, Varlaam. They made an extended rank, holding hands high. They bowed raggedly together, full of disenchanting goodwill, finally straggling away. We continued to demonstrate. Where was he? All the others returned, they bowed and curtsied, kissed their hands at us now that the spell was gone, and again they went, and we died away a little. But at once we were revived by more thrusting of the curtain—and then he was there.

But it was not Chaliapin. It was the Tsar Boris Godunov. The spell was instantly restored. His gravity was immense and imperial. This was no opera singer in costume but out of character, grateful for plaudits, pleased with himself and all of us. What we beheld was the ruler of all Muscovy. He still wore his long dark brocaded housecoat edged with marten fur, girded by a jewelled strap. His gold-stitched scarlet boots had turned-up Persian toes. On all his fingers of each hand were heavy rings somber with dark stones. He held his hands spread upon his breast. He raised his head to see far beyond the theatre. He heard nothing, though our applause grew and grew. Slowly his eyes seemed to focus within the house. He gazed at the topmost corners and rows, turning his head slowly from side to side. Dropping his head slightly, he swept the next lower balcony, and then poured his pale, burning gaze over the downstairs audience, and we felt the presence of a great emperor. And then, having taken the whole house, he slowly, slowly, opened one arm wide, then the other, to embrace and bless the city and the world, and at last, and only then, the Tsar bowed as one sovereign to another, and in a few superbly calculated steps backward, retired beyond the curtain. It was in itself a mighty performance.

x

In silent accord George and I sought the outdoor air under the gold-lighted canopy on Gibbs Street. He was pale and drawn. He nodded upward, lifting his fine chin in affirmation.

"A god," he said solemnly. "He is like a god. He *is* God!"

I could only agree silently, as I marvelled at George's entire absence of the self-preserving vanity common to most operatic artists. We were both so stirred that our usual habit of talk—gravely sarcastic—did not suit. Amid the after-theatre crowds we smoked a cigarette.

"The poor bastards," said George. "They don't know what they've just seen."

We heard a voice over our shoulders.

"Come with me."

It was Rouben Mamoulian, tall and splendid in his London evening clothes. He liked small mysteries, and so explained nothing, but led us back into the theatre to the door to the underworld. He said to me, "Your key," and I produced my master key. Once the door was shut behind us, he paused and said, "So, what did you think."

George inhaled sharply as though to govern himself, and replied, "I said it earlier. I say it again. He is a god. In my head I sang every word and note with him. I know how great he is. I love him and I adore him!"

Rouben turned to me. I shrugged as eloquently as I could. He nodded, then said, "We will give him a little more time. He will need time to come down from the heights." We looked our inquiries. He said, "We are going to meet him. —I will present you both. A gift of history."

Through the underground we took our time to reach the backstage elevator. Once there, we ascended past the stage floor where the crews were noisily striking the set, and went on up to dressing room 1. At the door stood a middle-aged Russian in a lopsided hat and a long black overcoat. Rouben and he exchanged a few words in Russian. He opened the door narrowly, went in sideways, and shut it. In a moment he reappeared and motioned to Rouben to enter. Rouben said, "Wait here," and disappeared within.

"I don't believe it," said George, "but I am actually nervous. It's almost indecent, the reverence I feel."

"I understand. You have it from inside Boris."

"I would kiss the hem of his robe."

"What would he do?"

"Probably belt me one."

After a long while of our uneasy banter, the door opened, and Rouben beckoned. We moved in and stood near the closed door while he continued to talk in Russian with Chaliapin.

But who *was* this?

The Tsar was gone. Stripped of his wig and beard, sitting naked to the waist at his dressing-room counter, facing the wall-wide mirror, was a great common hulk of flesh. He was rubbing cold cream on his face and wiping it away roughly with a stained towel. His face and body were uniformly pale. His hair was pale, rising in a quiff above his forehead. His eyes were pale and—amazingly—small, those eyes that had swept like beacons across seen and unseen multitudes a little while ago.

I was used to the artifice of the stage—how people went in and out of character, and yet retained from their stage presences something rich and strange when I saw them without makeup, yet alight with the thing that made them actors. But here: that shapeless lump of fish-white flesh sitting on his stool as though dumped there, his body slack with heavy contours like unbaked dough; his general pallor as though he were dusted with flour; the loutish cast of his eyebrow ridge; his puffy cheeks, wide nose, small mouth, and spade chin—all of these made me say to myself, "He looks as common as what: a baker: done for the day." Where was there any trace of the stiletto face of Mephisto, the dark eagle brow and the tortured lips of Boris? I stared at his wide mirror, seeing his profiled presence, and I saw emptiness after creation, and my dismay was, as I realized later, a tribute to the genius and the mystery of the making of great art with humble stuffs.

Behind him stood an elderly dwarf, his dresser, in what looked like gypsy clothes with a striped sash. He might have been a kobold out of Grimm. Chaliapin looked for something on the counter which was not there. He barked a command in Russian to the dwarf and the dwarf ducked away to a huge, old-fashioned trunk which stood with its lid open. To reach into it, he had to leap up and balance himself on his waist over the edge of the trunk, leaving his short, bandy legs treading air. Grunting crossly, he tossed things this way and that in the trunk and finally found what was wanted. He kicked his legs like a swimmer but could not find the floor again. "Feodor Ivanovich!" he shouted. Chaliapin half rose and stretched across to the trunk, still saying something to Rouben, and clutched the dresser by the seat of his pants, roughly set him down, and returned to the dressing table. The dwarf handed him the missing article, a bottle of cologne water. Patting some on his cheeks, Chaliapin leaned to the mirror. He hung his heavy head forward, waving it to and fro like a surly bear. He was running out of things to say. Rouben turned and motioned me forward. He introduced me in Russian, while I tried to look like what he might be saying about me. Chaliapin gave me a stare by way of the mirror, said nothing, and returned to his face. George nodded a silent "Well done," and braced himself for his turn.

Rouben then brought him forward and spoke a rather full introduction in Russian, while George managed a silent combination of operatic nobility and humble duty. Rouben, as he finished, said in English, with dignity and pride, "And so, Feodor Ivanovich, *this is our own American Boris Godunov!*"

On his seat, Chaliapin slowly turned. His face opened in a peasant's vacancy. His tongue lay loose on his lip. Silence expanded like a vacuum. Slowly he seemed to hear what Rouben had said. Slowly he focused himself. He made a leer at George, surveying him up, down, and sideways, staring him naked. He, Boris, the only tsar, swelled himself upward. At last he found voice. In a cavernous growl moistened by mucous and saliva, with a monstrous rattle of the uvula, he shouted,

"Boris? B-va-a-a-g-gh!"

It was a howling vomit of derision and dismissal. It smote George like a thunderbolt. He went white and then turned red.

"No!" cried Rouben. He motioned us to leave and as we went we heard him assail Chaliapin with passionate words, clearly defending George against the savage insult.

We descended to the stage.

"Come on, let's get out of here," said George, choking on set jaws.

xi

In a few moments we were out the stage door into the spring night, shocked into comradely silence. Aimlessly we walked the streets. George strode with his head in the air, his hands gripped painfully behind him. In the light of a street lamp I saw him work his lips and jaws in efforts of self-control. Based on his own ennobling experience of the role of Boris, and his worshipful feeling for Chaliapin's performance, he had imagined an ideal sympathy between himself and the great man: Chaliapin would receive him paternally, would smile with generous grandeur upon the stalwart young American at the outset of a career, and with a blessing—perhaps with a great bear hug—would elevate him as a serious fellow artist. . . .

"I don't know, I don't know," said George softly. His suffering was too deep for tears, and too private for open consolation. What could I say that would measure up to the power and authority of "the world's greatest singing actor"?

We wandered toward the Genesee River. At the bridge we paused and looked down into the black water, where late-night reflections gave tone to our moral and artistic sorrow. We were alone, and we felt alone—the streets were empty, the city was quiet, ours was the only catastrophe abroad long after midnight. Lights across the river were reflected in all their wavering mystery, and our thoughts wavered with them.

Then, after a long silence as we bent over the railings, suddenly George turned to face me. He took a deep breath and expelled it with force. He shook his head as if to clear away clouds of unreason. The faint city glow of deep night showed me a new set to his lips and cheeks.

"What do *you* think?" he asked.

"All right," I said, "I think he has the soul of a scoundrel. I think you should absolutely put him out of your mind forever."

"No," he said. "Do you want to know something? *It doesn't matter!*"

"What doesn't?"

"What he did to me. It doesn't matter—he is still the greatest."

"You really—"

"Come on. Let's go home. It's late."

In that humble act of acceptance George began to find his way back. We walked briskly uptown to our rented rooms, his in East Avenue, mine in Wyndham Street.

1925

D'Alvarez,

the Inca Princess

i

IN ROCHESTER, NEW YORK, at the age of twenty-one I was a vocal student at the Eastman School of Music, the scene designer for the newly formed Rochester American Opera Company, and a production assistant at the Eastman Theatre. My several jobs and, I suppose, a certain precocity in the culture of the arts, brought me membership in Rochester's charmed circle of the Corner Club. There at daily luncheons and after many an important musical or theatrical event I met the brilliant membership, which consisted of leading artists of the musical faculty of the Eastman School, along with a lively representation of Rochester's cultivated society.

One such occasion became particularly important to me. I was determined to write a novel, but I lacked my main character. She arrived one dazzling evening in 1924 in the person of the Peruvian prima donna contralto Marguerite d'Alvarez, who gave a magnificent concert in the Eastman Theatre. Afterward she was brought to the Corner Club for a post-concert party, and I was exactly ready for her. Here was the heroine I sought.

She was already a cult with me through her remarkable phonograph records, which despite the early shortcomings of acoustical recording technique caught a surprising plenty of her vocal opulence and emotional style. Her legend as a fatal woman off-stage was known to music lovers, and I could place her prophetically in the world of the criticism and the fiction of Carl Van Vechten. His characters were persons of extravagant styles and pliable morals, all set forth in unconventional prose in which everybody spoke without quotation marks, gratifyingly like those in French novels, and what they did was described in a beckoning mixture of common frankness and richly obscure polysyllables. Nothing could be more to my taste at the time, and when first I heard d'Alvarez in her concert, and, afterward at the Corner Club, when I met and talked at length with her, the encounter was like a confirmation.

Madame d'Alvarez was like a sculpture of overflowing womanhood by Gaston Lachaise, whose work I admired. Despite her great depth of bosom, width of arm, breadth of hip and thigh, she was beautiful; and when she spoke it was with a deep throaty voluptuousness rapidly expressed in English of the utmost theatrical elegance in pronunciation. As for what she said—nothing could have been more satisfactorily outrageous. It was an epoch reaching from Theda Bara to Nita Naldi in the films, but d'Alvarez made them seem like convent girls instead of vamps to distraction.

ii

As I came into the upstairs drawing room of the club after her concert, I saw her seated in the center of a yellow silk sofa, occupying it all but totally. She was addressing a fifth of a pound of Port du Salut cheese on a piece of French bread which she held above eye level. Her heavy black eyebrows, converged in a lofty angle of suffering and ecstasy as though in a moment of sex, drew her huge black eyes into a focus of deathless beauty, I thought, as I heard her say to the cheese,

"My God, cheese like angels' lips—divine, damp, and thrilling."
In one great swallow, it was gone.

This was how a leading character in a novel must sound, I was certain. On being presented to her, and speaking ardent compliments on her magnificent singing, I accepted her invitation to take the last edge of her sofa, while she continued with her consumption of a trayful of post-concert solids which had been set on a small table before her wide, shining knees.

"What was my best?" she asked in a speaking voice enriched by the crumbs and pastes, the sauces and dressings, the meats of sea and pasture, which in a continuous stream of nourishment invited and enlarged her appetite. She seemed, in fact, all appetites personified, and I was enlivened by the seductive aura of her presence.

"Oh," I said instantly, "the Debussy—*La Chevelure.*"

"How clever of you. You are right." (An inch-thick spread of pâté de foie gras between triangles of toast went down.) "I always sing it in honor of my darling. He never knows it."

She had sung it with such heavily breathed carnality and at the same time such beauty of tone and inflection—had acted the insatiate endurance of love's coupling with such elegance of gesture which her body enlarged—that she had made the belly go hollow with desire. The performance had been as frankly sexual as it was wonderfully lyric.

She had made me imagine explicitly the scene of which Pierre Louÿs had written, and to which Debussy had composed his song. In translation, then, something like this: *"He told me: 'I dreamed last night. I had your hair about my neck. I had strands of your hair like a black necklace around my nape and across my breast. I caressed them and they were mine. And we were bound mouth to mouth forever by the same hair, like two laurels, which often have but one root. And little by little, our limbs were so mingled that I became yourself, or that you entered into me like my very dream.' When he had done, he gently laid his hands upon my shoulders and he looked at me with a gaze so tender that I lowered my eyes, quivering."*

In the last lines, her impersonation of maidenly modesty had been so implausible that by its very artifice she managed somehow to increase the voluptuous intimacy of her effect. With a solemnity which must have excused its cheekiness I asked her my question, which she received as naturally as though youths of twenty asked it of her every day,

"You are in love, Madame?"

"My dear boy, insanely." (A forkful of shrimps dipped in *rémoulade* sauce.) "He lives in New York. When I am home between tours I send for him and when I hear his steps coming up my *escalier* I break into flame within myself, I become an awakening volcano, and then, as he comes nearer, I freeze, I become a goddess of frigidity whom he must reduce to her native fire, and when he at last enters my boudoir, I am like the moon—visible, glowing, but untouchable." (Four narrow sliced-chicken sandwiches held together, garnished with watercress and dressed with escaping mayonnaise.) "He has a waist like a wasp and shoulders like a grand piano." (A clutch of Spanish olives stuffed with peeled Moroccan almonds.) Her great restless eyes, black as smoky topaz with gold lights, roved the room and kept returning to me, and I must have breathed like the visitant in *La Chevelure*, for, looking at me now, she said, reading my thought,

"Yes, yes, isn't it?"

I shivered and she laughed gorgeously, pleased at having made her effect, and laying her hand, with its huge rings encrusted like sea deposits, on my tingling thigh, she said,

"You must come and see me when you are in New York. I scream with loneliness."

"Oh, no, Madame!"

"Oh, yes. No one is constant, I am so simple, all I ask is to be understood, perhaps you understand me. I feel that in you. I am never wrong when I feel, only when I think. —What is your life to be?" she asked. "You will be an artist." She managed to convey in that word an essential nature, using it so broadly as to allow of my existence in any of the arts. Before I could go beyond the word "aspirations," she said, "Let me tell you about mine. How wonderful that someone will listen."

"I have listened to you for years, Madame," I said, "through your wonderful phonograph records."

"Yes, they tell me something about my voice is suited to the machine. —But let me tell you:" and she went on to say, in a monologue with hardly a pause even when she dealt with her swiftly selected snacks, how she was the daughter of an ancient royal Inca house of Peru, how her father had been ambassador to Belgium, where the King after hearing her sing at a soirée—she was still a girl —had tried every imaginable method of seducing her, how she had run away secretly one night because she was virtuous and he was loathsome, how her family had finally consented to allow her to become a stage person, how Oscar Hammerstein had built his London opera house for her despite which she had never taken him in sin, how he had pursued her to America where he had created his New York seasons for her even while she still resisted him, how she had gone to the Chicago Opera there to endure ingenious snubs from the star of the company, Mary Garden, who was also the manageress, who seemed to sing through a narrow rubber tube, and then how she herself had had public triumphs in Chicago despite the accident at her debut as Delilah in the opera of Saint-Saëns, for at the top of a long flight of stairs where she had made her first entrance her heel had caught on a loose board and she had fallen and rolled the entire length of the staircase to the stage floor, only to rise as if nothing had happened, and had entered upon her first notes with such magnificence that the audience had gone mad, halting the performance in a demonstration of love. Why, she asked, was public love her fate, when God had made her for love in private?

She sadly swallowed a draught of champagne and held her empty glass forth without looking at it to a waiter who was passing with a wrapped bottle. He filled it while she gazed at me, working her circumflex brow up and down dreamily. Her lips darkly rouged almost to blackness made silently tasting motions. When I began to speak again it was in a shaken voice which I tried to control by asking a desperately trivial question.

"Madame, have you ever sung with Goossens"—pointing to the brilliant conductor where across the room he was conversing in abstracted charm with a worshipping group.

"Oh my God yes," she replied. "He is such a total musician, and so *soigné* besides. Not," she added with luxurious scorn, "like the man now conducting the New York orchestra, with whom I have sung. When that one conducts, he spreads his legs behind him like a Percheron stallion relieving itself in a great yellow stream splashing into a layer of straw in a byre on a farm in Brittany! How can one sing next to that?"

I had never heard a woman refer to such natural functions at all, much less in her extravagant particularity. I was momentarily muted, if fascinated, and in that moment someone else came to absorb her attention, which, turning to him with an enlarged grace and tumbling all her jewels and brocades, she distributed in the impartiality of celebrated persons. I must give way.

iii

George Houston, the singer, was across the room. A tall young man of splendid presence, he had a constant air of detachment except where young women were concerned, and, I thought, a strangely original way of talking which I tried to adopt when with him. We were close friends. Older than I, he had served as part of an ambulance unit in France during the war, which I had missed by several years. Now he was observing everyone at the party and he was ready for me when I joined him and began to repeat Madame's most extreme remarks. He listened gravely, taking air into his nostrils in little inward gusts, in an effect of comment. I relayed the scene of d'Alvarez awaiting her lover.

Houston said, "The poor bastard."

"It isn't his fault," I said.

"No, it isn't his fault. He's not a poor bastard," he said.

"She's an experience, all right," I said.

"A very foreign experience. All foreigners are experiences. Have a drink."

"No thanks," I said.

"We're all poor bastards," he said, "when we think of it. Let's not think of it."

"All right, we won't think of it. Have a drink," I said.

"All right." He raised his glass. *"Vivent les vulves,"* he said.

"Do you think he knows he's a poor bastard?" I asked over my glass.

"He knows. They always know. He pretends nobody else knows."

"You have to pretend sometimes," I said.

"That's right. Sometimes you have to. Don't ever pretend," he said.

"What am I to do about d'Alvarez?" I asked.

"Go up to her and fall on one knee and say, Madam, when can I sleep with you?"

"I've only just met her. She would think I wasn't showing respect," I said.

"All right. If you said, Madam when can I sleep with you, that wouldn't be showing respect. But it would be very fine and full of respect if you put it the other way."

"What way?"

"Put it any other way you like, so long as you put it. Putting it is the important part. It's very fine, too. —It's time we had another," he said.

"All right," I said.

"This is fine Canadian rye. *Vive le bootlegger,*" he said. "You must drink it truly and well. Never with soda, though."

"Why?"

"Bubbles," he said. "Bad for the aim."

Throughout countless such dialogues—the one I give is of course not remembered verbatim but the style and attitude are really how he talked and how through practice I fell in with his convention—we always preserved blank faces. I had never heard anyone talk like him; and when two years or so later I read *The Sun Also Rises* on its first appearance, I was astonished to hear Houston on every page, and I concluded that the author's generation and Houston's, returning from the war, echoed a system of expression common to alienated ambulance drivers whether they served in France or Italy. But at the time I had no idea that Houston was prophetically voicing an artificial style—like a dialect for a secret juvenile club—which later found its popular master.

As for Madame d'Alvarez, in a little while I said a decorous good night and left her—but not forever, for I saw her a few times in after years, and we had friends in common, one of whom—he was very handsome—had mailed her his photograph, asking for hers in return. She sent it with the inscription, "To Mr. Hunt, whom I should like to bite." She used to answer my letters in her huge handwriting —eight or ten words to a page—in purple ink on gray paper. Carl Van Vechten once told me that she had a fine technique for maintaining a correspondence: whenever she had a free moment she wrote a letter on a few pages, without salutation or signature, and filed it in her desk. It was composed of extravagant generalities in her most lavish manner. She had dozens of such pre-written letters available, and whenever she received a letter which required an answer, she would at random select one of her own stock, add a florid salutation and a passionate signature, and send it off. Readers who may feel that I have exaggerated her style should consult her autobiography (*Forsaken Altars*, 1954), whose tone more than confirms my own impressions. There is other delectable evidence. She wrote to me one time as she was crossing the desert Southwest in a Santa Fe train during a concert tour. The train whipped up clouds of dust which filled the air of her Pullman drawing room. "I feel," she wrote in violet ink on her gray paper, "that I am breathing the powdered souls of the pioneers."

She later figured in novels by Van Vechten under the name Claire Madrilena—in *Firecrackers* (1925) singing *La Chevelure* with "shameless effrontery," and in *Parties* (1930), eating "so much that one wondered how she found time to be witty." Even as late as 1972, Alfred Knopf told me at luncheon a story about her which had the unmistakable tone. He reported how she had told Van Vechten that Vicente Blasco-Ibáñez, taking her home one night in a taxi, bit her in the shoulder and left a gold tooth there.

In 1920 Van Vechten published a broadsheet about d'Alvarez in the *Musical Courier* which her manager used. It said, "I have never heard her sing any song in which she did not exhibit everything inherent in the music and sometimes a great deal more. For Debussy she has an almost mystic understanding . . . She has one of the most noble voices of our time," and "on the platform she becomes imbued with an ecstatic spirit, the contagion of which easily slips across the footlights into the vast spaces of any auditorium; her noble presence, her beauty, her eloquence, her passion, her intensity, her unconventional method of approaching her task (for she does not entirely forego the privilege of acting even on the concert stage) will reach the heart . . ."

iv

To resolve not my own earlier reaction to her but a renewed connection with this memorable woman, I will recall that during the Second World War, when I was stationed briefly in Hollywood, I lived at a lavish billet called the Château Elysée. The air was languorous and fine to breathe, and I kept all windows open high amid palm trees, and above jacaranda trees, plumbago and bougainvillea and scented groves, and so, evidently, did everyone else; for diagonally across from my place was another apartment hotel, from whose open windows I kept hearing unsettling sounds. They were loud, despairing shrieks, vocalizing on the scale, rising a half-tone with each repetition, and forcing me to shut my windows to avoid the most unmusical noises I had ever heard from a human voice.

My friend Houston was then living in Hollywood, directing productions of opera for a local company and also—so various was life in Hollywood—starring in low-budget films about cowboys and horses, both of whom he detested. One day while we were playing tennis I told him about the depressing screams from across the street. He said,

"Yes, of course, that is where Marguerite lives. That is whom you are hearing." In fact, he meant d'Alvarez. "She has Sunday soirées when people come to play and sing for her and she keeps promising to sing for them but never does. I'll take you."

We went the next Sunday evening. Houston told her I was her neighbor. With much grace of manner she swore she remembered me and our exchanges of letters, and she told me a new chapter of her sorrowful story.

A disastrous love affair in Paris had destroyed her voice, though she had not given up, but vocalized every day to recover it. She read my face.

"You have heard me?" I admitted it. "Then you know." I said nothing—she said it for me. "Alas."

She was in poverty, having to sell one emerald at a time to exist. Once or twice a year a film studio called her for a small role—I saw one humiliating movie in which she was made to play a shrewish comedy keeper of a boarding house.

"But they never ask me to sing in the films," she said sadly.

She was much aged, after two decades, but still vivid and interesting in her looks. I went to her evenings a few more times before my orders returned me to the War Department in Washington. Somehow, during the war, she managed to get to London and there she died before the war was over. I had come to know affection for her where before she had supplied me only with moments of preposterous comedy.

Anyhow, after my meeting with her in my extreme youth, I felt I must plan my first novel around her. In due course I had two hundred pages or so and I decided that my book was finished. I sent it off to the firm of Alfred A. Knopf, and drew a Borzoi on the title page of my carbon copy. Three weeks later I received a note on blue paper that said, "Dear Mr. Horgan, this is certainly not for us"—for the manuscript of my novel came back with the letter—"but we should be glad to see any future work of yours," signed Blanche W. Knopf. Because of the brisk professionalism of this, I already felt like a novelist—though without a publisher.

1 9 3 0

The Time I Couldn't

See Mrs. Fiske

MINNIE MADDERN FISKE was playing that season in *Ladies of the Jury*, which I'd seen and enjoyed very much. Her absence of beauty was a positive asset in the performance she gave—that extraordinary face so pointed with intelligence, those eyes so luminous and yet remote (the effect of the cloudy coiffure over her brows, I suppose, à la Bernhardt), the misty suggestion of musing on her thin little mouth, with its cat's delicacy. All these things made her expression one of hilarious wisdom. Add to it her voice, with its tones etched by acidulous irony, and you have a few of the elements which made her the greatest comedienne of her epoch. She not only impersonated the intellectual likeness of her characters, she managed at the same time to share with the audience a most flatteringly sharp *opinion* of that likeness. Like all the great theatre people, she instantly conveyed to the audience what it must think.

At that time I was trying to write a play. Every biography I read suggested to me a theatrical narrative of the most majestic proportions. It was a pity that every living person I saw did not do the same for me. Anyway, I had read Katharine Anthony's delectable book about Catherine the Great of Russia, and had written a play about the inexhaustible Empress. It was an ironic comedy, I thought. I thought that a play with both an occasional warmth and a great deal of brisk smartness in the dialogue, which had, to boot, an empress for its heroine, could only be a triumph. Like all tyros in this intoxicating profession, I spent much time casting my play with the great actors and actresses I had seen, even down to the court flunkies and minor prelates. Mrs. Fiske was to play the Empress.

How to proceed?

That winter I was in New York for Christmas, on vacation from my school job in Roswell, New Mexico.

"Why not let's get an appointment with Mrs. Fiske and talk this play over with her," I asked my agent.

"Do you know her?" she asked.

"No. I spoke to her backstage once in Rochester, and the other night I went back after *Ladies of the Jury* and was privileged to say something through a crack in the door of her dressing room. But—"

"We might as well try," said my agent, with some hardiness.

The next day she told me that we had an appointment to call on Mrs. Fiske in the dressing room after her performance that evening at the Erlanger Theatre.

I reread my play that afternoon and "saw" Mrs. Fiske doing it, very vividly—a great performance.

In the evening, my agent and I were to meet in front of the Erlanger Theatre just before the play was out. It was a rainy night. The clock I was going by had a certain malice. I had been at a party. I was late. My taxi was like a sewing machine, spending most of its energy in remaining stationary with its machinery running. The traffic was lovely to look at, all glistening and rainy, but so slow that when I reached the Erlanger, my agent was there alone. The theatre crowd had gone.

"I'm afraid we are too late," she said.

"Let us try, anyway. Here, this alley leads up to the stage door."

The street was almost deserted.

Faint rain, gold reflections of light, and here this velvety tunnel of an alley. We started up it. It had fire escapes with iron ladders, making angular compositions like constructivist scenery. Halfway up the alley, a single electric light burned above an exit door that was locked from the inside.

Out of the shadows through which we were hopefully going there came two small figures, walking with short steps, alert and modest.

We passed each other.

The single exit-door light saved us.

"It is Mrs. Fiske," I whispered, like a courtier. "Come!"—the accent of intrigue in Molière.

We turned. The two figures were nearly at the street. I ran after them. What to say?

I caught them, trying to be both social and professional.

"Mrs. Fiske?" I said.

My agent caught up. We four stood there.

It was Mrs. Fiske, all right. She wore a hat and a veil tied under her chin, like a Christy Motoring Girl of 1904, and a heavy cloth coat. Her hands were in her coat pockets. She was so very small and bundled-looking that she didn't seem at all the astonishing presence of the stage. She looked straight at me, and the streetlight shone past her veil, which left a triangle of face showing. Oh yes, it was she.

"Mrs. Fiske?" I asked again.

The woman with her, a taller, hovering guardian, said, "I am sorry, Mrs. Fiske can see no one. Can you give me the message? I am Miss McCarthy" (or McNulty—some such name), "her secretary."

I felt like saying, "But she *is* seeing me!" but instead I said to Miss McNulty, "I am Mr. Horgan, to whom you gave an appointment for tonight. I am sorry we were delayed—"

My agent took over Miss McNulty at this point.

"It is about the play, Mr. Horgan's play, which Mrs. Fiske agreed to consider, and we—"

"Yes, I remember," said Miss McNulty. "But Mrs. Fiske cannot possibly see anyone now."

Mrs. Fiske and I were looking at each other. I wanted to burst out laughing. So did she, I will swear it. Her triangle of face, with the brilliant, mischievous eyes, was full of comedy. In the next few minutes, she gave the most adroit, exquisitely sharp scene I ever saw her do. She preserved her official incognito—nay, her *established absence*—and while my agent charmingly wangled Miss McNulty, and while Miss McNulty ingeniously answered, Mrs. Fiske made silent comments on this elaborate exchange of news which was intended for her, and my, ears. She would nod tinily but sharply at a word of Miss McNulty's, close her eyes with the effect of a gasp at a proposal of my agent's, cock her head as if to "consider," shrug at me as if to say, "You see, we are both helpless. The affairs of the world run right past us."

"If we could see Mrs. Fiske for perhaps only five minutes, if not this evening, then tomorrow?" murmured my agent.

("What, more appointments?" "went" Mrs. Fiske.)

"I don't know," said Miss McNulty. "We are so very much engaged these days."

("Oh, frightfully!" Mrs. Fiske shrugged, silently.)

"Mr. Horgan won't be in town longer than a few days. He returns to New Mexico . . ."

("New Mexico! *Tiens!*")

"I could ask Mrs. Fiske tomorrow, and phone you."

("How sensible!")

"Perhaps we could ask her—now?"

"Oh, no, I *am* sorry, Mrs. Fiske can see no one."

("You see," "went" Mrs. Fiske, "It can't be helped. McNultyism triumphant," staring at me with inexpressible drollery.)

They say she always had the power to make everyone else act, too. I found myself doing it all: the shrug, the uprolled eye, the noiseless gasp—every means but sound and open recognition to exchange thoughts and conduct; in effect, a conversation. I have never had such a keen sense of communication with anyone, and I have never seen such eloquent merriment at the foibles and pomposities of human affairs as she had sparkling in her little, old, wise face where it lurked within the triangle frame of that ridiculous veil and the wide-brimmed hat hauled down by it.

It was finally arranged that the play should be sent to Miss McNulty, who would give it to Mrs. Fiske the very first chance there was, and there would be a reading, and then a report, with best wishes.

We left it at that.

As if she had personally guided the conference to its eminently sensible conclusion, Mrs. Fiske nodded and all but dusted off her hands and sighed with a sense of accomplishment. So, in silent quotation marks, she did the sentiment of decision and farewell, and the last diamond-like flash of style was the glance she gave me as she and Miss McNulty tapped hastily along to enter their limousine. It was a whole anthology of opinions, that glance, each one of which was as clear as possible, and they had to do with kindness, fatigue, infinite amusement, modesty, relentless cleverness, penetration, and a lifetime's accumulation of attitudes meaning goodbye. In other words, the great powers of art, revealed by a past mistress.

The next day, Catherine the Great went to Miss McNulty.

Several weeks later, Mrs. Fiske wrote a mysterious and fascinating letter from New York, on stationery belonging to the Hotel Kimball in Springfield, Massachusetts, which had much more style, somehow, than the "swank" paper a lesser star would have to use. The letter said, in part:

I have always been immensely interested in Catherine, but for several reasons I have always feared her as a heroine of a play. If your representative will call upon me some evening after the play during my present engagement at the Erlanger Theatre, I will explain to her just what I mean.

We never found out what the reasons were, but I imagine one of them, and the best one, was a tactful kindliness deserved by neither the Tsarina nor myself.

1 9 3 5

L'Après-Midi de
Mary Garden

i

ON TUESDAY MORNING, January 29, 1935, in New York, I awoke to a state of alarm mixed with elation. It was the publication day of *No Quarter Given*, my second novel, and Harper and Brothers was giving an all-out cocktail party for the occasion. In those days, the literary cocktail party was more of an event than it is now. All of New York's literary *gratin* turned out. Faces famous in caricature, minds tautly competitive, common charity disdained, the guests came to be seen and reported. The guest of honor was often said to be the least of the attractions. I had read all this in New Mexico, where I lived. Now about to be thrown in the thick of it, I thought how comfortable it would be simply to bolt. The dreadful day yawned ahead of me. How to get through it until five o'clock, when I must appear? Whenever the thought of the coming ordeal struck me, I felt the classic symptoms of stage fright—a tightening of the scalp, a thump at the solar plexus.

At breakfast, a sudden refuge in distraction faced me in *The New York Times*. There I found an item announcing that Mary Garden, the lustrous opera singer and actress, would present a lecture-recital in the Plaza Hotel ballroom at three o'clock that day. Her subject was Claude Debussy. Tickets could be had at a box office in the hotel. All my life—I was thirty-two—I had wanted to see and hear this amazing artist.

To mention Caruso, Melba, Farrar, Chaliapin, or, for today, Maria Callas, is to suggest the like position of Mary Garden in the international operatic world of her time. Much of her lore was known to me. I knew her voice through recordings. While still a vocal student in Paris she had won instant fame by brilliantly taking over the lead role in Charpentier's *Louise* when the artist singing the part became ill. On that night, Garden was established for life. She was twenty-three. Two years later Debussy chose her to create the role of Mélisande. Another triumph. As Massenet's Thaïs she inflamed her artistic success with her erotic enactment of the courtesan—a performance which gave the public its stubborn opinion, however mistaken, about how "daring" her private life must be. For one year she was general manager of the great Chicago Opera, grandly bank-rupting the company by the beauty and extravagance of her produc-tions. James Gibbons Huneker and Carl Van Vechten had written paeans to her which I had read. Here was my chance to attend this great artist, and also take my mind off my trouble for a good part of the afternoon.

But it would help to be with a friend. One came happily to mind—Natalie Hall, the operatic soprano. She and her mezzo-soprano sister Bettina were known for starring in a long-running Broadway operetta. I telephoned Natalie. To hear, to see, Garden? Wildly grateful. Could she bring Bettina, whom I'd never met? We would meet, all three, at two forty-five in the Plaza Palm Court. I telephoned for reservations and was asked to take up the tickets by half past two—the ballroom was selling out. My day began to look up.

ii

In good time I arrived at the Plaza, already somewhat insulated against my nervous state—but not for long. In the lobby was a portentous reminder—a large-lettered display announcing the day's events in the hotel:

MISS MARY GARDEN, LECTURE-RECITAL
3 P.M., Grand Ballroom
Second Floor South

And below that, ominously:

RECEPTION FOR MR. PAUL HORGAN
Harper & Brothers
5 to 7, White and Gold Suite
Second Floor North

There seemed to be no escape. At the box office I asked for my tickets. The young woman clerk shuffled them out and I was about to pay for them when behind her a tall, glossy, youngish man wearing a gardenia in his buttonhole snapped up the tickets, palmed my money aside, and said, "No, n'no, Mr. Horgan: with our compliments," and handed the three tickets to me.

"But why? Thank you, but I don't understand."

"I am Mr. Piza, Madame's manager. I have seen notice of your reception. My congratulations." Swarthy and elegant, he bowed like a South American. "We are delighted. Allow me."

Confused but elevated, I thanked him again and went to the Palm Court. There they were, the two beauties, one for each arm. Embraces. We made our way to the elevator.

"Garden: how exciting," said Natalie, the classic brunette, and Bettina, the glowing blonde, said, "Fabulous."

The ballroom was filling fast. We found our spindly gold chairs in a box on the right side of the room with a fine view of the small formal stage where a concert grand piano waited.

Suddenly the stage bloomed with light. There was a bated pause, and then, in a brisk and delicate stride, Mary Garden was before us on her way to the piano, followed by her accompanist, M. Jean Dansereau, a small, wiry Frenchman, and a self-effacing youth who would turn pages.

Everyone stood. She let them, and then, with all standing, she made a wide gesture showing the insides of her wrists, and leaned forward slowly in a bow that was not at all a grateful player's humble thanks, but a grant of permission to attend. In the bend of the piano she was now poised in command as the house settled. Already there was a sense of great occasion—how great, we did not then know, for it was her final appearance in public as a singer. As the newspapers noted afterward, many illustrious artists in music were present, including Geraldine Farrar, long retired from the opera, and Marguerite d'Alvarez, the Peruvian diva—both regarded in the past as rivals to Mary Garden, a rumor that Miss Garden had lightly dismissed. Rival? *Who?*

Small and delicate as she was, she had an affinity of countenance with the great cats, here refined exquisitely to retain the tiger's high cheeks above the fixed, meaningless smile; intent gaze; alert focus on all environs; thoughtless confidence of power; all supported by the gift of seeming beautiful at will. So, too, her movement, lithe, exact, gracile, was of the feline order. She was fifty-eight years old, she had abandoned the opera, and she was not any age. She was robed in who she was, which was enough to give the world.

Otherwise her costume suggested both theatre and salon, as best I can recall this, and all that follows.

She wore a close-fitting hat of black silk with a mesh of veil that came down just past her eyes—her eyes gleamed with a tigerish light in a little blue cave of shadow that put the years at a distance, and yet conveyed the vivid present. Her hair was a tawny gold. A floor-length fall of pale yellow satin, her gown was so tight over her straight hips that you wondered how she could step. A short-sleeved torero jacket in black sparkling stuff met long white gloves that reached above the elbows. A necklace of big pearls was looped once about her throat, with the rest of it swaying almost to her knees. How tall was she? A few inches over five feet, it was recorded somewhere; but she was a figure so commanding that illusion created height. By her valiant posture she seemed to tell us not to be nervous—all would be well, indeed brilliant.

And it was.

In the Hotel Plaza Grand Ballroom she was up to her old tricks —casting a spell, as she had done in countless opera performances. With peremptory grace she turned and gave M. Dansereau the signal to begin. Now they would give us songs by Debussy, a dozen of them, including the air of Lia from *L'Enfant prodigue*, the third of the *Ariettes*, *Je tremble en voyant ton image, Green, La Chevelure,* and *Mandoline*. M. Dansereau played the piano texts with a tonal intelligence equal to hers—by turns scintillant, brooding, declamatory.

How to be exact in describing a performance made of sound, that medium as fugitive as time? Her voice was without luster—she was past the age of brilliant tone. Perfect in pitch, it had at moments almost a *parlando* quality, in a timbre reminiscent of dried leaves stirred by air. But what expression, now smoky with passion, again rueful for life's shadows! What musicality; and what sense of meaning —the texts of Guignand, Bourget, Pierre Louÿs, Verlaine, Baudelaire, came forth in all the beauty and power of Debussy's description: "the spell of her voice . . . so softly persuasive." We were persuaded. Did any artist more fully know who, and what, she was? Was this the first attribute of the interpretive genius?

When the recital of songs ended with many curtain calls graciously acknowledged, Mary Garden remained on stage after the last one. She went right to work, saying something like, "Claude Debussy. The most fascinating yet mysterious public person I have ever met."

She then went on to speak for perhaps forty minutes, in an international accent. Her tone was conversational, emphatic when proper, beguiling when memory was tender; always correct as to the language, though when she needed French, the pronunciation made no pretense to sound native.

In particles, then: Debussy was "a very strange man," as she wrote fifteen years later in her autobiography. (Much that she wrote and much that she said in her lecture are merged in my memory.) She said he was not tall, rather stocky. Quite extraordinarily, he had *two* foreheads—yes, two, one bulging on top over which he brushed his dark hair, the other showing in the clear above his black brows. His eyes, dark, sometimes quite expressionless, were fascinating. You never quite knew what he was thinking. Things he said were original, quite. He was mad about women, though one didn't know if he ever loved anyone, really. People always wondered, of course, some even asked, if he and she had ever been lovers. The idea was preposterous —not that he did not make the attempt one day on a railroad platform in Versailles, but no, there was nothing to it. A perfect

artistic understanding, that was all, and it was enough. They rehearsed *Pélleas et Mélisande* for four months. Debussy attended, Mes-
sager conducted, they had forty orchestra rehearsals, unheard of. But
when the opening came, Debussy was not there, and in fact he never
attended a public performance. Some were offended. Not she. She
understood when he said that for ten years the opera had been his
life, and as he knew it best in that way, no other way was as real to
him. When the role of Mélisande became hers at his desire, the
author of the play, Maeterlinck, made a scandal, tried to have her
removed in favor of his mistress, Mme. Georgette Leblanc, but no,
Debussy held fast, he never gave in, Mélisande remained hers, then,
and for as long as she, and *she herself*, chose, in whatever opera
company she was singing. Debussy had a devoted first wife, Lily, who
adored him, she overlooked much, but never expected what happened, when he left her quite abruptly for a rich woman. Lily tried
to kill herself, and at that he seemed concerned, but in the hospital
when she assured him that she would now live, he shrugged and
simply went away, and that was all of that. A very strange man, but
yes, fascinating, a great pianist, though a poor singer when he sang
the part to everyone in a first reading—his voice was small and
husky. He adored Mélisande's voice (he always used that name
instead of Mary Garden) and he loved her voice so much that he
composed and dedicated to her a whole group of songs, the *Ariettes.*

I remembered this when I read in his letters that Debussy wrote
of her: *"Le succès de 'notre Garden' ne m'étonne pas; il faudrait autrement, avoir
des oreilles bouchées a l'émeri pour résister au charme de sa voix. Pour ma part,
je ne puis concevoir un timbre plus doucement insinuant. Cela ressemble même à
de la tyrannie, tant il est impossible de l'oublier."*

And she remembered what he said of her to Carré, the director of
the Opéra Comique at a rehearsal of *Pélleas et Mélisande* while she was
creating the character: *Je n'ai rien à lui dire*—he could suggest nothing
to enhance her realization of the role. But that was how it always was
with her work—she never *studied* how to do a part—she always
simply *knew*, it came from nowhere, and it was always the truth. At
the end of that particular rehearsal she heard him say to Carré,
"What a strange person, this child." Then in his baffling, remote

way, he picked up his hat and walked off—he was always doing that, suddenly walking out. . . .

She brought Claude Debussy before us and we believed. When she finished speaking, she allowed a long thoughtful pause; and then left the stage, not to return.

For two hours I forgot my coming trial, and when the lecture ended, my companions and I were in lingering thrall. I said we must try to go backstage to pay our respects, and as singers, the Misses Hall agreed with stars in their eyes.

At the hidden entrance to the stage, then, I presented us to Mr. Piza, who was on guard there. Could we say one word to Miss Garden of our perfect fulfillment?

"Ah, thank you, I'm afraid not. You see, Madame never receives after a performance. But I will tell her. Thank you."

"No, it is our thanks," I said. And then, in a leap beyond the bounds of the plausible, I added, "But you so kindly invited me to your occasion, perhaps you would let me invite Madame and your-self to my own party," and I mentioned the reception for my new book, already under way at well after five.

"Yes, I know, of course. But again—" Mr. Piza was extremely polite in excusing Madame from unscheduled and, in fact, unexam-ined events.

We sighed and turned away. I began to feel the familiar stress under my necktie again. Natalie looked at me and said, "You'll be all right."

By her concern she drove home my dread. I nodded. Compelled to a brave show, I took the sisters to the lobby where I bought flowers for us all—violets for them to hold, a dark red carnation for my buttonhole.

"Let's go up, then," I said, viewing the elevator with its brass lace as a tumbril. But the Hall sisters had to leave me: they must have an early supper to be ready for their evening show. With a gaunt smile I embraced them and saw them go; and then I ascended to the White and Gold Suite on the second floor, to be discharged upon a waste of polished parquet. Three lofty rooms facing the park were thrown into one, which at first glance seemed almost empty.

Where was the party, that clamorous huddle of people at cocktails, shouting each other down with a high decibel count thermally stimulated by their massed body heat? But as I looked about I saw that there *were* guests present—perhaps sixty or so—who were ranged tightly on little gold chairs lining the walls. A few were talking to others beside them, others sat silent, holding drinks. In the center of the floor was a Harper group of three persons, impassively waiting for me. I advanced upon Mr. Cass Canfield, the publisher; Mr. Eugene Saxton, my first great editor; and Miss Ramona Herdman, the charming publicity chief.

"You're late," said Mr. Canfield dryly.

"Not fatally," said Mr. Saxton with his perpetually amused smile.

The wallside chairs became aware and glanced in my direction, but no moves were made. The party seemed enclosed in ice. A waiter came our way and I acquired a martini.

Finally, "Shouldn't you meet people?" asked Miss Herdman.

She took me to the wall and walked me along to shake hands as we went. The guests looked briefly at me and returned to their self-absorptions. I had a sense that every known Van Doren was present, and I recognized other glittering names, for none of which, of course, was mine a match. The gathering, meant to be festive, was lost to the lifeless inane. Something had to be done if Harper and Brothers were not to endure a total waste. The case was so poor— a young writer from the far provinces facing his first New York public event—that nothing was at risk, even to my making a fool of myself. If nobody would talk to me, I would invade them in another persona. To play the host, I became a waiter. I took a tray of canapés and began to go down the rows of gilt chairs, offering a bite here, another there, which were accepted as intrusions or declined as interruptions.

iii

And then: there should have been a fanfare for tympani and cymbals. Glancing along the wall in my duty I had a sudden shock of peripheral vision which made me turn sharply for a direct view.

There in the central doorway of the party rooms stood Mary Garden, in her pose of permitting herself to the public. As there was no one to announce her, she was waiting to be received. Behind her were the members of her *cuadrilla*, extending the symbol of her torero jacket: Mr. Piza; M. Jean Dansereau; the female secretary, Miss Croucher (or some such name) in tweeds; a maid holding two fur coats and three large handbags; and hugging his music brief case the remote young man who turned pages. The great world was there for me.

I managed to set my tray down on a vacant chair and go to the doorway. Euphoria gave me character. Reaching the presence, I bowed like a Renaissance courtier and declared, I think ringingly, "Madame! You pay us an enchanting honor!"

With a piercing gleam out of her veiled cave, Mary Garden raised her right hand in a torch-like gesture and briskly demanded of her manager behind her shoulder, "Piza-who-is-this?"

"It is your host, Madame, Mr. Paul Horgan, for whom the reception is held."

"So it is. *Allons.*"

And so it was that I led her procession into the room, while all around us the murmur arose, *Look, look, it's Mary Garden!* which she acknowledged only by a slight lift of her shoulders. I heard Mr. Canfield inquire flatly, "Was she invited?" and Miss Herdman reply, "No, I made the list," and I, feeling like someone else, said, *"I* invited her" and escorted Madame to the precise middle of the room where in her habit of center stage she elected to take up her position. The *cuadrilla* ranged itself behind her. The gilt chairs were emptying fast as guests came about us to form a dense circle, though at a respectful distance. I was aloft in the translation of character which came to my rescue. As Harper and Brothers loomed a little nearer, politeness required that I say:

"Madame, may I introduce—"

"No-no," she interrupted in an elevated voice, "I will speak only to you," adding a smile worthy of Thaïs. An audience hush fell over the company. There I was, trapped with glory and fame. What could I, must I say, further?

"May I offer you a drink, Madame?"

She excused the banality with a crosswise wave of her forefinger.

"A cigarette?"

"Jamais—ma voix."

With the genius of desperation I knew I must play above my form. I said, "This has been an historic afternoon for the centuries, Miss Garden!"

"You attended my *séance musicale?*"

"Yes, Madame, the event of a lifetime of musical events."

"Lifetime?" She made a smile of devastating wistfulness. "A lifetime: how old are you?"

"Thirty-two. But—"

"How perfect—neither an ending nor a beginning! But my afternoon—?"

"Yes, the superb lecture. You hardly seemed to speak, Madame. You created pictures in the air."

"Pictures in the air. How lovely."

"Your text was astonishing. You spoke, not in phrases, not in sentences, but in paragraphs!"

"I did?" She commanded the *cuadrilla.* "Piza? Did you hear? Miss Croucher, write that down, make a note, so valuable, we must keep this."

She knew I was talking nonsense, but she felt the extremity that compelled it, and together we wrote our scene out of thin air in the ping-pong of drawing-room comedy.

"Yes," I said, "and the songs: never such musical line, never such penetration beyond what the poet meant!"

"Yes," she said, "poetry alone has never touched me, except to make me restless and nervous."

"Yes, good poetry is all nerves. When poetry is bracing, it is all bad."

"But then Debussy's music was always the right music for the words. Think of it: until we parted, but not as friends, he always said he was going to write an opera of Romeo and Juliet for me."

She spoke fast and imperiously, her voice a little edgy; and she made little steps in place, a miniature dance, to animate the scene and hold attention. Juliet invoked hazy romance. She measured me down and up with her veiled rays. I was only an underweight specimen at best, but. . . .

"Piza, look at him!" she declaimed. "Did you ever see a figure more *soigné?*" She danced a little near me and reached out her white-gloved hands and molded my flanks, waist, and hips, and cried, "Don't, you must promise me, don't you ever gain a single pound!"

From the always-growing throng of onlookers came a wordless murmur that meant, *Really!*

"Tell me," she said, "what do you write? I hope novels. I adore novels. When I want the truth I go to fiction."

"Yes, a novel, *No Quarter Given.*"

"No quarter: I never gave quarter. What is it about?"

"It's enormous. It's about—"

"What a novel I could write! Perhaps one day I shall. Though perhaps I have already lived my novel. One should never repeat. I shall never forget what someone said to me—was it Paul Bourget or Jacques-Emile Blanche? I forget—one should never repeat except in love. You will write many more books. I must have them all, I am an excellent critic."

And so on, and so on, as the minutes flew. Questions like sparks that died away, with hardly a pause for an answer; and *le tout New York* craned and stared for every word and gesture. I did what I could to keep the ball in the air, and I broke the law only twice—once when my sister Rosemary (to whom my novel was dedicated) arrived, and I introduced her to Madame. Again, when I saw an old friend appear despite a state of mourning for her husband's recent death—Mrs. Isabel Ames of New Mexico. I was touched that under the circumstances she came to my party and I broke ranks to go to greet her. In the piercing voice of an elderly lady used to coping with deafness in the family, Mrs. Ames said:

"They tell me that you are talking to someone named Mary Garden. Is she anything to the real one?"

"It *is* the real one," I murmured, trying to hush my friend.

"My God," cried Mrs. Ames, a lifetime of laughter in her endearing old face, "I thought she was dead years ago!"

Madame's management of this cheerful affront was masterly. Everyone had heard it. All leaned to see what she would do about it.

She simply grew tall, raised her gaze well above everyone present, and defied comment. The effect of vitality was immense. In an instant I was back in her service.

Finger on lip, she brooded a moment, and then: "I want to ask you something—you *will* do it, won't you: I want you to do it: you are the one to do it: I can tell, I can *always* tell, you are the one to do it."

"But anything, Miss Garden, of course."

"Then I want you to write a play for me—a delicious three-act comedy of manners, very high style, *gaie comme les hirondelles,* witty, blazing with epigrams, don't you know, yet with an undertone of sadness—not *sad,* don't you know, but *triste,* like a lovely day in autumn and full of love—*amusing* love, don't you know, nobody throwing themselves about, but so touching. And please: Mr. Horgan: give me just one little song to sing? the second act? perhaps, yes, I think, just before the curtain, so the *meaning* of the song will come to us in the *last* act! Do you think?"

With becoming extravagance I agreed to write the play. A book-news reporter or two made notes. Mr. Canfield loomed open-mouthed. Mr. Saxton beamed indulgently. The comedy was running down. Mr. Piza leaned across Madame's shoulder and showed her his watch, made a murmur about waiting obligations; and, facing me —"Ah!"—the white-gloved hand rose to the brow, deploring the second-rate demands made upon the numinous.

"I must go. Send me your novel, Hotel Pierre. I will read it. I will write you instantly about it. You have been gallant. We must meet soon again. Do not neglect my play."

She made a sweeping turn toward the exit, creating a parabola of knee-length pearls, and I escorted her away with the *cuadrilla* in tow. As I bent to kiss her hand, I caught a glimpse of the smile with which she made an open secret of the farce in our scene; and then she dutifully held a farewell pose in the elevator gates. The gates clanged shut. Behind me, the crowd had shifted to observe insatiably, someone started to clap, the ovation grew, and to farewell applause, Mary Garden's car descended with the effect of a great sigh of release.

I returned to the party. It was exploding in a clamor of talk. Everyone had the same thing to talk about. The ice was not only broken, it was shattered. I was besieged with questions—what else had she said; did she mean it all; had I known her before; where; would I really write her a play; tell about your novel; do you often come East from New Mexico. Suddenly, in the New York way, I had many ten-minute friends. Briefly I was a hero. Nobody left before nine o'clock.

iv

On the following morning, I went to Brentano's, where I inscribed a copy of *No Quarter Given* to Mary Garden and asked that it be sent to her at the Pierre Hotel. In hopes of a rapturous reply, I included my hotel address. Nothing came from her, either about the novel or about our future collaboration. After some days of growing realism, I telephoned the Pierre Hotel. Miss Garden had checked out days ago.

Any forwarding address?

"Of course not," replied the Pierre Hotel coldly, in defense of the vanishing point of celebrity.

1937

Garbo Observed

i

"BUT IT'S A JOB," George said, "and I am glad to have it."
Though it was not the opera theatre, or stardom in the long-running
romantic Broadway musical of his earlier days. He was my old friend
George Houston, and we had met up again in Hollywood. Over a
Sunday lunch at my pleasant small hotel in Bel Air, we exchanged
memories of our common experience of a decade earlier in the
Rochester Renaissance of the 1920s. But soon I asked, "What about
the job?"

"I am in a film called *Conquest* at M-G-M being directed by
Clarence Brown, and starring Greta Garbo and Charles Boyer. It's
about the famous affair between the Polish Countess Marie Walewska and Napoleon. She plays Walewska and he plays Napoleon. I am
the Grand Marshal Duroc of the imperial court. They are paying me
nine hundred dollars a week for fifty weeks not only because I'm
handsome but also because I am six feet two in height, and my job
is to stand around near Boyer to make him look as short as Napoleon. You have my permission to laugh."

"Wonderful."

"It's the movies . . ."

"Is it a good movie?" I asked.

"Too soon to know."

"Is it an interesting story?"

"In spots. I imagine that historically much of it is nonsense; but history never deters our scriptwriters. Anyhow, the part they're working on now is the high point of the film—the end of the romance, when he brutally tells her he intends to marry a royal princess to provide an heir for his reign."

"Is that the end?"

"No, in quick takes, Napoleon marries, has his heir, is exiled to Elba, escapes, is beaten at Waterloo, is exiled forever to St. Helena. She bids him farewell with her little boy—his son—and watches the British warship sail away with him."

"I see. —Does it sound a little thin?"

"So it is, thin, but gorgeous in all the production values: palaces, troops, uniforms, court balls, real M-G-M all of it."

"How is Garbo?"

"I don't really know, though they do say she is extraordinary in some takes. I only repeat what I've heard. I'm in very few scenes with her, nothing important."

"But don't you watch her in her other scenes?"

"No—it's the law that nobody is allowed near the set when she is shooting except those directly involved. No visitors, no New York bankers slavering over their investment, not even our supreme boss Louis B. Mayer, the African Tapir."

"But why all the secrecy?"

"It isn't secrecy as such. It's Garbo's way of avoiding anything like a live audience. They say she really is shy, in private and at work. *At work* is the worst, when she has to pretend to be somebody else who is called upon to do strange things, at which she herself refuses to be observed. —There's a case study there, somewhere."

"What is she like to talk to?"

"I haven't met her."

"But you're . . ."

"She doesn't see *me*—only the tall man in the grand uniform."

"Fascinating. I wish *I* could see her."

"Not a chance," said George. But he took on a remote look. Some scene was being played out in his mind. He crinkled a corner of his mouth and raised one eyebrow, and I had a hint of the sardonic Mephistopheles of his triumph long ago in the opera. Resuming himself, then, he said, "But we ought to try it."

"What:"

"They could only throw you out and threaten to fire me. I think you should risk it on the chance of seeing her on the sound stage, if only for a minute." He warmed to his work. "Great: we're going to rehearse tomorrow morning—it will be the scene where Marie Walewska, heartbroken, takes her leave of Napoleon after he reveals his plan to marry the Austrian girl. Something to see."

So it was arranged. He would meet me at the main gate in Culver City early Monday morning and while the sound stage was still empty he would escort me there and establish me far enough from the set to be lost in distance and dim light. There, he said, I just might, with any luck, see or anyway hear what would go on when they rehearsed the scene.

ii

The next morning we came into the vast gloom of a sound stage on the M-G-M lot. Once inside, I was blinded for a moment by the contrast—a flash of scarlet—between the California sunlight and the dim interior. Only gradually was I able to see where I was.

The sound stage was a building shaped like an enormous shoe box about the size of the drill area of a National Guard armory. Its central oblong space was taken up by a chest-high plateau of wooden platforms fitted together, the whole reaching from end to end of the interior. On each side, along the whole length, was a walkway, with doors at each end. The ceiling was defined by a grid of lamps and steel rafters. Only one or two lamps showed light but my vision was now adjusted to it. There was nobody to be seen.

When we reached halfway along the length of the walkway George said, "I leave you here. I'm needed in makeup. You can sit on the edge of the platform here. That's the set over there."

I followed his glance over my shoulder.

About forty feet away stood dimly visible a stage set of flats with the "fourth wall" open facing me. George continued:

"We'll be rehearsing in costume here sometime during the morning. You won't be too comfortable but it'll be worth it in case you can see action through the open side of the set. —Whatever you do, don't let her see you. You just might get away with it. Her dressing room is outside the far door on the other side. She comes along here when it's time. You just lie low on this side until she is safely inside the set." He added that unexpected persons were ejected at once. Ernest Hemingway had been thrown out; even, the week before, Garbo's friend Mercedes D'Acosta. "If we both survive, meet me for lunch in the commissary. *Bonne chance,*" and off he went into the perspective of "our" walkway toward the door by which we had come in.

I hopped up to sit on the edge of the platform with my back to the set. I felt absorbed into the emptiness and quiet of the place. Now and then an unexplained distant sound like a faint creaking of a timber only emphasized the sense of the vacancy all about. Every sense seemed to enact a new meaning of the word "wait." Why did I feel a little uneasy?

But I knew what to do. It was then, as now, my habit never to be without a book in circumstances that might involve waiting. With me that morning I had the first volume of Trevelyan's *The Life and Letters of Lord Macaulay* in the pocket edition. The type was small but my eyes were now fully adjusted to the lamps high overhead. I would be able to read in that strange isolation.

I'd been reading for half an hour or more when a sharp blade of sunlight cut along the interior and I saw an unmistakable figure enter through the doorway which I had used. I remember that I had the idiotic thought, *But she is supposed to enter by the other side.* The door closed behind her and she came striding along the walkway toward me where I sat with my legs dangling off the platform. She was swathed in a many-folded white robe. She unwound a light scarf from around her hair, which fell in marvellous waves by her cheeks. She wore enormous sunglasses. Garbo.

The jig is up, I said, for I could think of no escape. She was going the length of the building toward the door at the other end. She would have to pass close by me. Her law said that she was not to be seen. If I could not disappear, there seemed only one way to make sure that I would not "see" *her:* the nearer she came, the more intently I bent over my Macaulay. When she was almost upon me she took off her sunglasses the better to see who was there—and as she went by me at a distance of three feet, I turned the page, raised the little book closer to my eyes, and "saw" nothing. Once past me, she turned for a final look. I was still "reading."

In peripheral sight I saw that, oddly reassured, she went along in her square-shouldered stride. I directly watched after her now. She walked like the goddess of Samothrace, her robe clinging and swirling. At the far door, she opened it on yet another sweep of California light, and disappeared.

For the next unmeasured while, if I read at all, I read the same line or two over and over— *"Bulwer is to be editor of the New Monthly Magazine. He begged me very earnestly to give him something for it . . . I may possibly now and then send him some trifle or other . . . At all events I shall expect him to puff me well"*—and waited for someone to come and order me away.

iii

Nobody came—to me, that is; but after a long wait, a small group of men appeared in the twilight on the stage forty feet away and began doing things about the set. Suddenly with hushed booming sounds the great battery of overhead stage lights came on and through the open "fourth wall" of the set I could see most of the interior of a splendid chamber in the Schönbrunn Palace in Vienna —French doors giving on to balconies, great luster chandeliers, sumptuous furniture, tall Hapsburg portraits on the walls, including one of Francis I, the overthrown Emperor. I began to feel a welling of excitement and suspense at the atmosphere of *theatre*—myself in darkness, facing a zone of color, light, preparation, expectancy. More people arrived. The director, Clarence Brown, took his chair at the center of the opening. Someone called "Places!" Napoleon appeared and took up his aggressive stance in the center of the room. He wore his green short-tailed tunic, and decorations, white breeches, white silk stockings, and flat black patent-leather pumps. His forelock fell across his brow. His eyebrows scowled above his

Roman nose. Brown said quietly, "George," and a side door opened and the Grand Marshal Duroc ushered in Marie Walewska and withdrew.

A presence of joy itself, she flew to the Emperor's arms. They embraced passionately. She combined earthly delight with the delicacy and modesty of a young girl—she was bringing him tremendous news, the news of their coming child. He asked if she is happy. When she replied, her voice gave your heart a twist. It was as clear as still water, yet shadowed by its own depth. Unlike her voice in sound films, it had none of the electronic "ping" that faintly edges spoken words on the film track. Dove, low woodwinds, her voice, even when joyful, carried a hint of possible sorrow. Happy? She answered him, "I shall never be unhappy again," and thinking of his love and the child she will bear, "I shall never be lonely again."

Simple and elegant as a young willow branch, she brought him to a low chair where he must listen to her. She leaned over his shoulder, her face radiant with what she had to tell him; but before she could speak he jumped up with what he had to tell *her.* She was silenced by his abruptness.

"I am determined to marry again," he declared. With a great show of rational purpose, he went on to explain. He must found a dynasty if his reign is to continue and his Empire to survive. It will take a marriage to someone of royal blood who will give him an heir to save the future. He saw nothing of her shock and growing despair. She wilted. She gave the effect of closing petals. You could feel her blood grow thin, her joy seep away. He said he had chosen the young Hapsburg Archduchess Marie Louise to be his empress and give him a son. His regime will be legitimized.

Footmen interrupted, bringing in a laden supper table. They placed table and chairs and Napoleon waved them out. He brought Marie to be seated and took his own place and at once fell greedily to his soup.

Under the weight of the world she remained mute. At last he noticed something odd about her, and he asked rather impatiently, "Why are you so silent?" Thinking he had a notion of her concern, he assured her that his plans would make no difference at all to them —nothing is to change between them. In fact, if it were not for the stubborn need for royal blood in his scheme, he would make Marie Walewska his empress!—with an air that settled the whole matter.

Out of the depths she finally managed to say,

"This is a dead house, and you are going to live in it!" Her voice was a hardly inflected monotone. He was puzzled by her words, but a distraction intervened. The Grand Marshal Duroc came again, with a report. A young revolutionary condemned to death for his execrations against the Empire had been grandly offered a pardon if he would recant; but Duroc now reported tonelessly that, failing to recant, the youthful firebrand has been duly shot.

With righteous vigor Napoleon approved and dismissed the Grand Marshal.

Hearing all this, Marie was appalled. She cringed from what she saw and heard from the man whom she loved. Her grief broke forth. In anguish, she asked of him, "What has happened to you!" She gazed about in despair. Seeing the imperial Austrian portraits on the brocaded walls, she became a creature of flame. With a gesture like a flash of fire she pointed to the painted Hapsburgs and cried out, "These are your kind now! They are the dead in life! The liberator of Europe has become a son-in-law!"

The bitterness of her scorn bewildered Napoleon. She stayed his reach for her, and using the lover's name she had for him, she said in a grieving key, "Oh, Napoleoné! There was so much I had to tell you that I can't tell you now . . ."

She took up her long scarf and moved to the door.

"Where are you going!" he demanded harshly.

In a ghost of a voice, she said, "Where—" and the world turned into a wilderness for her as she vanished into it.

iv

There was a long silence; then from all the stage crew and the director applause broke out and I only wished I could join mine with it. The rehearsal was over. The lights dimmed down to a single work light above the set. Something extraordinary had taken place. People drifted away in silence. My feeling was with them in every way. I wanted not to move. My heartbeat was rippling fast along; my breathing was shallow. I had been taken into a play of emotion and given into the deliverance from self that true achievement in the theatre could make only in its highest moments. What had done it that morning was the acting of Greta Garbo, seen not in a moving photograph of herself, but in her physical presence. Her voice, the purity of her enunciation; the restraint of her gestures until the moment of her outburst at the painted imperial images; the sweet frailty of her body within its long, clinging simple gown; above all, the play of thought and feeling over her face whether joyous or grieving —all these elements came directly through the magnetism of her actual presence in ways that the camera could never register.

In after years, when at last I saw the complete film of *Conquest* I was sorry to find that, with the exception of the one scene I had watched in rehearsal, the film as a whole is nerveless and without style. Its absurd wrenchings of history are not the point—fiction has its liberties. But the script is trivial for the most part, and Garbo is evidently meant to say most of her lines with little interest or inflection. There is no special character in her movement, and amazingly she is costumed dowdily most of the time. Her partner, Charles Boyer, works at Napoleonic mannerisms—abrupt speech, rapid stride, hunched intensity—but without convincing effect. For the rest, production values are rich enough, with grand interiors, dazzling uniforms, masses of troops; but dramatic values are generally missing, and Clarence Brown's direction seems listless and unimaginative. In the film, only the scene of Marie's broken love affair has reminders of what I had observed—with bated breath—but they remain only reminders. I saw it all again, the palace room, the portraits, the tender beginning, the self-absorption of Napoleon, and on to the tragic conclusion and Marie's departure. It was all there, but it was *up there on the screen,* interesting, touching, but there, not here enfolding you like experience itself.

The actual presence of Greta Garbo was another matter entirely. On the sound stage she gave a performance as spellbinding as any I had ever seen in the live theatre. When she spoke her first word you felt a twist of emotion that made you catch your breath; and as the scene played out you became entranced beyond place and time—the effect that great acting puts upon its audience.

v

What made the difference? I was still brooding over what made the
difference when George joined me at a table in the studio commissary. Like many of the actors all about he was still in makeup but
wearing only a sports shirt and sweat pants and sneakers.

"We're going to shoot the scene after lunch, and they have to keep
my white pants and the rest all fresh. Did you stay? Did you see
anything? Did anybody see you?"

"Yes. *She* did."

"What!"

I explained how I was overtaken by her as I sat reading, and how
I made myself invisible with my book. He laughed out loud and said,
"Disappearing into your little book! What a lark! —Then what. Did
anybody come?"

"Nobody. I saw it all. I am still sort of shaken. —She was magnificent!"

He leaned back in his chair.

"Well, there you are," he said. "You do look a bit shook up."

"But I have seen all her movies and I admire a lot of them and she
is fascinating on the screen; but nothing like what I saw this morning."

What made the difference? —the difference between Garbo's
appealing presence on the screen and the transporting power that
Garbo, living, speaking, released through the luminous real air forty
feet away from you as you leaned forward to receive the magic of live
theatre?

We got into a discussion of the question, and I said that, for a first
answer, it was the difference between a photograph of a temperament and the impact created by a temperament physically present.
Everyone has felt and responded to the physical presence of a great
man or woman in public or private circumstance before they did or
said anything.

"Personality does communicate," said George, "even without
technique."

I was reminded of some of Rouben Mamoulian's words to me on
the subject of theatre technique. He cited two different approaches.
The first he illustrated by recalling the art of Sarah Bernhardt. She

was so great a mistress of her art that while remaining inwardly quite composed always brought off her great moments by incomparable technical control of voice and gesture to create the imperative of feeling in the audience. He told a story he had heard in Paris while directing a play there. Madame Bernhardt was playing a scene of heartrending emotion. The stage setting had a "fancy door center" (in the jargon of the old-fashioned stock company). In the midst of a searing speech she contrived a silence that left her words lingering in the air while she went to the door and clutched its drapery with a desperate hand. Leaving only her hand in view she went disconsolate out of sight around the opening. There, safely hidden, she commanded a stagehand, in a hoarse whisper, *"Une cigarette, pour l'amour de Dieu, vite, vite!"* It was handed to her, she took deep drags on it, and all the while, said Paris, she wrung the hearts of the audience solely by the tragic eloquence of how she played her visible hand against the fringes and velvet folds of the drapery on the door. Out of sight she exhaled her last draw on the cigarette, and slowly became visible again as though a new resolve made her bravely face life once more, where it seemed to be located at downstage center.

"Technique," said Mr. Mamoulian.

The other technical approach to the emotions of the audience was that of Eleanor Duse, who, he said, ravaged her body and soul on stage by entering into the very feelings that she must portray. Different ways—but the purpose was the same: overwhelming enfoldment of the observer within the illusion of the hour. Duse, though, was willing to risk her very being in attaining the intensity that her dramatic conscience required. In fact, she was known to have fainted on stage during a scene particularly harrowing to her sensibility. The curtain was brought down; an interval ensued; and when she returned to complete the act her reception was tremendous. . . .

Even the simplest moment could catch you by the throat when the actor's art was at its fullest. Long later, in Paris, I saw Edwige Feuillère play *Camille.* To Armand at a certain moment she spoke the word *"Ainsi"*—in context meaning something like, "Ah, must it be that way?" How she said it brought tears to your eyes and with a simple word created a sense of suffering that illuminated the whole play. I am reminded of it as I think of how Greta Garbo uttered the word "Where?" as she left the world of her love with a broken heart.

"Yet how much of technique is temperament, the natural endowment of the artist?" asked George.

Who could answer that with any precision? Much about Garbo was mysterious. We concluded that, unlike Bernhardt and Duse, she was not an intellectual creature. Her beauty, her voice, her *plastique* were as they were. Probably, we said, she was moved mostly by instinct, and when her acting persona was convinced by the situation and the nature of the character she was impersonating, and with the aid of strong but discreet direction, she found the way to moving expression. I added,

"If only she were capable of live theatre, she would command a response on different terms from those of her huge movie audience. However explained, her presence in person would in her own degree and kind make you think of all you had heard about the appeal of such artists as Bernhardt and Duse."

We turned to other matters—in a few moments George would have to return to resume his costume as the Grand Marshal and be ready for shooting the scene.

"I don't think we'd better try to repeat your stowaway performance of this morning," he said.

I agreed. In any case, I had to return to New Mexico that afternoon, taking with me one of the most rewarding moments of theatre that I had ever known, for which I gave him thanks.

vi

One morning many years later, Greta Garbo was taking her morning walk in New York, where she was living in retirement. A quick, heavy rainstorm had swept across Manhattan from river to river, and everything was still dripping as she turned into Sutton Place. A friend observed her there. She wore a soft hat that drooped about her cheeks, a belted raincoat, and large sunglasses; yet she was unmistakably who she was.

She came upon a little group of people who were gazing at something on the ground beneath a little sidewalk tree. It was a bird's nest that had been blown down by the storm. In it were two naked nestlings working their large beaks in hunger. Hopping before them and pecking at the little plot of city earth about the tree was a father bird. Peck, peck—but he found nothing. Greta Garbo paused and joined the onlookers for a moment. Then she said gravely, "He vants a v-o-o-rm," and walked on.

vii

Later still by many years, I saw her once more. I was the guest of Vera Zorina to attend the Comédie Française in their production of *Phèdre,* which they had brought from Paris as part of a gala New York season. The celebrated elderly actress Marie Bell was appearing in the great role. It was to be a heightened event, members of the audience feeling special in evening clothes and jewels, pleased to recognize each other as *le tout New York,* the occasion a crowning event of the year's metropolitan culture.

We had seats in the third row at the center. Before us in the second row were two empty seats. A minute or two before the house lights began to fade, two people hurried down the aisle to the empty seats. They were Greta Garbo and her frequent escort, George Schlee. She recognized Zorina, they exchanged air-kisses, and Zorina introduced me. I bowed like a boy in dancing school, and Garbo with a half-smile said to me in her low woodwind voice, "Halo-o-o," and sat down. She was directly in front of Zorina, so that I could see her half-left profile. Wearing a plain black dress, and older by many years, she still bore a version of her famous beauty. She settled a long-strapped handbag on her lap. The lights went out. The play came on.

Throughout the evening my attention was divided between the classically austere proceedings of the play and my view of Garbo's half-left profile so purely revealed by the light reflected from the stage. As for Marie Bell, I had been wondering whether her Phèdre would carry something of the piercing power, the fainting eloquence, the shuddering doom of guilt, and the unearthly voice that legend had recorded of Sarah Bernhardt's performance of the role.

Appearing in Act I, scene 3, with her "nurse and confidante" Oenone, Madame Bell was a small, rounded, slightly stooped old lady with a dim little face. She was draped, head, arms, body, with veils. Her voice was remote, faintly quacking, yet was mysteriously affective in Racine's stately measures. She was a gifted actress, deserving of the loyalty of her French following, and, mostly, throughout the evening, I was held by her power. But the end she had devised to turn us all to ice with moral horror was ruined for me and others nearby in the audience. It was ruined by an innocent distraction created by Greta Garbo in her second-row seat.

As Madame Bell enters upon her final tirade, confessing the guilty love that is destroying her, she works her way slowly downstage to the footlights, staring out above us at an infinity of sin. She is confessing to her husband the King about her incestuous love for his son, who is also her stepson. She extends her arms toward horrors in her mind, and she gives her lines—surely in what she must have thought an inspired piece of theatre—in a forced whisper meant to stop the heart; and in fact, the audience held its breath to hear every word. Tension was in the air until something had to go "crack!" Throughout the evening I had been attentive to the lovely line of Garbo's left half-profile, but now I attended Madame Bell as she advanced toward us in her great moment—and then I lost her.

I lost her because in the midst of the rising climax on the stage Greta Garbo snapped open her huge handbag and extracted her powder compact. Using its mirror in the reflected stage light, she critically examined her brow, her nose, her cheeks, her teeth, her lips. She powdered her nose and cheekbones and examined the effect from several little angles, lifted her head and felt the underside of her chin, restored the compact to the bag, and snapped the bag shut with a brisk little noise that did no good to the hoarsely whispered lines given out now at the footlights by the toiling old artist only a few feet away.

In a few short moments the play was over. Crouching, the occupants of the two second-row seats center hurried across their neighbors and up the aisle and away before the time for house lights and ovations.

1937

Frieda Lawrence

and the Tomb

IN SANTA FE, where I was spending the summer of 1937 in the rented second floor of Mrs. Shimp's cool stone house along the Acequia Madre, I was summoned to a pilgrimage by D. H. Lawrence's widow, Frieda. She was in residence at the Kiowa Ranch seventeen miles north of Taos.

If, more than a half century later, the energies of the lore and legends of the D. H. Lawrences have subsided to a decent historical calm, in the 1930s they were still at gale force, so that anything that was known in Taos this morning was known sixty miles away in Santa Fe by this evening—and *vice versa;* and by tomorrow was twice as vivid, for after all it was the creative artistic society of both ancient cities that made the world go round. . . .

Everybody knew that in 1924 the Kiowa Ranch had been traded to Frieda by Mabel Dodge Luhan, the rich manageress of emotional and cultural Taos, in exchange for the manuscript of Lawrence's novel *Sons and Lovers.* Some believed it was a far from equal exchange, since the ranch, a rundown set of shacks in forested acreage, might be worth $1,500, while the manuscript was certainly worth many more thousands. No matter—Lawrence and his wife moved to the mountain ranch and worked hard to make the place habitable.

Lawrence had a few happy, productive years there until travels to Mexico and Europe took over. He never came back; but some years after his death in 1930 Frieda returned to the ranch with her new companion, the Italian Captain Angelo Ravagli, who had left a wife and three children in Italy, and together they built anew.

Frieda, telephoning from Taos, said that I was to come to lunch. There would be other people—Aldous and Maria Huxley were staying, and Aldous and I could "do criticisms." After lunch we would all go up the hill "like pilgrims" to see the chapel tomb that Angelo Ravagli had built with his own hands to house the remains of D. H. Lawrence. "It will be all so nice—please say yes." (Frieda's spoken English sometimes had a Germanic cast to it, and she often heartily resorted to American slang, though, as her letters and other writings show, she was both original and correct on the page.) "It has been so long. You will not be disappointed in Angie's chapel."

Lawrence had died at Vence in the South of France and his remains, under his sign of the phoenix, were buried there. When the Kiowa chapel was ready, Angelo went to France to arrange for the cremation of Lawrence's remains and to bring the ashes back to their final resting place on the mountain in New Mexico. Despite their mortuary context, events that followed finally bordered on the comic.

In France, Angelo met bureaucratic troubles over the disinterment of Lawrence and the cremation that would follow, but finally he was granted permission by the authorities in Marseilles to depart the country with Lawrence's ashes; he sailed with them from Ville-franche in the *Conte di Savoia*. When he landed at New York he faced more trouble: the immigration authorities refused to permit the importation of Lawrence's ashes into the United States, citing the notorious charges of immorality against Lawrence made at the time of the publication of *Lady Chatterley's Lover* and the suppressed exhibition of his paintings in London in 1929. After vigorous protests by New York artists, including Alfred Stieglitz, the absurd impasse was resolved, and Angelo resumed his journey westward.

He was met at Lamy, New Mexico, the rail junction point for Santa Fe, by Frieda and a party of supporters, who made great jubilation on the station platform. The welcoming party then set out for Taos by motorcar. After twenty miles on the road they discovered that, in the joyous excitement of the trackside reunion, they had gone off without the funerary urn, which was left on the station platform at Lamy. Appalled, they turned back and raced to the railroad junction; there alone and safe by the tracks was the urn. The homeward journey was resumed. At Taos, Frieda proposed a visit to a friend before finally going on to the ranch. Arriving home she was vexed to find that the urn had been left at the friend's house in Taos. It was retrieved the next day and brought to the Kiowa Ranch at last.

But all horrors were not yet spent, as Taos lore maintained. In due course, a woman from the Taos Pueblo who was in the employ of Mabel Dodge Luhan heard disturbing news that she conveyed to Frieda. She reported that Mabel had concocted a plan with three friends to steal the ashes of Lawrence from his widow before they could be entombed in the chapel. Then in a flourish of victory they would carry them to the great world of nature, with its desert winds, its animal innocence, its mountain crests. There they would scatter his ashes to the great free forces so loved by Lawrence, as if to say, "There, Lawrence, and there, you Frieda, who plays the last trick now?"—for relations between Mabel at Taos and Frieda at Kiowa had long been kept at bitter distance.

For years Mabel, posing as their only "understanding" patroness, had worked every device, emotional and material, to separate Lawrence from Frieda. She had failed in the face of his decency and Frieda's love, which, though often tried by his irrational tempers, enfolded him safely all the way to the end. After the plot was betrayed, all plans for a ceremonial interment—distinguished visitors rendering *hommage à Lawrence,* Indians from the Pueblo paying reverence with their chants and dances—were cancelled. The cement crypt (as they called it) was rapidly prepared, and before Mabel and company could move, and in the presence of a few available loyalists, the ashes of D. H. Lawrence were set in concrete.

Such was the story as I recalled it motoring from Santa Fe to the San Cristobal Mountains for lunch with Frieda.

ii

The rough mountain road ended at the ranch. I parked my car near a picket fence that enclosed the clearing where the ranch was laid out. I saw two cabins, the near one a little larger than the other, both looking unfinished in their raw log-and-cement walls, flat roofs, general shack-like effect. There was a porch on the nearer cabin. In the blinding pour of the sunlight the porch was deeply shadowed; and from the shadow, as soon as I became visible, Frieda Lawrence, crying my name gaily in her frosted voice, came out to greet me. She was large, and made larger by the loose cotton garment that flowed about her. She blinked ready tears of pleasure against sunlight. Like a great child, at age fifty-eight, she showed her responses without measure. I had seen her fill a room with her exuberance; she now did very well with the mountain day.

Came a torrent of welcome, questions about my drive from Santa Fe, mixed with scraps of news, "last night a vonderful storm on the mountain," was my road muddy, we were going to have lunch first and then go up to see the chapel, you couldn't see it from here, it was just there, out of sight, over the crest of that hill, you climb the hill behind the level ground of the ranch, "Angie will be so bleased," come, we'll take a stroll to see everything before, Maria had a liddle headache earlier, it would be O.K. She was resting, Aldous was working, they would come oudt for lunch.

We walked out back. There were a couple of small sheds or outbuildings, a corral with I think two horses, random farm implements, the usual rural clutter. A pine forest loomed behind. A path led to a spring in the forest. Another showed the way to a sharp slope of the hill beyond which the chapel was out of sight. With startling immanence under the white sun, the San Cristobel Mountains showed their crystal-blue heights. Someone heard us coming and came from around the corral.

"Angie!" cried Frieda. "Look who's here!"

It was Captain Angelino Ravagli. He came stalking forward on bandy legs which were well developed by his years of active service with his regiment of the Bersaglieri, who took their marches at a hard trot, weapons at the port arms, cock feathers flying at the hat brims. We had never met, but he welcomed me with waving arms, a brilliant smile on his apple-shaped face. He was high-shouldered and stocky, darkly tanned in his open work shirt. He wore riding breeches and boots. He gazed about at the ranch site and nodding his head with pride indicated that it was one of the finest places in the world, which in its larger scale also deserved commendation. He was immediately likable. Having done his courtesy, he waved Frieda and me on with our stroll and returned to whatever job he was doing beyond the corral.

We turned and wandered back to the cabin. The larger one, to our left, stood under the shade of a tremendous pine tree to which Lawrence had given great devotion. To the right we saw the lesser cabin, where the Huxleys were staying. It consisted of two rooms and some rude plumbing. It stood silent and inscrutable under the noon light. We paused. Frieda put her arms across her heavy bosom in a pose that suggested woman's eternal sense of the tragic and told me in thickened voice, "Every night I take a liddle walk before going to bed, along the path there, past the Huxleys' cabin, where there is nothing showing, no light, no sound except something which tears my heart every time I hear it." It gave mine a turn for the way she spoke.

"What is it?" I asked.

"The typewriter. Aldous has been told he will be blind. In the dark, he practices typewriter so he can go on writing anyway, without seeing, to keep that marvellous intellect at work! So courageous and beautiful! It drifes me nuts to think of it!"

Her vehement sympathy excused her inelegance. In a brief silence we turned back to the big cabin, with its vast view of the desert miles away, and three thousand feet lower, where the Rio Grande gorge looked like a straggled line made by a pen on a bleached map. The view refreshed Frieda. In a letter inviting a friend to Kiowa she had expressed her feeling for the natural life of the place: "You can have a log cabin and you would like Angelino, he is so natural. One lives with the sun and the desert and the cowboys and the Mexicans, my bread is so good, and the vegetables, and the horses have just eaten a lot of corn, and the coyotes one gorgeous moonlit night tore a young sheep to pieces, and a weasel has bitten my two kittens to death. That is also nature sweet, pure and don't let's forget it!"

At the porch that Lawrence had built years ago she said, "Why don't you sit here and breathe the pine trees while I get started on lunch. My kitchen is just inside."

Frieda soon came to see how I was doing in all that mountain hygiene.

"Do you feel the altitude?"

"Perhaps, rather heady."

"*Ja*, I know. Aldous also. He loves it. The thinner and clearer the air the better for him. He has to be in mountains. He suffers from zose allergics, you know, smoke and smog, and he has to escape. Maria is just the other way, she wants always the sea level. Myself I am greedy, I love it all!"

iii

Frieda and I had met several times during her visits to Santa Fe, mostly at Witter Bynner's house. It was there that I first met the Huxleys when Hal Bynner gave them a welcoming cocktail party on their arrival in New Mexico. It was a crowded party, and conversation was difficult, but that did not matter, as everybody talked anyway without listening. Santa Fe delighted in celebrities, local or itinerant, and Aldous Huxley was an exciting visitor. Because of his great height—six feet four inches—he was almost a head taller than anybody else, and as he spoke in his soft and precisely articulated words, people watched rather than heard him. I was introduced to him and received a gravely polite recognition. In one corner of the room, almost alone, Maria Huxley was watching her husband as though hoping for rescue. I approached her; the one or two other guests who had been standing silently with her took themselves nimbly away.

She was very small and trim, smartly turned out in city clothes and accessories that looked deliberately alien amid the general Santa Fe style of mixed Pueblo Indian *cum* cowboy *cum* gentleman rancher or horse breeder *cum* all-but-unbuttoned poet or painter. Her face was a delicate triangle, wide at the cheeks and pointed at the chin. Set in critical inquiry were her great blue eyes. There was an impression of charm controlled by intelligence. The kitten effect was faintly heightened with a smile as I introduced myself. I referred to the party and shrugged as if to share what must be her view of it. She said something like,

"Not at all, poor dears, they are having a divine time."

I knew that she was of Belgian origin, that she had studied violin to the point of excellence, that she had been a governess in England, in which phase she and Aldous had fallen in love and married. I felt it a privilege—more, it was interesting—to meet them both, and my regard for his work was high.

In every generation there were a handful of writers each of whose every book as it appeared one acquired and read as a matter of course. People of my generation can remember how Aldous Huxley came to notice early with precocious poems written during his Oxford period. These were skeptical and ironic almost to the point of despair, but presented in a literary elegance that owed much to his admiration of the French poets of the later nineteenth century. They dealt with the sublimities of human aspiration, and also with the indignity of the animal nature of mankind, and their irony bore down heavily on the inexorable mingling of the two. When we saw his gangling young men reduced to self-torture in situations of hilarious inadequacy before the lusts of the flesh and the values of the prevailing society, we had a sense that we were watching the author himself writing his way through painful processes of discovery. He wrote in a mandarin English which rose far above the commonplace idiom of most mid-twentieth-century fiction; nobody else sounded a similar note that suggested at once enormous erudition, a delight in precision, a sense of the ridiculous, and a love of humanity troubled by an awareness of its barbarities. His essays more explicitly gave play to his fertile mind. His later poetry was destined to become old-fashioned, yet it contained a large rapture which more than elsewhere in his work permitted a glimpse of the deep emotional nature which his rationality of mind—an illustration of the tribal faith bestowed by the grandfather Thomas Henry Huxley—for the most part concealed. Those who knew him bore him love and respect. I loved and admired him through his work: he fought against cruelty, war as a social instrument, vulgarity as an ingredient of success, and he never lost sight of man's greatness even as he flayed the saving pretensions off man's failures.

Small talk was not working with Maria Huxley. I felt I should somehow say how much I admired her husband, and finally said so. I added that to my taste the writers of most consequence in the contemporary literature of Europe were Thomas Mann and Aldous Huxley.

"Why bring in Mann?" she asked flatly.

As I could think of no ready way to answer this, it was lucky for me that two painters, one beaded, the other bearded, came to pay attention to Maria Huxley. I excused myself. Frieda was at the party, and I joined the little coterie that attended her. She loved to recite common events of her day as though they were hilariously disastrous, and she was rewarded with laughter by those who listened and were delighted to be present at the creation of yet more Frieda legends, which of course would be flashed to Taos with the speed of light and be swiftly reflected back to Santa Fe as improved gossip. Between Santa Fe and Taos there was a sense of rival constituencies, and sensitive persons tended to be loyal to the powers, virtues, and dangers of one place or the other. Santa Fe was more worldly, more sophisticated. Taos believed itself to be animated by an energy of place that was actually occult. So it came to be that the atmospheric culture of Santa Fe and Taos could be likened to a cloud bank full of lightning strikes of gossip in constant discharge.

In the time I write about there was no energy of voltage greater than that generated by the direct acts of the Lawrences and Mabel Dodge Luhan and their respective loyalists. After only a few days at the Kiowa Ranch Maria Huxley could write to a friend in England that "Taos . . . is a nest of scandals and quarrels . . ." Many of these involved Mabel. Everyone referred to her as Mabel— "*May*-bel" — often with comic accent, mindful of her ceaseless bother about the lives of others. It was at one's peril, though, if anyone within range of Mabel's influence failed to recognize its malignity. She was sometimes referred to as the Morgan le Fay of Taos. By letter, she worked her aura at the Lawrences during their time in Australia to persuade them to come to her at Taos; and when they came, she tried to possess and to separate them, husband from wife. What defeated her were Lawrence's irritability at being possessed by anyone or anything, and the Valkyrian barrier of Frieda's long-suffering respect and love for him.

Long before he died, Lawrence detested Mabel. "It's terrible, the will to power of this kind of woman," he exclaimed to Frieda's younger daughter, Barbara, after reading Mabel's autobiography, *Movers and Shakers,* in manuscript. "She destroys everything, herself included, with her really frightful kind of will." Barbara added, "The manuscript seemed to fascinate him with horror." (After the publication of *Movers and Shakers,* with its scurrilous passages about many famous persons, many of them literary, someone asked Joseph Hergesheimer whether he was treated in its pages. "No, thank God," he said, "I neither moved her nor shook her.")

Like many people capable of damaging interference in the lives of others, Mabel had a sentimental streak about as sticky as that in a greeting card. During her early possession of Frieda's mountain place she had named it the "Flying Heart Ranch," and if she were to devise a brand for it, it would have had to be a heart with Cupid's wings attached. Similarly, her critical acumen inclined toward the spongy. After a quarrel with Thomas Wolfe in Taos during which in drunken eloquence he demolished her pretensions, she wrote him a letter—he showed it to me the next day at lunch in Santa Fe—in which she pleaded with him to be "as nice as your books . . ." She could not have missed his rhetorical character more entirely. Mabel the sentimentalist considered herself the bringer of light and life, but even her benefactions were self-serving. It was Frieda who was the life-giver through her open nature, her candor, and the outsized gesture of her simple being.

Seeing her at the ranch that day and during evenings at Witter Bynner's house in Santa Fe, I formed a private portrait of her. There was much about her to invite caricature. She seemed larger and more shapeless than she was, enveloped in a loose dress that was like a sculptor's sheet thrown over unfinished clay; and yet her body was so frankly itself that it could stir erotic wonderings. Her head and face were leonine, topped by pale hair, blond-gray, loosely piled as if ready to fall down. Her skin was ruddy over high cheekbones that accented the little caves enclosing her blue eyes. Like a cat's, her eyes were the chief organs of mood in her strongly modeled face. They stared fixedly at anything unknown until she had an opinion; then they could beam with light, or flood with tears of amusement. In anger, her eyelids would contract like little irises, showing only a pinpoint of turquoise blue. Yet overall her eyes deeply held a wounded aspect that was part of all that they might express, and now and then you had a pang of fellow feeling, as for an artless child who did not yet know how to dissemble.

She spoke in a bronchially clouded voice, in general loudly, at times explosively, with no thought for who might be listening over the shoulder. At the ends of her hefty arms her plump hands were either delicately expressive, making miniatures of any objects she handled, or lusty, as when she would slap her rolling thigh in high humor. She spoke rapidly, racily, often with high originality. Everything about her proclaimed abundant vitality, goodwill, and indifference to convention as befitted a daughter liberated from the social constraints of the minor German aristocracy; in her case, the family von Richtofen.

iv

"Come in and see my house," she called to me from the kitchen.

The kitchen, added to the cabin during Lawrence's time, had a pitched roof. Within, its walls showed unplastered logs. Five upright ranks of shelves held tin plates, crockery, and china. A wood-burning stove with a metal smoke pipe had a large oven where Frieda roasted her chickens and "baked twenty loaves of bread" at one time. Simple wooden chairs and table stood free. The living room opened off the kitchen. Its walls were plastered white. A small arched fireplace opened below a wide mantel along which knickknacks were scattered. Both rooms, and the bedroom beyond, in their rude materials and spare furnishings, suggested Spartan living; yet by some artistry for amenity they also spoke of comfort and contentment or, to relapse into the inevitable word in Frieda's context, *Gemütlichkeit.*

Within a few minutes the household assembled for lunch. Aldous and Maria greeted me gently; Maria went to help Frieda prepare food at her kitchen counter; and Aldous, seeing a book that lay on a table, took it up and moved to a window. There he stood with his back to the light and raised the book to within six inches of his face. Turning his head so that the better of his eyes faced the page, he read by moving the book back and forth line by line, a troubling promise of what must come. In another moment, to the intensely local sound of the rancher stamping the barnyard off his boots, Captain Ravagli joined us. He went to Frieda and threw his arms around her. At one and the same time she shrugged him away and inclined her cheek toward him.

Everyone had things to say, the food was plain and delicious, good feeling played over us, and I ought to remember brilliant passages of talk; but I don't. One thing is certain—there was no occasion for Aldous and me to "do criticisms," whatever Frieda meant by this. I quote what Maria had written to someone years before when they had all met in Italy: "Frieda is silly. She is like a child, but Lawrence likes her *because* she is a child," and Maria conceded that the relation between Frieda and Lawrence was "a great passion." Feeling was no less real between Frieda and Angelino, if not quite the same. In his uncomplicated virility he was her man and she welcomed his protection and responded to it tenderly. Aldous saw them clearly. Writing to his brother Julian from the ranch, he said, "The Capitano turns out to be a very decent sort of middle-class Italian—rather naif, at the same time intelligent and active. As far as one can judge he doesn't exploit Frieda: on the contrary, manages her affairs very efficiently."

But in the same letter Aldous shared his misgivings about the desert and mountain land of northern New Mexico. "The sky is full of enormous dramas of cloud and sunshine—with periodical thunderstorms of incredible violence. Boiling hot sunshine alternates with cold shade and icy nights. There are whirlwinds of dust in the desert below us and, after rain, the roads are impassable . . . The country is most astonishing and beautiful—but I don't know if one could stand it very long. I've never been in any place, except parts of Mexico, which gave such an impression of being alien, even hostile, to man. Humans crawl about in this savage, empty vastness like irrelevant ticks—just not counting . . ."

Perhaps their restrained views of the location of the ranch made the guests at luncheon less convivial than they might have been. Perhaps that is why the conversation yielded up nothing memorable. All was fond and friendly. In her turn Maria had written that "there was quietness and peace, and above all . . . there was Frieda whom we have always been very fond of and we liked her Italian friend the captain. So we stayed." They stayed three months.

Aldous began and finished a book—*Ends and Means*—that summer at the ranch, and Maria learned how to make bread in the wood-burning stove.

While the rest of us chattered Aldous had long moments of silence, when his whole figure seemed wilted and his thought far away and unreachable in exhaustion. And yet, if he came to speak, a wonderful change came upon him; he straightened up, his eyes took on light, his fine features glowed with interest, and you had a strong sense of the remarkable instrument of his mind. Much ironic humor underlay what he said. He marked his words with a sometimes comic fastidiousness—I remember that he pronounced the word "pseudo" in two syllables, sounding the *p* and framing the first two letters apart with his precisely chiselled lips. Maria—I knew by now that this was her manner, not her means of opinion—seemed rather remote. Angelo with scooping gestures of his bare forearms gave himself to the conversation. At the end of her table, Frieda presided so happily that her eyes showed again with watery light.

v

I always enjoyed telling over to myself one or another episode of her legend. When through the years I would be with her, most often at Bynner's, she always had tales to tell, and otherwise the local air yielded up plenty of news of her and her world. Hal Bynner had travelled with the Lawrences in Mexico, and his marvellous account *Journey with Genius* is filled with scenes both hilarious and frightening for the tantrums that Lawrence induced of which Frieda was most often the victim. Hal was a brilliant mimic, and his shrieking enactments of Lawrence in full fury, usually over trifles, reduced any company to helpless laughter. For example, Frieda was accustomed to an occasional unremarked cigarette until one evening in a public place Lawrence suddenly broke the convivial air with a steely-eyed glare and a choked scream, "Frieda, put it out!" She stared at him and calmly said, "Certainly not." He danced in his chair with rage and with fiery expletives ordered her again to dinch out her cigarette. "Lawrence, you fool! I have always smoked and I smoke now." More exchanges, rising in decibels and foulness of words until she was reduced to tears and Lawrence was coughing in exhaustion.

It was a scene repeated again and again under various pretexts, until it was tempting to see the Lawrences' behavior primarily as a web of absurdities. But equally true were the love they had for each other and their lack of pretense in public or private. Neither of them modified behavior to suit occasion. He would let go with hysterical scenes and she would give voice to her first response, however unconventional. What emerged was raw character—in Frieda's case, benign nature.

Hal and Frieda loved each other, and when he "did" his Lawrence scenes she survived lovably, as she always did in stories about her cherished and fondly told by others. It was the sheer outsize of her personality and person that called attention to her every aspect.

Another witness who had a good eye and ear for Frieda's effect was Santa Fe's Miranda Masocco (now Mrs. Ralph Levy). This witty and observant friend recently reminded me of details of an episode that demonstrated Frieda's happy indifference to her surroundings. The scene was the music tent at Aspen during one of the summer concerts. Miranda accompanied Frieda to a chamber-music program that featured the sonata for flute and piano by Norman Dello Joio, featuring Albert Tipton, who was the first flutist of the Cincinnati Symphony Orchestra, with the composer at the piano. It was a brilliant event. Both artists were prominent figures during the distinguished summer music season at Aspen, and Albert Tipton, probably to his embarrassment, was everywhere noticed because of his extraordinary good looks.

As Frieda and Miranda arrived, their passage down the aisle gave many in the audience a chance to marvel at Frieda's costume.

"She always wore versions of the same thing," said Miranda. On her loosely coiled hair Frieda wore a purple yarmulke. Over a volu-

minous Mexican blouse of white cotton embroidered in bright colors
she wore dyed vegetable beads and an Indian silver belt. Her muslin
skirt was magenta pink, of the kind worn by Navajo women. In a full
bell-shape, it had a thousand pleats, which the Indians created by
tightly wrapping the skirt when wet around a broomstick and letting
it dry. Unwound, the pleats were fixed in place, and when the wearer
strode along she gave a fine flare to the skirt. On her feet she wore
always a pair of satin ballet slippers. In the cool air of Aspen she
threw over her shoulders a great black Spanish shawl weighted with
long scarlet fringe and blazing with embroidered flowers an inch
thick. All this was in wild contrast to Miranda's chic—her burnished-
bronze bangs, plain black blouse, and beautifully cut slacks, and her
wide Inca cuffs of pure beaten gold.

The tent-auditorium was already settled into proper silence; the
flutist and pianist were exchanging nods of readiness but decided to
wait until the latecomers settled themselves upon their rattling
wooden benches down front.

As quiet descended again Frieda had her first look at the artists—
at Albert Tipton in particular. The piano was about to sound. The
flutist was raising his platinum instrument to his lips, when Frieda,
narrowing her eyes at him, exclaimed in her robust wheeze, which
carried well in the perfect acoustic of the music tent designed by Eero
Saarinen,

"My! Isn't he handsome!"

A few in the audience couldn't help laughing, and one or two
people applauded. The artists had to lower their hands from ivory
and metal keys and wait for silence. They were again poised for the
music when Frieda, extending her interest, declared,

"He is like Tarzan! He should be wearing a leopard skin!"

Another collapse of decorum on stage and in the audience. More
people caught on to who was making such merry commotion and a
buzz of voices rose with her name for a moment. But silence again
succeeded, and the sonata was about to be launched when, in the
classic three-time convention of the folk tale, Frieda cried,

"It is not fair, zat he should be so handsome, and bplay the flute
also!"

At this everybody had to laugh, including the afflicted artists. But, as it must, silence held, and the music finally made its entry and prevailed. Miranda told the anecdote with humor yet with affection, as people did when speaking of Frieda. It was not always so when they raided the copious anecdotage of Mabel and Lawrence.

Frieda, as I heard her tell it, delighted in making ridiculous the time when Mabel on a visit to Buffalo was quizzed by her mother, old Mrs. Ganson, who was at her desk working on monthly bills. She came on one that she held up.

"Mabel? What's this?"

"It's a bill from my doctor," replied Mabel.

"Why, it's for ten thousand dollars! Is it correct? Who is this man A. A. Brill?"

"He's my psychoanalyst in New York."

"And you want me to pay it?"

"Of course."

With a sharp sigh of exasperation, to which Frieda gave full value, Mrs. Ganson said bitterly,

"Well, I'll pay it, but so far as I can see, you have not lost a single pound!"

As Santa Fe heard it, however, it was Mabel who settled the account of ten thousand dollars with Dr. Brill by giving him the manuscript of *Sons and Lovers,* which at the time was appraised at that amount.

I met Mabel only once, in the most brief of encounters. One day the clerk in the Villagra Bookshop at Santa Fe introduced me to her. She was shorter than I expected, and thicker, and her eyes were shadowed by her black Pueblo Indian bangs. Never taking her probing glare off me, she asked the clerk whether Mr. So-and-so had come in yet—"he was to meet me here." The clerk replied, "Oh, yes, he left here five minutes ago." Mabel, not changing her fixed gaze, said in a grimly earnest voice, "Well, I hope he falls down and breaks his arm," as if she really meant it. I flinched away from her eyes and the spell she had cast upon the unlucky man, and made my escape.

I never met D. H. Lawrence and was sorry for that, as so many busy reports about him were in the air; but I was absent from New Mexico while he was at the Kiowa Ranch with Frieda. When they left for a journey to Europe they were hoping to return; it was not to be, for he fell ill and died in France, and Frieda eventually returned with Angelino instead. But later I encountered the demonic side of Lawrence's energy in the form of his paintings, which were exhibited at the La Fonda Hotel on the Plaza in Taos. Admission was one dollar. Many tourists were glad to pay it for the lubricious delights to be seen in the exhibit.

In his final years abroad Lawrence took up painting in oil and watercolor. In due course there were enough pictures for a one-man show, and in June 1929 an exhibition opened at the Dorothy Warren Gallery in London, with Frieda in attendance. Gorgeously turned out in a gown of her own design, she carried a sheaf of lilies. There was a message in this—the lilies were meant to demonstrate purity, even the purity of the paintings, which presented nothing but totally nude male and female figures. Thirteen thousand people came to the show, and so did the police, for public outcry arose in much the same terms as that which not long before had greeted *Lady Chatterley's Lover.* "Arrogant obscenity" was the general verdict.

But lilies or no lilies, and despite Lawrence's obsessed philosophy of the phallus as the source of man's very nature and splendor, his paintings, like so much of his writing, had the same thrusting sexuality that reflected not so much a rationalization of healing innocence as a morbid fixation upon the subject. The nudity in his pictures was aggressive: great thighs were thrown at you; arms and ham-like buttocks and swollen melon-like breasts bumped into each other in the random compositions. Phalluses and mats of pubic hair were defiantly visible. If the subjects were literary, historical, or allegorical, their treatment was loutish and technically absurd.

In any aspect of drawing, design, and the handling of paint, the pictures revealed the worst kinds of amateurish incompetence. Worst of all was the prevailing color in Lawrence's palette. For his flesh tone he settled upon a chalky and sickly pink, much like the color of a popular digestive remedy. From figure to figure it varied hardly at all; in fact, the same pink was flushed through many of the backgrounds, as though these pictorial celebrations of the erotic had been brushed with Pepto-Bismol. In startling contrast were the rude patches of pubic hair painted in dead black. Actually, it was this detail of the female anatomy more than any other that had outraged guardians of decency in London. Three weeks after the exhibition opened, the police raided the gallery and took away thirteen of the paintings. Quite properly, outcries against censorship were heard, and Frieda and others moved to recover the missing pictures. They were returned undamaged, but with the provision that they and the rest of the show never be exhibited again in England.

Eventually they came to America with Frieda and years later ended up in the Taos hotel as an attraction with a racy reputation that pulled in many tourists. One who came to see them there was Rebecca West, who was on a visit to Taos. The cognoscenti of Taos were breathless for her opinion after her visit to the gallery at La Fonda. They had to be satisfied with Dame Rebecca's laconic response. "What pink friends he had," she said.

Santa Fe heard this masterpiece of evasive indifference to titillation and scandal—probably nowhere more gleefully than in the house of Witter Bynner in College Street. Bynner was admittedly the presiding genius of Santa Fe's cultural life. In his early youth he had embarked on a career as a lecturer to cultural clubs and associations then burgeoning across the nation. His first engagement was in Pittsburgh. He was paralyzed with stage fright during the introduction given by a provincial litterateur who salted his remarks with knowing references to the leading literary figures at the turn of the century in the United States. His crowning gem was his reference to Witter Bynner as "William Winter," a famous critic of the day. The error was enough to resolve Bynner's stage fright with a stroke of inspiration: as he rose to speak, Witter Bynner said with gallant modesty, "Ladies and gentlemen, I greatly fear that I must be the Witter of your discontent . . ."

Years later, as he came to Santa Fe to give his lecture, he was suffering from a heavy cold which in the next day turned into influenza with its attendant risk of pneumonia in the high altitude of seven thousand feet. He was obliged to enter St. Vincent's Hospital. By the time he was done with a week's convalescence in the ancient mountain capital he knew that there he would live out his life. He bought a small adobe house which he enlarged from time to time; there, a tall, energetic, witty, and generous poet, he entertained constantly for visiting writers, artists, and other persons of consequence, assisted by his companion Robert Hunt, an architect and poet who only sparingly used his talents. On many an evening after dinner when a few guests were gathered, Bynner presided over readings by local writers, himself included. He read magnificently in a rich, dark voice. Others had their turns.

Frieda was sometimes present on such evenings. I recall one in particular when I was there also. Hal Bynner had a special treat for us that evening. He had found, I don't know where, a volume of poems so ambitious in their vision and so misbegotten in their arch sentimentality and limping technique that on this evening he must give us a hilarious reading from the text. It was a book called *City and Country's Joy, Grief and Romance*. It was published in 1929 by the International Press—clearly a vanity house. The author was Jessie Adeline Phelps. A frontispiece showed her face in profile emerging from a crescent moon. From a contents of over 185 pages, Hal had chosen a poem twenty pages long called *Magnificent Mansion of Love*.

After lamenting in a prose prologue how hard life is with "heart bleeding from useless love-dart wounds," the poetess embarks on six hundred lines descriptive of her dreamed-of love house. Her cumulative effect is like the fumes of cheap perfume. Her experience of the beautiful is limited—you think of the greeting-card culture and the crudest St. Valentine conventions; and yet her vitality is so remarkable—she says that she gave two hours each to her daily sessions as she worked on her epic—that her catalogue of architecture, furnishings, ornaments, landscaping, accessories, sound effects, and all, along with her marvellous confidence in her taste, casts a spell.

> . . . it seems that thousand kewpies
> Govern ev'rything that's there.
> Ent'ring through great front doorway
> See the fountain there named *bliss*
> By bronze man and woman featured
> Partaking of first soul-kiss.

Hal recited the verses, going from climax to climax of innocent crimes against sense, prosody, and use of time, leading us all in applause and laughter. But it was when, nearing the end, he gave voice to a certain line that he brought relief to our aching responses. Jessie Adeline Phelps listed

> Lawn tennis and fine golf grounds,
> Horses and saddles for hunters,
> And some educated hounds . . .

At which Frieda exploded. "Educated hounds!" she gasped. *"It is too vonderful!"* And she laughed so hard that we laughed now at her instead of at our poetess.

vi

In 1937 when I went on my pilgrimage to see Lawrence's entombment chapel at the Kiowa Ranch above Taos, I took along a copy of the Rydal edition of Frieda's fascinating autobiography, *Not I but the Wind.* I was going to ask her to autograph it for me. Lunch was over at half past two. Knowing what was still to come, but not how long we might be about it, I thought it wise to fetch the book from my car and ask her to sign it now. She took my pen and put my name and hers, and then she gave me a wicked gleam and wrote, "From one educated hound to another." The others wondered why she and I had a fit of laughing; she let them.

And then, "So now, everybody!" she cried, "to the chapel! Angie, take them up the hill."

"Won't you come?" he asked

"No—" It was so steep, she would go quite out of breath, no, she would wait for us to return and tell.

We took to the path behind the house and began the ascent. It was a steep hill, and from where we toiled until perhaps a third of the way up we could see nothing on top; but as we progressed, and paused to breathe and to look up, we could see by stages the front of the chapel come into view; first a pitched roof at the apex of which stood a sculpture of a phoenix, Lawrence's signum of resurrection out of fire; then under the roof overhang a small round window; then the white plaster walls of the front, and its long wooden door, and finally a cement doorstep. I was walking with Angelino, the creator of the whole structure. He turned to me, rolling up his shirt sleeve and making a great biceps for me, and said in simple pride, "I build! I build! Up da hill, and up da hill, I bring sixty *sacco cemento,* and I build *la capella!*"

And there it stood on a little grassy plateau. Behind it was another hill thick with pine forest that rose to the dense blue sky broken by vast sunlit cumulus clouds. The setting was superb. Angelino went to the door to undo its dime-store padlock. I had no desire to be irreverent but my first thought was profane: the chapel looked like a one-car garage. I stood aside with Angelino to let Aldous and Maria enter first. When in my turn I entered, the likeness held until I examined the decor.

Under the pitched beams and wooden roofing long pine boughs had been twined to make a Gothic ceiling. Their needles were dried to a dusty bronze color, and most had fallen to the floor. Into the far wall another small round window was set and on it was painted a symbolic likeness of the sun with rays. A wrought-iron vigil lantern, unlighted, hung before it. Below this, against the wall, was the tomb.

Angelino had made the tomb itself with more of his *cemento.* It stood, a solid block perhaps three feet high and four feet wide. The effect was that of an altar. In its frontal panel were painted the initials DHL; painted green boughs supported them. On the upward surface were Indian bowls filled with seeds. To either side were tall candelabra holding each a single tall candle. Recessed in the wall above the tomb was a niche with a rounded top. Within it reposed a fox carved from redwood. The wood shone again with high polish. The fox's head was turned back over its shoulder. A large knot in the redwood, having defied the sculptor's chisel, deformed the fox's throat as if with an exophthalmic goiter. We later heard that the fox was a commemorative gift from a devoted reader of Lawrence's works in Denver.

There was little more to see. Out of respect, we paused for a while. Speaking for myself, and supposing that the Huxleys might be thinking along the same notion, I couldn't help feeling a qualm of guilt at admitting the gap in quality between the exalted and loving intention of the place and the finished fulfillment: guilt, because, though you had respect for the former, you saw the terms of the latter as inept, and, in certain details, even funny. My profane thought went even further—the chapel on the mountain and the *Magnificent Mansion* of Jessie Adeline Phelps both referred to, if they could not express, profound human responses to the sublime . . .

At last we turned to go. Angelino indicated a slanting wooden shelf near the door on which was an open ledger-like book, with spaces for name, address, date, and Comments. He waved us toward it. Aldous Huxley shrank back, murmuring that he and Maria had already made their entry in the book some time before on an earlier visit to the chapel. It was my turn, and I wrote my name, address, and date, thinking of nothing respectful enough to put in the last column. Angelino reproachfully put his thick forefinger on the Comments space. I clicked my teeth at my own forgetfulness, and wrote, "Wonderful," and he nodded solemnly. He then set my attention on a framed document that hung above the guest book. It was an important part of his responsibility in the whole memorial affair. The document stated in official French that permission was granted to Captain Angelo Ravagli to remove the ashes of the deceased M. David Herbert Lawrence from the port of Marseilles on embarking by ship for the port of New York, signed (with a flourish) by none other than the *Directeur des Pompes Funèbres de la Port de Marseille*.

Descending the hill we were soon in cool shadow, for high mountain cleavages lose the sun early. The descent with its sharp incline took all our attention and we said nothing. It was time for me to start back to Santa Fe.

Frieda, lounging in the rough wooden chair that Lawrence had built, received us gaily.

"So, what do you think now that you've been there?" she asked. "Maria?"

"—Again," murmured Maria, but she added a sound like "M-n-n" that could only mean that words were not enough. (But in a letter published long after, she had already written that Angelo's chapel was "childish.")

Frieda nodded comfortably at this, and said, "Aldous?"

He bent down and then straightened up, and looking far into the famous view of the distant desert, he said, in a masterly straddle of truth and perjury:

"Yes, it has the most extra*or*dinary feeling!" and his voice rose to falsetto in the great Oxbridge manner, and fell back.

"*Ja!*" exclaimed Frieda with joy, and turned to me expectantly. I could only quote the guest book: "Wonderful!" I said, then went to her and took her hands and kissed her cheek, saying I must be off. As I turned to say goodbye to the Huxleys and Angelino, Frieda found her word for the chapel. She beamed upon us all until her turquoise-blue eyes were all but irised out, and in a wheeze of *Gemütlichkeit,* she said of the chapel tomb up over the hill,

"*Ja,* I think Lawrence would have loved it—it's so *homey* . . ."

1940

Luncheon for

Somerset Maugham

i

IN THE EARLY SUMMERTIME of 1941, on vacation from my school job in New Mexico, I came to New York to recharge my cultural batteries. On my arrival I began to make a number of appointments by telephone, to make the best use of my limited time. Among the first I called was Daniel Longwell, the editor of *Life* magazine. I had met him through Peter Hurd, whose paintings of the Southwest he featured in the magazine, and I now hoped to see Dan and Mary Longwell on my own account. He was one of the most dynamic, knowledgeable, and engaging men I ever knew, and Mary his wife, who was a staff editor at *Time*, complemented his brilliant energy with her quieter but no less appealing style.

"Just arrived?" he said in his staccato manner. "Lucky you called, delighted, have you come to lunch today, Somerset Maugham coming, other interesting people, love to have you, Mary will be pleased."

"Yes, thank you, yes," I said.

"Good. Look for you. One-thirty, River Club. Great. Come a little early. Talk. See you."

Such instant hospitality was like him. He knew that meeting Maugham would interest me as a younger writer. Moreover, I enjoyed thinking how I would return home with a report of this meeting for a neighbor of mine across the park who was an intrepid lion huntress. She collected shamelessly. One of her assaults was directed at Maugham, to whom she wrote asking for his autograph. There was no reply. She wrote again, and again, referring each time to her earlier requests. At last came this: "Dear Madam, oh, very well, here it is, W. Somerset Maugham." The weary tartness of this accorded well with the likeness I had formed of him from other anecdotes and countless passages in his plays, stories, novels, and essays. *Of Human Bondage* I had first seen at the age of twelve among books that my parents were reading. I did not read it until much later as a school-boy, but then I came to know Philip Carey well, with his self-shaming limp, his rancid passion for Mildred, the lowborn waitress, and his fatalism, which was shocking to my Catholic confidence. I followed his books quite regularly. It was possible to enjoy equally those that were of literary merit and those that went evenly along as magazine entertainment. By 1941 he was, of course, a world figure and surely one of the richest living authors. He had lately been in the news because of the story of his hair-raising escape from his villa at Cap Ferrat just before the Nazi invasion overwhelmed France in 1940.

Some weeks before my New York vacation I had read in the *Saturday Evening Post* Maugham's four-part serial account of the sacri-fices, privations, endurances, and danger of his dash for freedom before the Nazi horde and the spineless collapse of the French government. It was a grim story, told evenly, yet spiced with anec-dote and lighted by a power of will and courage that seemed surpris-ing in one so famous for his fastidiousness, esoteric taste, and syba-ritic style. The conditions he had to meet and survive were all too true of what happened to civilized life in the conquering drive of the German barbarians. Supplies were suddenly scarce—Maugham had to shop as a hoarder. His house was insecure—he had to take refuge on the old fishing boat that served as his yacht and sail up obscure estuaries in hiding. But soon enough it was clear that he must leave France. He must find passage to England. This was arranged on a coaling ship that would sail from Cannes to Liverpool by way of Portugal and Algiers—a fraught journey of more than two weeks in waters infested by enemy submarines. It would be interesting now to meet not only Maugham the celebrated writer but also Maugham the survivor, who could be the emblem of what the Hitler war could portend for us in the United States if we should be drawn into it.

There were those among us who would loudly choose the appeaser's peace in order to stay out of the war; there were others, no less eloquent, who thought our best chance of avoiding the conflict would come through our giving aid to Britain, which could then serve as our shield. I was a strong interventionist. Through the prospect of meeting Mr. Maugham, the war suddenly seemed personal. I hoped he would tell us all about it. I wondered how it was that Daniel Longwell knew Mr. Maugham and whether (here I was reminded of Mr. Maugham's occasionally rebellious way with pronouns) he was inviting him to write war articles for *Life*, which he could do so effectively, and if so, whether he had already asked him, or was about to ask him today, once an excellent luncheon had put him in a grateful mood so that he could not but accept his invitation.

ii

I came "a little early" to the River Club on East Fifty-second Street, where I was shown into a large, airy, paneled room closely overlooking the East River. Dan Longwell came forward—seemed to spring forward in his hearty energy—to welcome me with a few staccato words. I had heard that the top executives of Time Inc. all spoke in somewhat the same manner, loyally echoing the speech of Henry Luce, the founder and presiding genius of the firm. In contrast, Mary Longwell, soft-voiced in a horn-like tone, gravely gentle in manner, spoke from a fine mind in repose. Dan now led me to meet four other guests who also had come a little early.

They were William Allen White and his wife, from Emporia, Kansas; their daughter-in-law, Mrs. William L. White, whose husband was overseas as a correspondent; and Dr. Foster Kennedy, a British psychiatrist. We all made our manners at each other and settled in for light conversation. Reflections off the river wavered across the high ceiling of the handsome room. The long windows were open. River airs stirred the curtains. Occasional shipping on the river—tugs and barges, pleasure boats, an oil tanker—animated the candid summer day.

Mr. White seemed to have an equally candid air. He was a rotund gentleman, pink-faced, white-haired, who beamed with an open countenance upon the world. I think I remember blue eyes and an alert smile. I had never seen him before, but his fame as editor of the Emporia *Gazette* was national, and his championship of Great Britain's heroic stand against Hitler drew millions of supporters. He was easily loquacious in his high prairie voice, with its underlie of good humor and wit. His wife was a comfortable mid-American lady who could smile inwardly over her husband's great, self-earned position as a leading voice of national opinion. With Dr. Kennedy they exchanged views of Britain's acts of survival under Nazi bombs. Dr. Kennedy was elegance in person—tailoring, trimness of figure, leanness of face under flat, shining hair. His idlest remark was framed with precision.

I thanked Dan for his invitation and noted my interest in Mr. Maugham. How long had he known him?

"Years ago I was his editor for a while at Doubleday's. I've only seen him once or twice before—remote, you know. Mixed feelings. But interesting. Escaped France ahead of the Nazis. Now here in the U.S."

"Yes, I know."

"What are you writing?"

Before I could answer, Dan's small-eyed glance across my shoulder was a signal. He saw his last guest halted in the doorway, and he went rapidly forward to greet him. Dan suddenly was a courtier, unbending slightly, showing a deference that the editor of *Life* was more accustomed to receive than to give. He shook hands with Mr. Maugham and brought him into the company. Making the introductions, Dan seemed a trifle off his form. I thought I understood why. The presence of W. Somerset Maugham was, amazingly, powerful for so small a man. He was narrow-shouldered, carrying one shoulder higher than the other, slim, almost apologetic in bearing as though to state shyness. He was quietly tailored in a close-fitting double-breasted dark suit. His necktie was subdued. He held his hands against his waist. His face was pale, with deep wrinkles coursing down beside his wide mouth, which was permanently turned down. His eyes were startling—large black pupils unwavering under pouched lids, upper and lower. His fixed gaze seemed to enter, diagnose, and judge person or object, all without emotion. If his manner was diffident, still, his effect was subduing. Weariness underlay a polite air. If he smiled, he dropped his lower lip slightly, revealing small teeth distinctly separated. His thin, dark hair was brushed straight flat back above his high white forehead and seemed to draw his dark eyebrows up in angles of discomfort, as though from a chronic headache. To meet Dan's introductions, he came forward with short, fastidious steps. I had expected him to limp, but then remembered that where Philip Carey limped, Maugham stuttered.

". . . Mr. and Mrs. William Allen White. Mr. White is chairman of our Committee to Defend America by Aiding the Allies—editor of the nationally esteemed Emporia *Gazette* . . ."

Mr. Maugham had a brief, silent struggle with this information, which was plainly new to him, but he recovered to imitate courteous awareness and approval. "Mm: y-yes, of c-course," he said. He did not shake hands, but only pressed fingertips.

". . . Mrs. William *L.* White, daughter-in-law. . . ."

A brief body inclination.

"Dr. Foster Kennedy, your countryman, I believe."

Dr. Kennedy inserted his monocle on being introduced; Mr. Maugham let his dangle on its thread. It was the first time I had been in the presence of two monocles.

Turning to me, Dan, whether playful or nervous I never knew, said, "And this is Paul Horgan, the leading novelist of Roswell, New Mexico."

I had by then published ten books, some of them in England. The town where I lived, about thirty thousand in population, domiciled no other novelists, so far as I knew. But any consideration whatever of my credentials threatened to exhaust Mr. Maugham. He fixed upon me his dark, plum-like gaze and again murmured, "Y-yes, of c-course," and turned to sit down in a huge armchair facing the river.

While Dan and Mary kept the conversation afloat with trivia of the day, Mr. Maugham sat bolt upright with his knees smartly crossed and looked from one to the other of us as we chattered, and though he had nothing to say, he seemed to be the presiding presence of the party. His small frame contained so much reserve of experience, opinion, and fame that a silent expression of these was all that was required of him. There was no hint of rudeness in this detachment—only a stated position, laid over the air of bitter weariness that was so deeply marked in his face.

In an effort to meld him into the idle conversation, Dan asked him about his trans-Atlantic flight on the Pan American Clipper from Lisbon of some months ago: did he enjoy flying? He replied that he had never flown until a few months before, and only then because he had volunteered to give safe conduct to official dispatches that had to be spirited out of France to England. Flying, he said, had always seemed "an un-n-necessary risk." But, after all, what were risks for in wartime? he seemed to say.

"Do you like to fly?" I asked Dan, whose coverage of the weekly world required much air travel.

"No, no, not at all. Keep thinking Newton was right, Newton was right."

General laughter, to which Mr. Maugham wryly contributed a smiling downturn of his grape-colored lips.

iii

In the authority of his polite reticence Mr. Maugham made all attempts at conversation by the rest of us seem false and diffuse. It was lucky when luncheon was announced. Dan and Mary led us to an adjoining private dining room where the River Club's famous knack for elegance was fully demonstrated. Plenty of flowers, ranks of sparkling glasses, a comfortable armchair for each place, and a cadre of waiters waiting like footmen. As we sat down, Dan gave his quiet rippling laugh as a prelude to an announcement.

"I am going to give you the philosophy of our first course," he said, "terrapin in sherry. Quite a culinary comedy-comedy. You see . . ."

And he went on to say that there was only one place in North America where the choicest terrapin were to be found—a certain cave on the coast of North Carolina, where terrapin abounded, "almost secretly." Took particular skill to gather them. Before dawn, actually. Terrapin were not stupid; elusive, clever in fact; touch and go. Finally caught and brought out. Pack 'em in ice. Off to the airport. Fact is, the ones we were going to have had been caught that morning, had been flown to New York, just now popped into the boiling water, only matter of hours since the catch before dawn.

As he finished his history, waiters served the terrapin in sherry in large soup dishes. Mr. Maugham and Dr. Kennedy examined the terrapin through their monocles. The heavy soup spoons began to ladle. I feigned joy but the famous dish repelled me, in what seemed to me a revolting mix of reptile and fish; and I watched Mr. Maugham as he took his spoonfuls in a steady rhythm. I couldn't say why, but something about this absorbing of nourishment in order to continue the course of a disappointed life seemed full of pathos, and a parable of human life at large. I cast back to what I had read in the *Saturday Evening Post*—his account of his precarious escape from France just ahead of the Nazi obliteration of all that France meant to him. How, in the stoical frailty of his presence as I saw him, could he have withstood so well the risks and hardships of his flight?

Once bound for England on board the overloaded collier, he took his share of duties, shelling peas and peeling potatoes amid the ship's grimy layers of coal dust. He thought ruefully of his house as he had left it—"no flowers in the living room." He had gone through the rooms to say goodbye to his bookshelves; to take a last look at his Gauguin painting on glass that he had bought off a native in Tahiti; to pick up to take along a typed transcript of holograph entries of what later became *A Writer's Notebook* and to destroy the original pages; to choose for reading on his voyage Plato's account of the *Trial and Death of Socrates*, Thackeray's *Henry Esmond*, and *Villette* by Charlotte Brontë. It was his habit always to start his morning with "serious reading" and later, on board, the trial and death of Socrates assumed extra significance. On a coastal collier built for a crew of only thirty-eight, there were five hundred others like him trying to escape. There were lifeboats enough only to take on the number of the crew. What, he wondered, what to do if one were cast into the sea—the Mediterranean could be stormy, there were enemy submarines about. He asked a doctor on board. "Don't struggle," said the doctor. "Open your mouth and the water pouring into your throat will bring unconsciousness in less than a minute." But rather than drown, he was willing to think of suicide, and he kept with him a little bottle of suitable pills. He could contemplate using the pills though he still had books to write and things to do. But anything was better than being taken by the Germans in their inhumane genius. It was good to record that he met with "wonderful kindness" on board. Several of the wretched lot fell ill, one poor old woman died, and "three went off their heads." The rest had to wash in common tubs of unchanged water used by dozens of persons, a levelling experience: "There can be few class distinctions among people who are all equally dirty." Ordinarily even a slow boat would take only a matter of a day or a night to voyage from Cannes to the west coast of England; but the collier, in an evasive route by way of Algiers and Portugal, took "three weeks to the day" to reach Liverpool, where the exhausted passengers were kindly received. A while later, Mr. Maugham took a plane from Bristol to Lisbon. There he boarded the Pan American Clipper at nine o'clock in the morning and arrived at New York the next day soon after one o'clock. He noted that he had three dollars in his pocket and, he added, "I ordered an old-fashioned."

iv

Finishing his terrapin in sherry, Mr. Maugham laid down his spoon. He touched his lips with his napkin, and with a slow turn of his sleek head he surveyed the company and made one of the two memorable remarks that he offered during that little party.

"N-now that we've eaten it," he asked, "wh-why is it so-so expensive?"

As there was no answer to this except by general nervous laughter to convert it to witticism, the conversation went on without Mr. Maugham for a little while. I was still held by my thought of how amazing it was that this small, obscurely wounded, seemingly frail man had survived an ordeal foreign to all his habit of life. At a proper moment and in simple concern, I said, "Mr. Maugham, after all you had to go through to come to this country, I hope you are comfortably situated here."

He turned his unlighted, penetrating gaze upon me. In the second of his remembered remarks, he said, bringing together with wan elegance the extremes of his recent experience, "Y-yes, th-thank you. I am at the R-ritz, where they give me r-rates, as I am a r-refugee."

1 9 4 1

Peter Hurd:

Artist at War

i

SOMEONE HAS CALLED IT "The Living-Room War"—that conflict in the Persian Gulf which we watched at home through pictures
that talked and we wondered how much of the truth we saw, as our
feelings sought to share the experience of our armed forces in the
desert. The experience was fleeting, gone with the electronic pulse of
the recording film.

In earlier wars, the sights and the feelings have been stayed by a
more personal talent than that of the camcorder. Combat artists, war
correspondents, however they were called, have accompanied the
fighting forces to draw and paint the common lives of soldiers and
sailors and fliers; and what is preserved is the recording artist's feeling
about what he has seen and perhaps suffered in doing his job. He has
served history—and also he has honored the anonymous dignity of
human beings at hazard, and their rituals of duty, character, survival,
or death.

In 1942 the brilliant American painter Peter Hurd was recruited
by both *Life* magazine and the Army Air Corps to go overseas in
World War II as a war correspondent-artist—this after his first
assignment by the magazine to record Marines in training at Camp
Elliott, California. Hurd was offered a captain's commission in the

army, but the editors of *Life* believed he would have more freedom of movement as a civilian assigned to the air arm, and *Life* prevailed.

Leaving his ranch in New Mexico and its fine hacienda and his enchanting family—his wife, Henriette Wyeth, the exquisite painter, and two children—he was aloft in April 1942 on a Pan American Clipper flight for Fownes, Ireland, Bristol, and London. The drone of the airplane's four engines produced a curious state of mind. "Though I am perfectly aware," he wrote, "that it is not a dream I am experiencing, yet it is more like an ether dream than anything else I have ever known . . ." Here was war's reality of disruption, and the echoing void of the unknown future.

ii

In Hurd's letters and journals of that time* and my own memories of it, I find him vividly again; for we were lifelong friends, ever since our days as fellow cadets and classmates at the New Mexico Military Institute in the 1920s. His present World War II military assignment seemed proper on many counts—he would do a lovely job as an artistic correspondent. He had always had a strong, even a romantic, flair for the profession of arms—he had spent two years as a West Point cadet, resigning only because the urge to paint was stronger than the appeal of panache. But he retained something of the *beau sabreur* in his bearing; on his studio chimney piece he displayed a great trophy of swords; his dashing horsemanship and ardent polo playing suggested cavalry. There was a temperamental affinity between his wiry figure and the quick, nervous line of his pen drawing that promised well for his on-the-scene observation of soldier life.

In England he was dismayed by the bomb damage in London. Soon enough he found his way in British style, which he liked. Attending a press conference held by Dwight Eisenhower, he was gratified that the General "had no woof-woof qualities about him" such as the high military sometimes displayed.

*In preparing this memoir I am indebted to *My Land Is the Southwest: Peter Hurd Letters and Journals,* edited by Robert Metzger, 1983. (Permission to quote granted by Estate of Peter Hurd, copyright owner.)

Billeted with an American pilot as tent mate, he was given entire freedom to see and draw what interested him. He went on practice runs in the great B-17-E bombers, and drew his crew mates at work, and, looking down from the co-pilot chair, the lovely countryside. He was moved by the individual as well as the collective character of the American airmen he lived with, and he painted many portraits that reflected a heroic undertone in the perilous lives that they made light of.

One British officer in the station with whom Peter was acquainted was the Duke of Buccleuch, whose estate was nearby. A jeep, with a GI driver from Texas named Jenkins, was assigned to Peter to drive him about his work. A favorite Hurd story came of this. On their ramblings, Jenkins kept hearing about "the Duke's" woods, "the Duke's" farms, "the Duke's" great house, and more, all of which made him thoughtful. One day the Duke himself needed a quick ride and Peter took him aboard. Jenkins, feeling neighborly, said to Buccleuch, "In my hometown in West Texas we've got a big ol' family name of Duke, same's you. I've just been wonderin' if you's any kin to them?" Managing shy regret, the Duke replied, "I'm afraid not, actually."

Peter once spoke to me of the poignant mixture of hope and dread that he felt awaiting the return of the bombers from their lethal missions. In November 1942 he wrote to me that "in this curious attenuated life on a bomber station deep-seated friendships spring up quickly—and although the shadow of death is constantly palpable— the actual fact is a hideous shock." He felt it deeply when a young navigator whose portrait he'd been painting failed to return—"a hell of a good boy . . ." He wrote of "the fated look on these boys' faces," and later, as he looked back at "these boys," they seemed to him like "a band of legendary heroes . . . their faces haunt me." Rooted in his regard for the humanity of these men was his sense of purpose, when he wrote, "I'm terribly conscious of my mission and of its *potential* importance as a valuable document." As a great respecter— and lover—of fact in both life and art, he was wonderfully articulate in both language and drawing. Such was his abundance of temperament that he could find the kinship of fact and feeling through that broad stripe of the romantic vision that was also true of him.

iii

Peter Hurd and I never met overseas. For the better part of four years I was held in a dawn-to-dark staff assignment in the Pentagon. But his letters—to me and others—take the story forward. After about six months in England he returned to his ranch at San Patricio to flesh out his field notes for *Life* magazine, which would soon publish a comprehensive album featuring his airman portraits and aspects of life on a bomber station. On his way home he paused at Chadds Ford, Pennsylvania, where his family waited to greet him amid the vibrant clan of his father-in-law N. C. Wyeth. There Andrew Wyeth, in his late teens, already a master of watercolor painting, persuaded Peter to go out painting *en plein air* with him. The days in the field observing Andy at work laid the foundation for Peter's watercolor technique.

To be home again—like Antaeus, he took renewed strength from touching his own earth: "I want much to go nowhere for a time to stay on this ranch during growing season . . . We are planting like fiends . . ."

But the summons came again, this time for a longer and more colorful odyssey. The war was truly global. At every stage he made field drawings, his touch growing surer. His rapier-like pen line seemed to sting the paper, his filled brush to color the scene as immediately as air and light. He was still a civilian but holding the assimilated rank of captain with all its privileges. Everywhere, it seemed, he encountered old fellow cadets of West Point, and though grateful for his lifelong freedom, he could not help revealing now and then a hint of nostalgia for the soldier's life that he had given up in his youth.

Again, he was away from home for half a year. The farthest reach of the second journey took him to India. When at last he began his return, he wrote to me that he would stop in Washington: we must meet. It was a high reunion. He came into town and put up at the Mayflower Hotel. I joined him there for dinner and a long spellbound evening. He was trimmer than ever, hardened by the vagaries of risky, inconvenient travel in every sort of military aircraft. His traveller's tales were too rich and recent to be contained. He talked and I listened during those hours of recaptured friendship, and I saw much of what he talked about: for he opened his portfolios and brought out his field sketches in their profusion. All over the hotel room he strewed dozens, hundreds of small, sparkling papers that magically held scenes, persons, and climates of his flights and stations, throughout half a year.*

First destination outbound—a beauty pageant and dance in Puerto Rico to crown a beauty queen in the name of the United Nations. On to Hispaniola, to see and record an air show for the President. Flying by bomber to Aruba and Curaçao, the crew on patrol against enemy submarines. Over British Guiana he saw jungle so high and dense that he was sure no light penetrated as far as earth. And always the work—he had learned from the English months that "the least, most inconsequential note may later serve to evoke the feeling of the moment." On a jungle river in South America he went with a search party looking for a lost B-24. Always "the weeks ahead with much *going.*" He painted the rust-pink mountain of Ascension Island in the South Atlantic. At Accra, West Africa, when the plane circled to land over the surf, he saw a score of black children playing in the surf, and he painted them in a marvellous little air-viewed watercolor, all blue-green water, joyful little black bodies, bone-pale beach. I saw it at the Mayflower, and I craved it. He gave it to me. With the local garrison he played polo, riding "chunky little horses . . . like the horses Velázquez painted." From Kano in Nigeria he went on to Khartoum in Anglo-Egyptian Sudan; and soon it was Yemen, and other stations of Arabia, where it was "strange to feel yourself shunned and hated as an infidel in these Arab lands." In a big Douglas four-engined transport he flew over barren sand to Masirah, and from there "on to India."

Even in my synopsis, with mere mention of Cairo, Iraq, Suez, Jerusalem, Tunisia, Algeria, Morocco, and his varied lengths of time along the way, the great passage sounded like a narrative proper to Scheherazade.

During an "amazing three weeks" there was relief from the rattling flights of continent-hopping. In Jodhpur he was the guest of the

---

*The collection of over two hundred fifty of Peter Hurd's war sketches is being held intact at the Hurd–La Rinconada Gallery at San Patricio, New Mexico.

Maharaja Umaïd Singh in his rose-pink palace. Polo in the cool of the morning was the order of every day. When Peter moved on to Jaipur, yet another Maharaja put him up in "a little guest palace all my own with nineteen servants in green livery and a coach at my disposal with two grooms before and two footmen behind . . ."

In India he commissioned the making of a treasure. It was an exact replica, done in silver of a density purer than sterling, of his favorite little Winsor and Newton watercolor box. He had it made by an Indian master craftsman, and he carried it ever afterward. On its lid was deeply engraved his familiar signature, with its gallant flourish.

iv

After six months the homeward turn came again, by way of a pause with the Fifth Army in Italy, which was fighting its way up the peninsula against fierce Nazi resistance. Here he encountered his first ground combat. As he spoke of it to me at the Mayflower, the experience possessed him still.

Later, in a letter to Andrew Wyeth, his words about it gave forth the intensity and depth of his feeling. "One day in the middle of May/1944/ after a jeep trip to the front from Naples I found myself smack bang in the middle of a battle—a frontal assault by tanks and Infantry . . . I think I could make you feel how it was from my view . . . from the eye of a scared worm . . . I hadn't the least desire to paint or draw it. It was too vast, too horrible, too paradoxical to be paintable (by *me* at least) a . . . a phantasmagoria of shattered buildings, dust, smoke, orange groves, teller mines, the smell of dead bodies."

In the midst of the horror he came upon a scene that was so poignant to him that when he described it to me I received an impression so strong that after the war I was able to write a short novel about it. I called it *To the Castle*. What he saw was "the unforgettable sight of a tired-looking chaplain talking quietly to his men—who sat on a pile of rubble waiting to be called up to support our advance just a mile beyond us. He was whittling aimlessly on a stick talking inconsequentially apparently, but in that overwrought atmosphere every word every gesture seemed full of overtones of 'who is to survive the coming ordeal, who not?' " (The soldier's immemorial bargain with death was no more than a caprice. It possessed us daily in our Living-Room War.) The battle itself gave Peter an abstract sense—it might all be a "sham." He remembered being careful not to *show* any signs of fear or concern so that when a shell landed nearby he was the last one of the four in the jeep to scramble out and flatten down in the dusty road.

He was with the Fifth Army in Italy for less than a week, "an outsider," free to leave whenever he chose. It was hard for him to imagine what it must be like to be held there week after week. He wrote that he would never again "be astonished at man's character being altered or at least temporarily warped after that kind of experience. Boy, let's try to remember this when those poor bastards come back—those that do." War: always new, and always the same. . . .

At last, and again, he was home in November 1944 on his own healing earth. After some weeks of recuperation he was at his easel, completing another comprehensive collection of war reports for *Time–Life.* He created an artist's document that placed him as a peer of other Americans who recorded in their art the faces and facts of war—Winslow Homer with his unforgettable drawings of the Civil War; William Glackens and his drawings of troops training for the Spanish-American War; John W. Thomason of the Marines in the thirties; Tom Lea with the navy in World War II—who saw war both as a genre and as individual men under fate.

By springtime 1945 he was again an independent man giving and taking his share in the general creation. "Spring is such an exciting time here. For the past month we have been wrapped up in the minutiae of existence in the country. The birth of calves and colts; watching the young seedling sprout and the orchards bloom."

1942

Captain Wilder, T. N.

i

AFTER MANY YEARS of hoping to meet Thornton Wilder I was unwittingly provided with the power, and the style, to do so by the Honorable Henry L. Stimson, Secretary of War during World War II. In July 1942 I arrived at Miami Beach, Florida, to inspect the Army Air Corps Officer Candidate School. My credentials had preceded me. I was therefore conducted immediately to the office of the Commanding General. The General already knew that over the signature of Mr. Stimson I was declared to be an "Expert Consultant to the Secretary of War," and further, all appropriate personnel were charged to provide me with every convenience and cooperation in my official mission. The ultimate authority—the eye, the disposal power of the Pentagon at its highest level—was the terror of commanders in the field. I, a civilian, as its embodied agent, was assumed to hold a direct channel to the ear of the Secretary, with his control of high careers in the army.

The result was that splendid, if slightly nervous, courtesies were extended to me, even to charming reproaches—"If only we had known in advance, Mr. Horgan, my wife and I," said the General, "would have wanted to give a little dinner dance for you at the

Officers' Club; but in any case we'll hope to be seeing much of you while you are with us."

The VIP suite was reserved for me at the club, there would always be a car with driver, the chiefs of all sections would be advised of my schedule of inspection, and if I required any special demonstrations, I had only to ask. If I had not before been in Miami Beach, perhaps a tour of the area might be attractive? The Officer Candidates—a splendid group of six thousand of America's best young men—went through formal dress parade every afternoon at four, and the staff would be honored if I should agree to "take" the parade on which-ever of my afternoons I might designate. Meanwhile, the aide would be my "guide and counselor" throughout my stay—and, continued the General, how *was* the Secretary, so remarkable at his age (he was seventy-five) in his heavily burdened post which he executed so brilliantly—it would be a kindness to be remembered to him if the occasion should present itself on my return to Washington. And so, until a quiet dinner this evening?

It was easy to fit myself into such anxious comforts; and I decided that in accepting them quietly I would the more efficiently see my job done. Living a fraud imposed from without, I enjoyed the concealed comedy of it, and went briskly about my business.

My official purpose and my official status were much less grand than they were assumed to be. A few weeks earlier I had been summoned to Washington to be commissioned in the army as a captain, AUS, with the charge to write and produce an information film for troops on the Officer Candidate system, with a view to recruitment. I was to be attached to the film unit commanded by (then) Major Frank Capra. The papers for my commission were slow in being processed; in the meantime, my Pentagon boss, Colonel E. L. Munson, Jr., sent me out as a civilian to travel across the nation to all twenty-odd Officer Candidate Schools to prepare my script describing what each branch of the army offered—and required— toward the making of second lieutenants in ninety days of training. It was Colonel Munson, a virtuoso of War Department maneuver-ing, who arranged for my awesome credentials. My expenses were to be paid, and I would receive in addition one hundred dollars per diem as an "expert consultant." There must have been dozens of us so titled going about our jobs, bearing the famous letter signed by Mr. Stimson. While it lasted, I made the most of my grandeur.

Miami Beach was an early stop on my tour, which was to take me from coast to coast. There was no phase of OCS training that I did not observe, including mess halls, where I became a connoisseur of that equipment known as the "deep fat fryer," which mess officers seemed particularly proud to demonstrate. At the end of my tour I was to proceed to Hollywood, compose my shooting script, and then lead film crews to all the OC Schools once again, this time to shoot the film.

On my second day at Miami Beach I was escorted to the Officers' Club to have lunch with the Commanding General. It was a blistering-hot day, but on the patio there was gently chattering shade under palm trees as air from the sea brought a drying coolness. I was seated at a round table with three generals and a staff colonel or two. At the next table were the three aides to my generals, well within call. By now we were all easy with each other. Conversation was full of enthusiastic shop, sensible and intelligent, ranging across activities of the school and service gossip.

One of the generals, in passing, said to his neighbor, "General" —generals enjoyed addressing each other by rank—"General, did you happen to hear last night's Cultural Lecture?"

"No, General, matter-of-fact, my wife and I spent the evening catching up on our correspondence. Who was the lecturer?"

"Let me see, I believe it was a Captain Wilder."

"Is he with the candidates?"

"No, he is one of the retreads."

"You see, Mr. Horgan, in addition to the young candidates, we have people who have served in World War I and are here for refresher training."

A spark of surmise. I asked, "What is Captain Wilder's full name, General?"

"Why, I'm afraid I don't know." He turned to the next table and called to his aide. "Buck, what is the full name of that Captain Wilder who gave the lecture last night? Were you there?"

"Yes, General. Captain Wilder, T. N., sir."

Thornton Niven Wilder. I must have lighted up.

"Do you know him, Mr. Horgan?"

"No, but I have long wanted to meet him." The General's face showed polite curiosity as to why. I added, "He is one of the most brilliant and distinguished of our living authors."

"Really!"

"Oh, yes—" and I recited a few titles: *The Bridge of San Luis Rey, Heaven's My Destination,* and everyone knew *Our Town.* "Would it be possible for me to meet Captain Wilder?" I asked.

"Why, of course. The retreads have their daily parade every afternoon just after the candidates' own parade. You'll be reviewing the first formation this afternoon. Captain Wilder's contingent will parade immediately after on the same field." The General turned to his aide. "Buck, set it up to have Captain Wilder fall out and report to Mr. Horgan right after the retreat officers' parade."

"Yes, sir."

Report to me? I choked into my napkin.

At four o'clock the General's car (with its two white stars on its little red plate) delivered me and the aide to the long freeway of a golf course, which, like so much in Miami Beach, had been converted to wartime use. The golf course was now a parade ground. Six thousand officer candidates were marching to their initial parade formation as I was shown to the reviewing post. There awaited the commandant of the OCS and his staff. They ranged themselves to my left in the order of diminishing rank. As Secretary Stimson's stand-in, I wore invisible stars, and I was prepared to take the honors of the parade.

Commands came thinly across the wide greensward. It was a humid, overcast day. Tropical heat soaked my seersucker suit. The march-past began. The end of it was not even in sight in the moist distance. I took the salutes—national colors, squadron colors—with my hand over my heart. The band played, happy dogs danced along ahead. The wave upon wave of featureless pink faces going by, the scissors flash of chino legs clipping past made me giddy and I tensed my knees to keep control. Remarks were not out of order between the spaced salutes.

"Very fine," I said to the colonel on my left.

"We've done better, sir. But on a day like this, with their strenuous schedule, the ranks become a little ragged at times."

"Well," I said forgivingly, "you've clearly done a superb job with the training. I am honored to attend this."

I meant it. For all the fraudulent aspect of my honors, I was moved by the thought of the war, the country gearing itself up to it, and those faceless but invaluable lives marching by. When the last squad of the last platoon had made it past the reviewing stand, my feeling was no longer comic.

The aide brought me back to efficiency. He pointed to a small white circular pavilion with dome and pillars in the Greek style that stood a hundred yards away at the end of the freeway.

"See that little temple, sir?" he said. "That's where Captain Wilder has been ordered to meet you after his parade, which will follow in a little while. You just go up there and wait for him. If you're warm, you can have a Coke; there's a machine there—sort of a golfers' old rest stop. Jump in the car, sir. It will wait for you up there until you dismiss Captain Wilder."

Ordered? Dismiss? The innocent absurdities continued.

ii

There were benches in the weathered wooden pavilion, and there I rested, drinking a Coca-Cola. Through the flaking pillars I had a straight long view of the parade ground from its upper end. Presently I saw the formation of the officer refresher group march into sight out of the mists of late afternoon. It was a company-sized group. From my distance they looked like toy soldiers going through their evolutions as if they had windup keys in their backs. They formed first in line, then in column, and then into a faraway march-past. They executed a great square-about once more. I imagined Captain Wilder anonymously doing his part as a component of that collective moving machine, and I wondered what he would be thinking about. The column came into line facing the reviewing officer and halted.

A tiny pantomime took place in the distance.

The company commander gave an order, too far off for me to hear. The troops stood at ease. He addressed them, probably with what the army called a critique. He gave another order. The troops came to attention. Another order, and from the rank in line a small figure stepped three paces forward. The commander pointed to him, then pointed to the pavilion where I sat waiting. A final order, the small figure saluted, smartly turned left face, and began to march toward me on the slightly rolling green freeway. Behind him the company was dismissed and drifted away at will.

In the perspective, the small figure persevered. It walked rapidly in a swinging stride, as though executing a parade all alone, *hut-two-hree-faw,* with unflagging vitality that suggested civil good nature and independent dignity, projecting the character of Thornton Wilder. He was assuming himself as he diminished the distance between us, and I went through the peristyle to meet him.

Yards away he opened the beam of his smile and extended his hand. He carried the effect of many traditions—he was Emerson, Teddy Roosevelt, Don Quixote, Montaigne, Catullus, Jefferson, Aeschylus, John Evelyn, and George Brush, all in one, and his khakis were sweated through as we shook hands and drew into the domed shade of the temple.

"Oh, oh, let me demilitarize myself!" he said, taking off his soaked overseas cap with its captain's bars and shaking it.

"Would you like a Coke?"

"Bitte."

With trifling ceremony he lifted his bottle to my health, and then, as he drank a full swig, his near eye held a long appraisal of me, as though deciding how he must see me. Evidently no adjustments were necessary. He gave an energetic breath and with his total smile he said something about our meeting at last, after years of sporadic correspondence, mutual friendships, and news through our common editor, Eugene Saxton, at Harper's. He was in beaming health, trim, squared at the shoulders, tanned by Florida, and perfectly equal to the farcical rigors of being a retread.

"Isn't it killing?" he said, mocking the dated slang.

"?"

"This whole thing—marching, sir-ring, the treadmill! What are *you* doing with it all?"

I explained my mission, my pending captaincy, how I'd found him, what a pleasure, and the rest—and was he comfortable in the anonymity (like T. E. Lawrence's) in the effacing military world?

"You can imagine?"—meaning he was enjoying it, though not in an uncritical way.

We had little time. The afternoon was expiring damply. I said, "Can you dine with me this evening?"

"No-no-, you will dine with me. Do you like French cuisine?" I did. "Then I know just the place. Now I must shower and change."

"I, too. I have a car—I'll drop you off now and come back."

We were driven to his small hotel, which had been requisitioned as barracks, and as he left the car, he said seriously, "Give me half an hour—but please: promptly. I must be back at eight o'clock for study hall."

Study hall? When I laughed he made an extra gleam of opinion through his glasses and dashed into the hotel.

At dinner he did the ordering in French without a glance at the menu, nodding his imperatives at the waiter. As in everything, he had a command presence, as the army would have put it. Because of study hall, we could not have wine—at least he couldn't, and I refrained.

He was smart and exhilarated in a fresh uniform; and if dinner was mostly his monologue, I can remember only its theme—not many particulars. But the burden was that the juvenility of the military sometimes ceased to be amusing. One of course conformed to everything, however absurd, and with good cheer. At the same time, the ancient military habits of training, discipline, hierarchy, detachment from human compunction, and the dangers of authority too often vested in those incapable of wielding it sensitively or even sensibly went far beyond the materials of farce. In my notebook of the time I wrote down my immediate impressions of Captain Wilder in his unaccustomed circumstance.

Mannerism: the bright, charming, nibbling at ideas and words, each so good, and the sudden arrest in place, the gaze, so unwinking, so straight, so accustomed to truth in its most wary haunt, and that was, in self as well as outward . . . The selfless and strict and humble work (for such as he) to take on in middle life a new attitude and suffer its absurdities and inconveniences because it was an agreed-upon method of serving an end bigger and better than any one . . . This was the real lesson. What it entailed: the alumni caperings of fat Babbitts—the ambient insensitiveness—the poor and earnest idiom of adjustment.

He felt it rather a relief to be able to share one's view of all that with someone still outside the system—and how good to be looking forward now to a *soufflé au chocolat* that would appear in a few minutes.

"All this," I said, "makes me feel like a visiting uncle, taking his nephew out of school on a pass before study hall." He was half a dozen years older than I.

"Yes, yes, I am the eternally aging student."

I asked him what would follow his present course of training.

"My next assignment is already scheduled. In a few weeks I go to the Air Corps Intelligence School at Harrisburg."

And what would his job be after that? Prepare manuals? historical records of the air services? that sort of writing?

"Never!" he answered in a subdued sort of shout. He kept his smile, but it became severe and his heavy brows seemed to bristle. "Never. *I shall not write for my country!*"

Feeling like a traitor to literature in my assignment of writing and producing an information film to recruit officer candidates, I welcomed the *soufflé* as it arrived. We dispatched it swiftly. Captain Wilder kept an eye on his wristwatch, and all too soon we were back in the two-starred staff car and at the door of his billet. He made a hearty farewell, all voluble thanks, enthusiastic references to postwar encounters, and was gone into the Miami Beach flocked stucco Spanish-type entrance at two minutes before eight. *(Notebook: "An admirable and painful discipline from without for an artist of finest grain, used to imposing the strictest form within.")*

By noon the following day, I was done with my local duty and on my way back to Washington, where the Secretary of War was ignorant of my return. In a few more days I resumed my tour, to be received at a dozen more OCS components with the familiar luxuries and blandishments, which I gladly suffered—until I reached Fort Sill, Oklahoma, and the field artillery. There in the course of inspecting the deep fat fryer and other points of pride, I was overtaken by a telegram from the Adjutant General of the army announcing my commissioning effective immediately, with orders to report to Major

Frank Capra's army film unit in Los Angeles. In a single official puff, the empowering spell of Secretary Stimson was dissipated. I became one of perhaps a quarter of a million captains in the army. No more starred cars, orderlies, VIP suites, clever little dinner-dances at the club, deferential messages for Mr. Secretary. Under somewhat more difficult conditions, I got on with my job, glad, even so, to be in uniform.

iii

The postwar years went by without my seeing Wilder for quite some time; but I read him whenever he published, and about him, as he made his distinguished acts for style and culture. At the Goethe Festival in Aspen in 1949, on one day he simultaneously translated into English from the Spanish of José Ortega y Gasset, and on the next did the same from the German for Dr. Albert Schweitzer.

When Wilder gave the Charles Eliot Norton Lectures at Harvard in 1950–51, the *Atlantic Monthly* published the first three out of six scheduled to be given. I found these to be of such spirited originality, so brightly illuminating of central problems in our classical literature, and of the strong but sometimes stumbling energy of our American nature, that I wrote to him, hoping for publication of the next three lectures. He replied that they were not ready to be published—they needed more work; but he was pleased to have my response. In fact, I was told by others that in giving the lectures, particularly the final three, he did not use fully prepared texts but, dramatically striding the platform from side to side, spoke from notes, or sometimes quite spontaneously without any notes at all; and I wondered if the missing three pieces had been extemporized, never to be recovered by him in usable form. Anyhow, the first three finally appeared in his posthumous book *American Characteristics*, edited by Donald Gallup, and many of the key concerns of these magnificent essays can be seen in embryo in his *Journals 1939–1961*, also edited by Gallup and published even later. No critical historian of our literature can fail henceforth to be instructed by these diary entries.

Down the years, my path occasionally crossed with Wilder's. One day in Washington I was descending in the elevator of the Hay-

Adams Hotel for breakfast. At a floor lower than mine, he entered the elevator without seeing anyone. Standing in front of me, he went out first and into the dining room. I felt sure that he would not, no more than I, welcome a recognition before breakfast. When I followed after a brief delay, it was to take a table two removed from his, along the same wall, but facing away from him. Behind me I heard him order breakfast—a burlier voice than I remembered, commanding *"café au lait,"* and when the Hispanic waiter did not understand: *"café leche, café leche,"* barked out, *"café leche!"* as *The Washington Post* was whacked open with impatience.

Judging by the instructive little sounds of silver, china, glass, newsprint, I decided when I might venture to turn and greet him. He was just finishing. His greeting was warm. We had a second cup together. He was heavier than Captain Wilder, but as keen as ever in the moment. His speech was more rapid, punctuated by staccato intakes of breath that made witty even the simplest remark. We traded *bavardage* briefly, and then because his energy seemed geared to pressing affairs, I got up to go and said, "Sometimes I think of writing to you, but I wonder if Harper's is the best address. How to reach you at home?"

Like a schoolmaster he pointed to my vest pocket and said, "Your-book, your-book," readying me to take dictation.

When I had my pocket diary open and pencil poised, he said, "T.N.W.—50 Deepwood Drive, Hamden, Connecticut."

"What a nice sylvan address," I said idly, as I wrote.

"No-No. It's *kitsch.*"

The word was then entering critical slang, and I was not familiar with it.

"What is *kitsch?*"

"You don't know what *kitsch* is?"

"No."

A sharp little breath as he pondered how to define it. Then he brightened with a comic light in his eye, and said, defining by illustration, *"Thaïs is kitsch!"*

I laughed at his method and meaning, he joined me, we said goodbye.

A while later in New York I was entering the Century Club for lunch and met him coming out. After light greetings, I said, "I have something to tell you."

When he gave attention it was with an almost quivering alertness, as though he were creating and drawing out what was said to him: arcs of heavy eyebrows, dancing gleam of eyeglasses, inhaled exclamatory breaths marking intervals in what he heard.

I told him that since our Washington encounter I had reread his novel *The Ides of March,* which I suddenly hungered for on my travels *(a quick little drawn breath of pleasure),* and had to find a copy in a secondhand bookstore, as it was out of print *(ironic breath meaning "yes"),* but the interesting thing was that it seemed almost everyone I ran into was *also* rereading *The Ides of March* with high admiration *(flex of brows),* and I was delighted to report this to him.

With the friendliest teeth imaginable, he said, "Ah, yes, tell me, how-are-they-doing with *Black Beauty?*"

iv

I had hoped to see him again in the summer of 1962, for as the organizer of a symposium in honor of Igor Stravinsky's eightieth birthday to be given by the Santa Fe Opera, I wrote to Wilder asking if he would give one of a series of lectures on phases of Stravinsky's achievement. All of the composer's operas would be performed by the company. Others who had agreed to speak were Milton Babbitt, Carlos Chavez, Thomas Messer, Roger Shattuck, and Virgil Thomson.

Wilder replied from Germany, forecasting a retreat into an out-of-the-way village in Arizona where he would spend almost three years (one of the results of which would be his penultimate novel, *The Eighth Day,* a work that is like the harvest of a lifetime's wisdom).

Dear Paul

Thanks for your letter and the honor of the invitation it extends.

That will be a great occasion: first to hear so many works of the great Master; and to be among those immediately extending our gratitude and admiration to him.

Your invitation comes, I am sorry to say, at a time when I can no longer accept it. In May I am going into a real retirement, long overdue. To live as a real hermit in a state adjacent to yours. I expect to live so for about two years and a half. —To loaf, to read, to learn Russian, to refresh my Greek, to hold my tongue—and finally to do some writing.

I feel sure you will understand this perhaps better than most and I ask you to express it diplomatically to those of your committee who sent me this generous invitation.

All cordial best to you,

    ever

      Thornton.

But once or twice during the exile he broke away to visit Santa Fe for a day or two. During one of these moments I happened to be in Santa Fe, and he telephoned to invite me to dine with him the next evening. With every regret I had to say that because of research for a piece I was to write I was obliged to leave early the next morning for Phoenix and Tucson.

"Yes, you-must, you-must," he said, so fast that it sounded dismissive.

By the time I returned, he was gone—back to his hermitage in Arizona. We did not meet again until several years later in Connecticut, when an old and protective friend of his, Mrs. William Sloane Coffin, of New Haven, telephoned me at Middletown asking me to come with only two others to join Thornton Wilder for an evening at her house.

He arrived last and set himself at the edge of a sofa. He held and rarely sipped from a glass of whiskey. He was older, heavier in figure, but not in style or spirit. Seeing him again—it was to be for the last time—I had a sense of summary. His very presence was an assertion, not aggressive, simply vital. Of some people it is said that they wear their learning lightly. He possessed his dismissively. His thought raced, and his speech with it, though always with clarity and dramatically accented point. Not serious about himself, he held a lyrical and tragic view of life, though most often he played everything through comedy, even farce. If his natural climate of mind and spirit was his great residue of the Mediterranean classical world, he searched for the universal in the American vernacular style of life and expression.

His energies of personality had their confirmation in his elderly physical substance and social bearing. Not tall, he was compactly assembled and tense with strength. His head was large, and under heavy brows his eyes behind glasses were bright and dark. He wore a clipped mustache that accented his smiling mouth. His smile was comradely whether it covered opinions damaging or confirming. In flashes of courtesy he took each person present with individual address. To me, at a moment's lull in the general talk, he turned and exclaimed, "Great Paul!" and allowed a small silence to convey something warm and regardful that moved me.

Mention came up about his recent birthday—the seventieth. I can only repeat what I have recorded elsewhere. He told us with great gaiety how Goethe declared that "each of us is born with some inner resonance that for all our lives tells us what our ideal age is, no matter what our years may say." Thornton rayed us all with his smile and said, "I was an old man when I was twelve, and now I *am* an old man, and it's *splendid!*"

1945

Michelangelo's Morning

i

IN THE ARC OF A SINGLE DAY I was taken from the greatest celebration of life created by the art of man to man's ultimate triumph in his craft of death.

ii

We finished my brief army mission in Rome late on a Sunday afternoon in August 1945. Our overseas branches were winding down after V-E Day. I had made a portfolio of messages to their families from officers and men that I would relay by telephone or mail when I got back to Washington. On the morrow I would be leaving.

Lieutenant Colonel Hutchings Salisbury of the Rome headquarters, who acted as my guide and host, drove me back to my billet after the last meeting. As we drew up to the Hotel Excelsior he said briskly, "Well: good to have all that done with. You have nothing further scheduled here. Your plane leaves for Paris tomorrow at three, from Ciampino." He was a distinguished architect from Old Lyme, Connecticut. As a young man he had been a Fellow of the American Academy on the Trastevere, and he knew Rome well. "Is there anything you would like for me to set up for the morning? You haven't seen much of Rome itself these days."

"Yes," I said, "but I suppose it would be impossible."

"Oh?"

"I know it is closed for the duration, but I hate to think of leaving Rome without ever having seen the Sistine Chapel. Would there be any chance at all?"

"Oh, well, if you care for that sort of thing, I can try—you never know with those people. I'll come around in the morning, say nine o'clock, if you can be ready. Till then." In his dismissive way he drove off.

Only a few Allied soldiers were drifting about St. Peter's *piazza* that next morning. At the entrance leading to the Sala Reggia in the Vatican we were received by a tall, slender man with a scholarly look about him. Salisbury introduced him. "This is Dr. Redig de Campos —he is curator of paintings in the Vatican collections. He has very kindly agreed to open the chapel for you."

Equally impressed by Salisbury's powers of management and the generosity of de Campos, I made my thanks and we proceeded into the palace through twists and turns I could never have memorized. Presently de Campos unlocked a double door and motioned us through. We entered and turned to our right to face a high grille of wrought metal with gilding, and darkness beyond. In a moment he touched light switches and a slow bloom of subdued light came over all and we saw the Last Judgment at the opposite end of the Sistine Chapel. In a gesture that said, *Please,* de Campos brought us through gates in the grille into the chapel.

"Well, there you are," said Salisbury. "How much time shall I give you? Half an hour or so? I'll come back."

"Good God no, two or three hours, anyway, don't you think?"

De Campos instantly warmed to my feeling for the place. He nodded eagerly and said, "I shall come back at half past eleven in case I can be of any assistance." He was a South American, as his accent in English made evident. Salisbury shrugged, accepting the schedule. They both left me. I was alone under Michelangelo's ceiling.

My eyes adjusted slowly to what seemed to be electric lighting at

half strength—no doubt under wartime restrictions. The high windows were all blind, sandbagged against bombing. My first emotion
was perverse. To be there by myself, in the ghostly silence and under
the thronging splendor of the populated firmament above, bore upon
me like a burden. I was alone in the center of a dead calm, like that
of the hurricane's eye, in that vacant chamber of arrested energy on
ceiling and walls. I clapped my hands softly to break the spell. The
returned sound was flat and remote. For a moment I wished I could
leave—what right had I to this stunning privilege? My efforts to see
gave me a sense of strain. My eyes watered—I would not admit to
tears. A lifetime of awareness from childhood on had given me a
sense of Michelangelo that now converged with his astounding mas-
terwork, and I took refuge for a little while in fleeting recollections
of intimate moments out of the past. My German-born grandfather
brought home from his journeys abroad albums of engravings and
sheets of reproductions of the very works which I now gazed at. A
framed print of the Cumaean Sybil used to hang in my parents'
house with another, of the painting by Ingres of Pope Paul VII
presiding in splendor in the Sistine Chapel, where I now sat on the
steps of the altar. Best of all, a copy of the heroic Florentine *David*
stood on the shore of the Park Lake a few blocks from our house in
Buffalo. This was an immense bronze, in the size of the original. The
huge hero stood facing away from the lake toward the Albright Art
Gallery and the Museum of the Historical Society—two of my childhood haunts. On many an afternoon after school I roamed about
those classical temples imagining myself their inhabitant; and then I
would go down to the lake to see David, and often to sit down on the
granite base that supported him, and eat my apple, or read my book,
or simply stare with him, the benign giant, at childhood's empowering invisible. As I grew older, even to late years, I acquired books that
brought me drawings by Michelangelo, his sonnets, large photographs of his sculpture, his letters, many biographies, and critical
studies. In my modest scale, he, the mightiest human creator, became a companion in thought, whom even thoughtlessly I held to as
a polar star of reference, if intimations of the sublime, under God,
should touch my life.

In the twilight of the chapel, I took in the ceiling, slowly walking the floor end to end. The surface of the ceiling disappeared. Its painted universe seemed to dwell there of itself. The first overall impression was of sumptuous textures, of tapestry-like muted colors (this before the restorations of the 1980s), and of the great stilled drama of passionately loved figures in their narrative of creation, sin, redemption, and the power of human beauty. A wonder: it was impossible, seeing the likeness of these, not to think of the ideas and beliefs from which they unfolded into form. As the art historian Tolnay wrote, "By means of this dynamic exaltation of classical forms Michelangelo could arrive at his supreme aim: to make a new second world—a transcendant reality." Michelangelo's own words, describing the Belvedere torso, can speak for his own achievement: "This is the work of a man who knew more than nature."

On the altar wall the immense doomsday theme sumptuously unrolled from heaven to earth. Much has been said of the *terribilità* —"the frightening power of sublimity"—that suffuses Michelangelo's dramas. They make the more impact because their dread sublimity is framed in elegance raised to the ultimate power . . . I saw, but did not linger over, the great panels on the side walls—master works by Botticelli, Signorelli, Perugino, Ghirlandaio, Cosimo Rosselli—any one of which would ask for exhaustive study. They gave their splendor to the total richness of the chapel; but it was Michelangelo's hand, eye, and soul to which I had come to pay homage.

But everything has been said about the Sistine Chapel. I only know that my morning alone there was the greatest of gifts to my inner life—the summit of my aesthetic, religious, and historical experience.

iii

Michelangelo was not yet done with me. I had no sense of the time passed in the chapel when the others returned to take me away. They brought a third person, who was introduced as Dr. Fritz Volbach, curator of ancient fabrics in the Vatican Museum. He was small and gray, ingratiating and shy. Like de Campos he was curious about this United States officer who paused in his duties for half a day to commune with Michelangelo.

"Enough?" asked Salisbury.

To ignore this, I turned and thanked de Campos with so much feeling that again he kindled to my response. He read me well. He said with an air of sudden inspiration,

"Would you like to see the last paintings of Michelangelo?" I would, most assuredly. He added, "The two chief Apostles. They are never open to the public."

He was speaking of the murals that depicted the Conversion of St. Paul and the Martyrdom of St. Peter. They decorated the side walls of the Pauline Chapel, which was reserved for the Pontiff's private use, including the ceremony at which in creating cardinals he distributed their scarlet birettas to them.

Dr. de Campos led us out through the immense, ceremonial entrance doors of the Sistine Chapel. We entered the Sala Reggia and passed under a great valance of white marble carved in every fold of drapery upheld by *putti*—a fantasy by Bernini. Then, to the right, he unlocked doors and brought us into the Capella Paolina. It was a medium-sized room, rather narrow for its height, and it was furnished for the most part by luxuriously carved wooden panels, pilasters, and moldings of mellow wood in natural color. To our left was the painting of the Conversion of St. Paul, and, on the opposite wall, the Martyrdom of St. Peter.

They are narrative paintings—imagined depictions of events of central importance to the history of the Church. De Campos let us look in silence for some while. I had known reproductions of the paintings, but nothing prepared me for their scale and color. They are of great size; their colors show pale values thinly washed in, with outlines in evidence; their figures and fittings are sparely drawn. The whole texture of the panels is factored down to the simplest essentials; the familiar Renaissance love of gorgeous detail is not there. The information and the action seemed to have been breathed upon the walls, to remain almost as abstractions. Where it came from I could not say, but into my mind came an echo of the attenuated spareness of Beethoven's final quartets. The genius of that condition lay in its release of powerful emotion through most restrained means.

Paul lies on the earth, felled by a bolt of belief from Heaven. His horse rears. His soldiers—Paul was a soldier named Saul—are dumbstruck. He is blinded as he raises his face to the divine ray of realization.

Redig de Campos pointed to Paul's face and asked me, "Who is it?"

Still maundering over my recognitions, I said, "St. Paul."

"No, no!—of course, *yes*. But *who* is it?"

I stared at him.

"Look at him! It is himself!"

I looked and it was. De Campos turned swiftly across to the opposite fresco and exclaimed, "And there, and there"—pointing to two of the figures attending to the carpenter's job of nailing a fellow man to crossed timbers upside down—"also self-portraits! And remember the flayed man in the *Giudizio Universale*—again his own face! Wonderful! The great artist always sees, he feels, as autobiography, everything he touches!"

And in truth the "frightening power of sublimity" in those final testaments seemed to make plain that Michelangelo suffered what he painted—some blinding self-realization in the shattering epiphany of St. Paul; some guilt as humanity's witness to the torture of St. Peter. . . .

Such contemplations were interrupted by Colonel Salisbury's wristwatch.

"Look here," he said. "It's past noon. I've arranged for you to attend an audience of the Pope. We'd best move along."

We retreated from the Pauline Chapel, and as de Campos locked the doors, Dr. Fritz Volbach, with an apologetic smile, handed me a small brown booklet which he had been holding. He had inscribed it "Souvenir from the Vatican," and by his modest air, it was plain that he was its author. It was a monograph on medieval fabrics entitled *Stoffe Medioevali, Città del Vaticano*—published in 1943, after his escape from Vienna and the death camps. I have it still. To keep fresh my memory of the wonderful kindness of Redig de Campos I later acquired an English translation of his monograph, *The Frescoes of the Pauline Chapel in the Vatican*, published in Milan and New York. I still have this scholarly work also. On that day I took leave of their authors with full feelings.

Salisbury hurried me off through the Stanzae of Rafael with

scarcely a glance and into a great chamber called the Sala Clementina where a papal throne was set up facing a standing audience of perhaps three hundred Allied soldiers of several nations. Helmeted halberdiers of the Swiss Guards marched back and forth behind a railed barrier in front of the throne. Saints and martyrs of the painted baroque looked down upon us, it seemed, for almost an hour while we waited. Deep into the pause I looked at Salisbury with inquiry— should we wait any longer? We stayed, and suddenly there was a clang of halberds and Pope Pius XII strode rapidly to his throne, seated himself, looking very small in its massive grasp of velvet, gilded wood, and carved papal heraldries. He spoke in French, Italian, Polish, and English to these veterans of the recent polyglot liberation of Italy. His arms made stylized arcs of welcome and praise, and after a quarter of an hour a final gesture turned into the triple papal blessing, as everybody crashed to kneeling, and so remained until he was gone.

iv

I boarded a C-47 of the Air Transport Command at Ciampino airport, the only officer in a complement of enlisted men. The plane was full. The flight clerk, a young sergeant from California, handed me a typed schedule—something of an unusual feature on military flights. We would land at the army airfield at Marseilles for evening mess; depart for Paris at 9:28 P.M.; land at Orly-Paris at 12:52 A.M. Fuselage windows were no longer to be blacked out.

The day faded with our northward flight. I slept away the afternoon. After we took off later from Marseilles I could look into the darkness and see the little lights of France far below. They kindled a sweet melancholy love for the nation and its recently long-suffering people.

Later, as we were approaching Lyons, the plane began to shudder, then drop in dead air, then halt its fall with a wrenching impact. In seconds we were in the worst electric storm of my life. Thunder and lightning played wildly with the airplane. In my thought, as in everyone's, was the question, were we going to make it?

In the midst of that airborne tumult, the sergeant came through the cockpit door. Innocent of his dramatic timing, he knelt down next to me and said, with the hearty omniscience of the radio news listener,

"Sir, we thought you would want to know this. The captain has just had a radio bulletin—today the United States dropped an atomic bomb on Japan."

1956

To Meet Mr. T. S. Eliot

i

ON A FINE SUMMER DAY IN 1956—it was Thursday, June 4—I touched the door buzzer at the New York apartment of my friend and editor Robert Giroux in East Sixty-sixth Street. It was answered by T. S. Eliot, who was staying there as Giroux's guest during a brief visit to the United States. I had been invited to luncheon with him, and I was there to make his acquaintance, and presently to bring him to join Giroux and the other guest, Jean Stafford, at the Carlton House restaurant in Madison Avenue.

He stood in the open door for a long moment, regarding me silently from his stooped height. I gave my name and hand. He accepted both. He was in shirt sleeves and tie, with waistcoat and trousers of a dark gray suit. His head, sleekly haired, seemed small for the length of his frame. His eyes were gray, powerfully taking, under lids slanting aside. Cavernous nostrils in his great nose suggested a hungry indraft of life. His mouth was wide, his chin strong and balled. The general effect was that of composed good looks at the service of sober good manners.

Gravely, he now extended his long forefinger, pointing to the small peephole set with its magnifying lens in the apartment door—a

discretionary device common enough to thousands of domestic door-
ways across the land.

"What.is.that?" he asked in a measured quantity.

"That? —Why, it is a little optical peephole to let you see from
inside who is there outside," I said, wondering if I should be more
facetious.

But, not smiling, he said, "Let us try it. I will close the door and
try to see you through it."

He closed the door. I stood outside a couple of feet from the door.

In a moment, he opened the door and said, "So that's it. Now let
us change places while *you* try it."

He stepped into the hall. I stepped into the apartment, closed the
door, and fixed my sight at the peephole. Instead of his head and
shoulders, what I saw was the magnified eye of T. S. Eliot peering
at me through a wash like undersea light. He had his face against the
door. His gaze was steady, watery, disembodied, piscine, and unnerving. In his own long time he backed away and touched the door
buzzer. I let him in. He said, now with a delightful, whole smile to
declare the little comedy, "There! May I come in?"

If the scene were meant to break the ice for strangers meeting, it
was a success. It trifled with the irrational, it forced two exchanges
of identity or position, and it required that good manners hold in the
face of deliberate nonsense. In no time we were off and running in
the easiest small talk—so small that I don't remember any of it,
except an anecdote that occurred to me as we walked down Madison
Avenue. How it came up I can't say, but somehow prizefighting was
the topic, and I said,

"While I was in the army I had occasion to report to Fort Riley,
Kansas, in 1942, on an inspection tour. Army post gossip is always
lively. At Riley they talked about Joe Louis, who was an enlisted man
in the cavalry. It was the time when Nazi propaganda was putting
out stories of racial unrest in the United States; Hitler was promising
a better life to Americans of color after he won the war. There were
Negro troops at Riley, some of whom were showing signs of disaffec-
tion. Joe Louis was asked to make a statement on public radio and
news film. He rose to it in sleepy eloquence. He said, 'There's

nothing wrong with the United States that Hitler can cure.' "

Eliot stopped stock-still on the sidewalk and hunched his wide shoulders in a slow, periodic laugh. When we reached the Carlton House he was still smiling over the mood of the anecdote, and after we were settled at the table with Robert Giroux and Jean Stafford, he repeated it to them. Bob Giroux's laughter conferred a convivial mood; his hearty cheeks reddened like a schoolboy's. Jean Stafford smiled like a wise and pretty housecat. She was in one of her days to be pretty. Tightly chic in smartly cut tweeds, and wearing at an angle a sly little saucer of a hat, she made the perfect luncheon companion. She began with a little laugh that said something was coming, and in her adolescent boy's voice and in her dangerous drawling mode that yet had something innocent about it, she told *her* prizefighting story.

"I have a Joe Louis for you, Mr. Eliot." He leaned into the story like Old Possum himself. "It begins," continued Jean, "with Jersey Joe Walcott at the camp where he was training to fight Louis in a week or two. The press was there in numbers. The fight would be a wowser. Newsreel cameras put out film showing the Challenger in the ring with his trainer. In almost all the shots, Jersey Joe was dancing around, mostly backward, demonstrating the fanciest foot-work in the world, backing and spinning away in the prettiest way. The next pictures on the newsreel showed a reporter asking Joe Louis what he thought of the Challenger's tactics. The Champ replied, 'He can run, but he can't hide . . .' "

A great success with the guest of honor. The luncheon went along in good spirits, to the relief of those of us who knew of Eliot's private troubles at home—the incurable mental illness of his wife, her place-ment in an institution, his act for separation, his own periods of depression that resulted. In our day with him, despite the light-hearted moments, we could feel an underlying lowness of spirit, however politely he dissembled it. He seemed a quieted man. Some-thing rueful was threaded through the outlines of his greatness as a poet and his position in the literary world. For the sake of civility, the undertone was hushed; but even the structured farce at the peephole seemed to suggest that he must make a special effort to manage such a trifling outgoing as saying hello to a new acquaintance. Were there muted calls upon our unspoken empathy and—even on first acquaintance—our concern?

ü

Two years later, in April 1958, I received a telegram at my home in New Mexico from Lon Tinkle, the professor and critic at Southern Methodist University in Dallas. It told me that T. S. Eliot would be coming to Dallas on Friday, April 25, to give a reading at the university, and it was further announced that I would be on hand to introduce the poet on that evening. I was of two minds on receiving this. I was nettled at not being asked beforehand whether I would agree to introducing the poet—yet who, if not Lon Tinkle, could more confidently put me to work? For years, as the literary and cultural arbiter of the Southwest he had supported my writings with acclaim and approval, and he and his family had become my close friends. I must agree with good grace to be on hand for Eliot's evening.

But more—I had been following with delight and astonishment the news bulletins that told of Eliot's wide American tour, now in progress. His public readings were breaking records for attendance everywhere. At the University of Minnesota he had drawn a crowd of fourteen thousand to the indoor stadium. Twelve thousand gathered to hear him at the University of Texas in Austin. These seemed unlikely responses to the esoteric quality and metaphysical climate of Eliot's poetry and criticism and plays, not to mention his famous personal avoidance of overemphasis in any direction. The whole adventure of his immense popular success was intriguing. I wanted to see him again, and to meet his wife—for after separation from his first wife and her death he had married again. I went to Dallas to do my duty.

We came together in a quiet place off the lobby of the field house at S.M.U. just before eight o'clock in the evening. We could hear the sustained shuffle and hum of a great crowd entering the building. The Eliots were accompanied by Robert Giroux, who had brought them from New York, President Willis Tate of the University, and

Lon Tinkle. Holding a collected volume of his verse, Eliot was calm
but remote, harvesting his resources for the ordeal ahead. Valerie
Eliot held his arm. Her broad smile spoke for them both. It was
enough. She had the conveyed charm of complete happiness. Forty
years younger than he, she had long hoped as his secretary that one
day he might marry her. She saw him loyally and discreetly through
many an ordeal. He came to rely upon her. He came to love her.
They were married on January 10, 1957. On their return from their
wedding trip in the South of France, their friends saw that they were
both transformed. The change in Eliot was extraordinary. He was as
carefree as a boy, and as carelessly demonstrative. He held hands in
public with his wife, and caressed her when he felt like it. He show-
ered goodwill upon anyone. His energies seemed boundlessly renewed—witness the gruelling speaking tour now going on. When he
smiled now it was like a personal benediction without a trace of
diffidence. If he was called upon for a word in public, say to the press,
he would consult his wife with a lifted eyebrow to ask encourage-
ment, and gaining her smile and her little nod of worshipful confidence, he made benign noises for the world to hear. He was a happy
man and he did not care who knew it *pace* peepholes.

At thirty years of age, Valerie Eliot was full-bodied and graceful,
with a pretty face in the fresh English way of high color, smiling eyes,
and ready gaiety. In the Dallas field house she bore herself like a
royal consort. Her dignity was easy, and it was always there, but she
made of it a means to reach people and let them be comfortable in
the presence of her husband. To support her high color she dressed
in pastel colors, with many accessories and appendages that wanted
graceful management, and got it. Fine bangles, light furs, perimetric
hats that yet did not veil expression; and always the smile of genuine
pleasure that meant to share an occasion and bless it.

At one minute before eight President Tate led the concert party
out into the echoing field house where seven thousand people filled
the floor and the balconies. Valerie Eliot went to front-row chairs
with Lon Tinkle and Giroux. I followed Tate and Eliot to the
platform, where we subsided for a few moments. Eliot wore a fixed
smile but saw nothing except his interior concentration upon what
must come, with its nervous heightening as he waited, while the

crowd gradually went silent. Now Tate asked Eliot if we might proceed and was given a stately nod. Tate nodded to me. I went to the front of the stage and declared, "Mr. President, ladies and gentlemen, Mr. Eliot"—my entire introduction. I turned to receive him at the lectern. He bent toward me in grave acknowledgment, set his book on the lectern, put on his shell-rimmed glasses, and waited for a long breath. I went down to the floor with Tate, where we took our seats.

Then followed a performance of such unexpected power, splendor, and eloquence that it became for me one of a handful of significant emotional events without equal—Chaliapin in *Boris Godunov*, Gielgud and Richardson in *Home*, Feuillère in *La Dame aux camélias*, Scofield in *King Lear*, Toscanini leading Siegfried's *Funeral Music* and *Journey to the Rhine*, Winston Churchill saving the decent world by radio through the instrument of the English language, Stravinsky conducting his last performance of the *Symphony of Psalms*. . . .

Eliot began with early poems—*The Portrait of a Lady* first—that twilit interior picture of love imagined, remembered, lost, and forever claimant. His voice here was meditative, caressing, yet faintly mocking in the character he projected in the lady's words. He read so quietly that we had to strain a little to hear—exactly the effect he wanted, for so capturing us, he held us in his power then and throughout in all the changes of character and mood in the poems. They came in their chronological order: *The Waste Land* entire; passages from *Ash Wednesday*, *Sweeney Agonistes* . . .

What was astonishing was his transformation from a tall, private, underemphatic gentleman with perfect manners to a public master of theatre who created scenes in the air and a variety of speaking people in all their various accents. To "neutral" passages he gave an elevated bardic voice, slow-paced, with mellow tone as evocative as that of a hunting horn distant beyond a hill. For "character" lines he quickened the pace and flattened the tone in mimicry that made us see who spoke. In moments of fatality we were waved over by a sea of human sorrows. And in all his modes it was the power in his strong, grainy voice that held us.

We were held even when a new and unlikely hazard threatened his reading. The April weather over the central plains of Texas began to turn violent. The wind rose and sang about the walls of the field house. Intermittently for the better part of an hour a storm rose and fell and rose again. We strained again to hear, but Eliot raised his voice and the poems even in their veiled nuances held sway and we heard. The unlined roof of the building bore the tattoo of heavy rain. Lightning flashed against the steel-webbed windows. Thunder rolled rampant. Eliot read on, serenely overriding the storm outside. People could not help stirring apprehensively in their chairs. Eliot read on.

The storm had been muttering its way toward the Gulf of Mexico when Eliot announced *Little Gidding,* and updrafts from the warm April rain-soaked land struck high ice in the clouds, and hail fell. It fell like bullets upon the thin vaulted roof of the huge chamber. Against that assault of hard sky action, he read his most attenuated of spiritual abstractions. He read it in a long crescendo, raising his voice against the beating on the roof, pulling us forward in our seats not only to hear him but to be with him. His voice took us individually and together, and we were lost with him, so that when he came to the universal, abiding, sweet commonplaces of

> the source of the longest river
> The voice of the hidden waterfall
> And the children in the apple-tree
> Not known, because not looked for
> But heard, half-heard, in the stillness
> Between two waves of the sea . . .

it was his enfolding stillness that we entered into against the rattling hail. We breathed according to the pulse of his closing lines:

> And all shall be well and
> All manner of thing shall be well
> When the tongues of flame are in-folded
> Into the crowned knot of fire
> And the fire and the rose are one.

He closed his book, removed his spectacles, and made one step back from the lectern, and the storm broke indoors. Over the long hour the audience had been fixed and silent and—despite the weather outside—entirely absorbed by the emotional power of the poems and moved by the elegance of their delivery. Now in one great mass everyone thundered to stand; they clapped with raised hands; they yelled, they whistled—Texas unbridled. They held him, and held him, while he bent toward them again and again in self-effacing acknowledgment. I gazed about. Their faces were alight with the contagion of feeling brought out by the poems, and renewed by the ovation that fed back upon themselves.

I remember one individual celebration of joy. In the balcony near the platform sat a black woman on two chairs. She was immensely fat. She was wrapped in a huge garment of fuchsia pink cloth. Her eyes were closed. Her columnar arms were raised above her head. She waved her hands upward like fans of jubilee. Her broad face was transfigured into a mask of ecstasy. In the din I could not hear her but clearly she was crying out "Glory!" Everything about her suggested a nearly old woman of the working class and primitive religion. Her dignity was capacious. Yet it was not social condescension to wonder how much she may actually have understood of the sometimes wry, sometimes erudite, often half-expressed ideas and metaphors she had heard. What was superbly plain, and lovely with the honor of poetry's inexplicable powers, was the consuming happiness of that transported being in the balcony.

Willis Tate went to rescue Eliot from the platform. Exhilaration was still Eliot's state when his wife joined him. They embraced. No longer was this the man made ill by troubles he could not assuage, the poet who had only art to love, the tea-time visitor who was snubbed by the shrewish diarist of Bloomsbury for his pallid longing and self-doubt. Privately and publicly he was now a fulfilled eminent man of his epoch, splendid to see.

A festive supper party followed the poetry reading. Tinkle had gathered a dozen or so people in a private room at what then was the best restaurant in Dallas—La Vieille Warsovy. The Eliots had no shyness about showing their love before others. Seated together, like royalty, at one side of the long table, they held hands like young honeymooners. They exchanged open secrets of comedy, pleasure, and understanding in company. She was protective among crowds, and he wanted her to be. When she spoke for him in measured accents of responsibility, like a proper consort, he silently confirmed all she said by a smile and an inclination of his head. He took pride in her harvest of new friends whom she made everywhere. She admired him dearly, and he would do anything to bring her pleasure. Her quick, gleeful, pretty smile delighted him. The four decades of age between them was no separation; it attracted fond marvelling by those who saw them so compatible.

Wine flowed at the Old Warsaw. On Eliot's left side was Lucy Hunter, a young matron of Dallas society who was chosen to sit there for her intelligence, charm, cool gaiety, and high humor. He took to her with comfort and as the night went on he became convivial to a degree. Their exchanges were lively, during which she addressed him as "Mr. Eliot." Unexpectedly he leaned to her and said, "Call me Tom!"

She put her hand to her throat and exclaimed, "Oh! I couldn't! You were required reading!"

The supper party went right along.

A day or two later the Eliots were to return to New York with Robert Giroux, their old friend, editor, and guide. There were local ceremonies to supplement the triumph of the poetry evening. Eliot sustained himself amiably through addresses and customs of honor, however outlandish they might be under the self-celebrating habits of genial Texans. When made a deputy sheriff and presented with a "gold" badge, Eliot let them pin it on, and—to please his wife, who innocently saw it as a serious distinction—he wore it as though it were his Order of Merit bestowed at Buckingham Palace. In another investiture a civic worthy came up to Eliot bearing a large round box. Without indication of what he was about to do, he reached out and snatched Eliot's superb Homburg hat (from Lock's in St. James's Street, London), took from the box a fawn-colored ten-gallon hat, and placed it on Eliot's head. Attending admirers cheered, press flashlights went off, and Eliot with the courtesy owed to scheming children accepted the tribute for the pleasure it gave his wife. He wore it to the airport, where I was among those who saw him off. He wore it arriving in New York. When with Valerie Eliot he sailed for home, he still wore it as he took ship.

iii

In later times, under medical advice, T. S. Eliot had an annual midwinter vacation on one or another Caribbean island. A chronic respiratory disorder grew more troublesome with the years, especially under London weather during the dark months. With Robert Giroux and Charles Reilly, their close friends of many years, Eliot and his wife made a companionable little circle that came together to enjoy perfect privacy and anonymity for a few weeks on warm beaches facing the blue-green sea.

With the turn of the 1960s, foreign travel, including the weeks on winter islands, became more difficult for the Eliots. His health declined. Heavy public engagements were out of the question. Moreover, currency controls in Britain restricted her citizens to a limited amount of money that could be taken out of the country—was it twenty-five pounds? Sources of funds had to be found abroad by British travellers.

Eliot's physical troubles were worsening. He needed to find the tropics in 1963, with a planned stopover in New York on a journey to the islands. Some months earlier Bob Giroux telephoned me, asking for my help in finding a not too arduous assignment for Eliot that could bring him both the reason for travel out of England and enough United States revenue to pay for it.

At that time I was director of the Center for Advanced Studies at Wesleyan University. My first notion was to propose a fellowship of two or three months to Eliot, but that would require him to remain in residence, and so to be exposed to the fog, blizzards, and heavy snows of a Connecticut winter. It then occurred to me that possibly the Wesleyan University Press—this was almost thirty years ago, under a previous administration—might consider engaging him to serve as its European correspondent, with a view to finding and recommending new works in England and on the Continent which the Press might consider for publication. It seemed a reasonable and properly professional notion. Eliot was after all not only an eminent author and critic—he was also an editorial director of Faber and Faber, a leading English publishing house. In an annual visit to America, with a suitable stipend, and expenses paid, he would attend the Press's editorial meeting to discuss his findings. I believed the suggested plan held a possible solution, bringing relief to Eliot, and to Wesleyan critical guidance of the highest quality and, not least, honorable prestige.

To my amazement, the Press people were doubtful, yet I had to respect their honest qualms: would so world-famous a figure as Eliot perhaps overshadow the independence and self-respect of a small university press? Was it also possible that the arrangement might too patently reveal itself as a mere convenience, if not a subterfuge, to justify a journey to the United States primarily for the private advantage of T. S. Eliot? All such policy debate seemed to me to threaten an opportunity for a distinguished editorial collaboration. But I had to let the matter soak for a while in its common advantages.

Finally, the Press agreed to a one-year trial run. The treasurer of the university met in New York with Robert Giroux, and in an entirely courteous discussion, set up the terms of Eliot's engagement —continuing reports through correspondence, a most generous stipend, and Eliot's attendance at the Press's meeting scheduled for December 16, 1963, at Wesleyan University, in Middletown, Connecticut.

iv

It was a hard winter day. The sky was dark and low. Snow lay beside roads and streets after an earlier fall. Giroux was bringing the Eliots from New York in a limousine. Eliot would be taken directly to the meeting, which Valerie Eliot and Giroux would attend from the sideline, without participating. Without saying so, they were worried about his state of health. Mrs. Eliot wanted to be nearby in case she should be needed. The meeting lasted close to two hours, adjourning at about half past noon. I was waiting for the three of them to come to my house on the Wesleyan campus for lunch before returning to New York in the hired car.

When they arrived at my door Eliot was in a state of near-collapse. Giroux and Valerie Eliot had to hold him as, bent double, he emerged from the car on slowly articulated limbs. He breathed in shallow, whistling takes. Coming inside, he looked at me but could not speak, but gave me a rueful smile instead. We took him to a sofa in my living room, where he sat crouched into his laboring breath. We gave him a glass of Scotch. He sipped it carefully. A droll gleam came into his eye. He held out the empty glass for another. He straightened up somewhat. He found his voice. He looked about and smiled at my profusion of pictures and books. We talked quietly until lunch was announced, and when we went in, Eliot walked at his full height, holding his wife's hand as if to assist her instead of the other way round. Watching him lovingly, she lightened everyone's spirits as he grew more easy.

There was no visible concern now. There was wine. A toast was given by Bob Giroux that set just the right tone. Eliot murmured a simple response, and by his inflection turned it into wit, so that we all laughed. At this he sat erect and gave an embracing smile. The talk eased into a sustained flow. Color came into his gray cheeks. The food was right. Conversation built into a four-way dialogue of interest, amusement, and charm. Eliot led it. His exhaustion fell away, and as it did, his wife became an image of relief and pride. He had a second helping. The wine came round again. His slow-paced laughter marked stanzas of talk. His eyes glowed. The clock was stopped for everyone. The luncheon lasted for almost three hours, until the mid-winter afternoon was falling toward early dusk.

In the living room, on the table near his coffee cup, Eliot saw a copy of his *Collected Poems*. He took it up and wrote, "Inscribed for Paul Horgan, after a memorable lunch Dec. 16, 1963. T. S. Eliot" and drew a great three-inch slash underneath that spoke of high spirits.

It was time to go. As the Eliots put on their coats Bob Giroux said to me aside that the meeting had been difficult. Throughout all the preparatory months, Eliot had corresponded with the Press, and now he proposed and discussed a number of literary projects for the editors to consider. Civility and mutual respect prevailed, but the atmosphere was joyless, even though each party honored the good faith—and the uncertainties—of the other. Nothing was resolved. The one-year trial was over. Eliot would never return.

At a little past four o'clock the winter day was dark as night. We all said goodbye, they entered the car, and I watched them away—

my last glimpse of the Eliots, and T. S. Eliot's last time in the United States.

v

He died in London two years later on January 4, 1965. I heard the news with that sense of shock which briefly makes things seem unreal. It was unexpected that I should feel his death so intimately. The key to my response was the affection, as mysterious as it was true, that persisted in my thoughts of him. Amid the abstractions and attenuations that shaped so much of his poetry and his life was a sense of his presence. When, by turns, I think of his work and his days, it is a presence that remains with me like a design for an unfinished portrait of someone I had once known.

1 9 5 9

The Vatican's
Hundred-Year Proviso

i

NEARING THE END OF MY QUEST, I drove into Rome during the early afternoon of October 31, 1959. I arrived with high hopes but low expectations. At work on the research phases of a biography of Jean Baptiste Lamy, first bishop and archbishop of Santa Fe, who was a Frenchman born in the Midi, I had gone first to Paris. There the office of Cardinal Feltin granted me access to any archives pertaining to Lamy—but there were none there. At Lyons I was received by Cardinal Gerlier—hero of the French Resistance—but all he could tell me was that any matter concerning Lamy had been transferred with all the Lyons archives to Freiburg. But undoubtedly there were copies in Rome—surely I was going to Rome?

It was true: the great prize lay ahead in the archives of the Vatican, consisting of the central documentary record of Lamy's life, particularly during the years 1851 to 1888. It was, I had already been told by prelate and historian alike, a prize that I would never see—because of the unbreakable "hundred-year rule." The ancient and inflexible proviso of this rule decreed that public access to archival materials less than a hundred years old was forbidden. I would be working on the years from the 1850s to the 1880s—a span of four decades closed to me under the hundred-year ban; yet these were the four most important decades of Lamy's life. If I could not have access to those years in the archives, there would be little point to my going ahead with my biography of him.

But even in the face of a lost hope, such as I had been assured of by all who knew, it seemed to me that if I were going across Europe collecting my notes, it would be gross neglect of duty not to throw myself against the official walls of the Curia in Rome, though my defeat were inevitable. In fact, letters to prepare my way, even if certain to prove useless, had been sent off to Rome by my own archbishop, Edwin V. Byrne of Santa Fe, who had a keen interest in seeing that the life of his first predecessor would be written. Archbishop O'Connor, rector of the American College in the Via Umiltà, was informed that I would be coming to Rome and would appeal to him for proper introductions. Father Philip Caraman, S.J., of London, had also prepared my way with requests for help from his fellow historians in the Jesuit establishment in Rome. He had also advised me to appeal directly to a certain Very Reverend Father Frederick Heinzmann, M.M., procurator general of Maryknoll, and rector of Maryknoll House in Rome, who in mysterious ecclesiastical tradition could open—or close—many doors in Roman corridors.

But none of these measures, I had been promised, would be of the slightest avail, and I must be prepared for the worst. The last case which anyone could recall in whose behalf the proviso had been waived was that of George N. Shuster, president of Hunter College, and that was done by direct order of Pope Pius XII himself, who had asked Dr. Shuster to write the history of the Vatican in its troubled years during World War II. The work was never written, and, so far as I knew, nobody since had been granted the waiver. Still, if I insisted on trying for myself. . . .

ii

As I entered Rome through appalling traffic, the top was closed on my car—I had rented a little Fiat convertible for the drive from Paris —and a cold rain was falling. Under a dark sky the building stones of Rome were wet and darkened to a somber rust color. I was tired from the long drive and my spirits fell under the overcast day. Was

I on a fool's errand? But here I was and I should pause to catch my breath—and, in any case, nothing could be done in Rome on Saturday.

I claimed my reservation—two small, square, cold marble rooms —in the Hotel de la Ville on the Trinity Mount above the Spanish Steps. I went to have lunch next door on the roof garden of the Hassler Hotel. The view was fine—a scattered splendor of baroque domes and finial lanterns washed by the silver light of rain. In a corner of the restaurant the King of Denmark was lunching with a small suite. "Europe," I thought. After lunch there were two errands; one, to call at the American Academy for mail, and two, to surrender my car to the rental agency, for what I had just seen of Roman streets, cars, and drivers made it plain that I was no match for their brilliant chaos. I then retired to my rooms for a long nap. At eight o'clock, as a matter of discipline, I ventured out to dine at the Hotel Excelsior. After dinner I went into the almost deserted bar to take a cappucino, and recognized a small, thickset man with a drooping mustache as the author of *A Streetcar Named Desire*. He quickly made away with a small brandy and left. A pair of American tourists came in to sit at the bar, a man and a woman. The bartender said to someone else who came to sit along the way, "Tennessee was here. Just left." The American male exclaimed to his companion, "What? Did you hear that, Tennessee Ernie Ford was just here! Wish we'd seen him!" "America," I thought.

Late the next morning I went to Mass at St. Peter's, and under the echoing sound of the human throng in that enclosing world-space I was for the moment relieved of my anxieties and hopes. It was enough for the moment to be lost in humility and glory. But late in the afternoon I could no longer put off coming face to face with my purpose. I rang the telephone number of the Maryknoll House and asked for the Father Rector.

"This is Father Heinzmann." I gave my name, and he said, after a pause, "So you came anyhow." I remember well enough how it went from there, in substance, if not literally.

"Yes. I have a letter to you from Archbishop Byrne of Santa Fe, and I would like to deliver it, and to tell you how I have been proceeding so far."

"Ah, Mr. Horgan, it cannot be of any use—it really is a shame you came to Rome looking for what cannot happen!"

"So everybody has told me, Father, but I had to try."

"I suppose so. —Where are you?" I told him. He said, "Yes, it's not too far away. Well, if you can find a cab, it is raining hard, come and see me here," and he gave me the address. "You can hand me your archbishop's letter, though I wrote to him weeks ago advising that you spare yourself a trip to Rome. I do not mean to be unwelcoming, but you do see:"

"I know. Thank you. I'll come right along."

iii

It was dark as night as I drew up to Maryknoll House. He was waiting at the door. We went into a low-lighted, chilly room and sat in a panelled corner. I handed him the Archbishop's letter. He opened it, read it swiftly, laid it aside, and said, "I've no doubt you would make good use of the Lamy material. It is sometimes a great pity that excellent work has to be sacrificed to what is, when all is said and done, a prudent and proper rule."

Clearly, he was a man of the upper officer class; direct, well spoken, with ready charm and serene authority. He was tall and trim. His energy showed in repose. He wore rimless eyeglasses that doubled the light of his eyes. In the rather dim reception room where we sat, those points of optical light were bright. As he continued to discourage me, he was friendly.

The hundred-year proviso, he said, however frustrating to scholars with immediate needs that overlapped the forbidden time frame, was actually a prudent and perhaps even compassionate policy. In many a case, the central concerns of the Church often had implications that were not to be executed or judged or subjected to political stresses until a long—a century-long—time of seasoning, as it were, could test their legitimacy. Contexts changed, nuances of papal policy might or might not respond, and the continuity of the essential Faith must at all costs be protected. Again, immense amounts of the archives had to do with individual and personal matters; inevitably some of these might carry implications of scandal, or other quite innocent suggestions whose untimely revelation could, without the proviso, unjustly affect living individuals. Finally, all scholars were not equally gifted in the art of historical perspective. These—a spark of humor winked from his lenses—were protected from their indiscretions by the proviso.

"But I suppose these reflections are of small comfort to you, Mr. Horgan."

"I'm afraid not, Father. —But could you arrange for me to see Archbishop O'Connor at the American College? I understand he does wonders for visiting Americans with serious requests."

"Ah: I'm afraid not: he is in the United States for the annual conference of bishops. However, before he left, he answered Archbishop Byrne's letter about you, urging that you be advised not to come to Rome, as nothing could be done. I saw the correspondence."

In that cold, rain-hushed, dimly lit room, something made me unwilling to close my own door on my hopes, and, mainly to continue the conversation, I said, "What is the location of the archives?"

"You are staying at the Hotel de la Ville at the top of the Spanish Steps. You go down the steps to the Piazza di Spagna, turn left, pass the American Express, and a few steps beyond, across the way, is the Palace of the Propaganda Fide—a fine affair designed by Bernini. All the archives of the Church in far countries are there. The Prefect of the Propaganda Fide is Cardinal Agagianian, a splendid man and a fine scholar. I see him frequently in the interests of my missionary Order."

"I recognise his name. He was a strong candidate for the papacy at the recent consistory, was he not?"

"Yes. He is now close to the Holy Father"—John XXIII.

"I see."

A long moment. Then, "What led you to undertake this work on Lamy?"

I suppose I sounded rueful as I described the background of my lost cause. I told of my boyhood visits to the Santa Fe of 1915 and after—its Old World airs, primitive utilities, and everywhere evidences of the life and work of the French bishop who had come there in 1851. His hospital, schools, college, cathedral, all spoke of public mercies. His personal presence also seemed real to me, because Santa Fe friends of my parents grew up knowing Lamy in their childhood when he came visiting. He would bring fruit from his famous garden, and presents for sick children, and he even came to plant young trees in their front yard—anything for growth. Then there was the great scale and splendor of the landscape of New Mexico and the Southwest to write about as part of his life. There, in his diocese larger than all France, he lived the travelling life of the frontiersman, days and nights of hardship to which even in his frail constitution he was equal. The more I read and heard about him as I grew up the more I saw him as a man of both spirit and act who contained historical horizons that defined the great Southwest land I came more and more to love. With all that, there was, to be sure, my affinity as a Catholic for the Bishop's place and effect in the Church. His most appealing aspect, perhaps, was that of the mitred occupant of one of the most august offices on earth who at the same time travelled his time in a hard and beautiful wilderness as humbly as any Mexican *paisano* on his bony burro. In a word, character. In pursuit of my subject I had already been all over the Southwest, and the Rocky Mountains, and to Europe; and there were more places to go—the American Middle West, the Gulf of Mexico, Arizona and California, and deep into Mexico itself; for I must see every place where he had himself been; or so I had planned. . . .

Another long moment. Then, with a little breath of impatience governed by a sense of duty, Father Heinzmann said, "Well: since you have travelled all this distance, perhaps we owe you an attempt, anyway. I'll try to look into a way at least to state your case. But I beg you not to expect—"

He opened his arms to confirm the stalemate, smiled with great friendliness, and showed me out into the dark cold wet street where my taxi was awaiting. Though my thoughts grew darker with the night as I reviewed our conversation, my immediate notion was, "What a charming individual."

iv

I was awakened early the next morning by the bells, near and far, of Rome. It was in the scheme of things that I should hear Mass next door at the Trinità dei Monti. When I returned to my hotel room my telephone bell was ringing—short, insistent jabs. I answered.

"Hello, Mr. Horgan. Father Heinzmann here. I have arranged for you to see Cardinal Agagianian for a few minutes later this morning." There was a little excitement in his voice. "He has just gone to the Vatican for his usual audience with the Holy Father, after which he will return to his office at the Propaganda. What you must do is prepare immediately a memorandum of your project, as much as you can describe in two pages. Include the sort of thing you told me last evening, and give an outline of your credentials, including honors (don't be modest), and your previous experience as an author. You have a typewriter? —Good. Now get to it, and don't leave your room. I am to call you back when the Cardinal leaves the Vatican. You must then go at once to the Propaganda and wait for your appointment with His Eminence."

"But I don't know how to find him."

"True. I will meet you at the entrance to the building. You cannot miss that. Be sure to have your paper ready within the hour."

"Yes, and Father, thank you, thank you—"

"No, no, nothing has changed. Now get busy!"

I typed for perhaps forty minutes, reaching over into a third page, when my phone rang.

"Heinzmann here. He has just left. He will be at the Propaganda in twenty minutes. You must go there at once. Are you ready?"

"I have only another paragraph—"

"Cut it short. I must go now myself. I will wait for you."

I joined him within the great arch of the entrance to the palace. He led me up a long *scala* of shallow marble steps to a high second floor; down a wide corridor like a drawing for an exercise in grand perspective, and into a great square anteroom whose walls were lined with I'd guess fifty people, waiting with their petitions, whatever they might be. We were received by an official in a sort of uniform and personal bearing that proclaimed *majordomo* of the office. He bent deeply before Father Heinzmann, who said to him, "This is Mr.

Horgan from the United States. He is to see His Eminence at once, *before* all these people. Is that clear?

"Yes, Father."

"Has His Eminence arrived yet?"

"No, Father."

"Good. Now"—turning—"Mr. Horgan, your paper?"

I gave it to him. He did not glance at it, but handed it to the *majordomo*.

"You will hand this to His Eminence before he sees Mr. Horgan."

"Understood, Father."

"Very well. Thank you. —Mr. Horgan, I leave you. Telephone me after your interview. God bless."

Superb in his fierce authority, which was accented by his thick upbrushed mustachios, the *majordomo* pointed me to a high marble doorway leading out of the anteroom. As we passed all the longing suppliants on the wall chairs, he disdained their pleading looks, and took me through a door opening upon a lane of red carpet that led past a row of towering windows to a far door forty or fifty feet away. Halfway along, he bowed me into a great gilded armchair in a deep window embrasure and returned to his thronged anteroom.

The grand reception room where he left me alone was coldly splendid, with its walls of green silk brocade against which hung huge papal and curial portraits. The lofty windows were draped in heavy moiré silk of cardinal scarlet, the hue of rank. Chandeliers of festooned lusters took up the light of the windows. It was a clear day over Rome. I was put in mind of the Palazzo Farnese setting for Act II of *Tosca*.

How long must I wait? Affecting composure I did not feel, I took from my pocket a small book, *Sybil*, by Disraeli. I opened it and began to read without taking in anything. I had hardly turned a page when in a peripheral flash I saw the entrance door open upon a waft of scarlet silk. The *majordomo* stepped ahead. Holding my memorandum pages out before him like a banner, he led Cardinal Agagianian along the red carpet in a two-man procession. They came briskly. As they passed me, I rose and bowed deeply, in silence, like a courtier. They vanished through the far door, which was faced with leather and studded with bronze rosettes. The door had barely closed after them when it came violently open again to reveal the *majordomo*. With a commanding scowl and with both hands he waved me forward. In a few seconds I was alone with the Prefect of the Propaganda Fide.

Standing by his plain, flat-topped desk, the Cardinal extended his hand. I kissed his ring. In excellent English he said, "Do sit down, Mr. Horgan," and indicated a chair facing him at the end of the desk. He took his own seat, and without preliminaries, held up my memorandum and asked, "This is your paper?"

"Yes, Your Eminence."

"I shall read it."

He was a figure of style and authority, of average height and weight, with a full-fleshed face and a rather lean mouth. Behind his spectacles his eyes were large, very dark, and luminous, declaring his Armenian race. In a random recollection I thought he somewhat resembled Pope Pius XI of decades past. He read rapidly, leaning his brow upon his right hand. Midway into my second page, he paused, faced me with an intent narrowed look, and with a finger on a typed reference of mine, he asked, "You *are* a Knight of St. Gregory, Mr. Horgan?"

"Yes, Your Eminence."

"Under which papacy and what cause?"

"Pius XII, 'for services to literature,' " I quoted from the citation.

"Thank you."

He resumed reading. When he finished, he took up his desk telephone. "Send Father Kowalski to me," he said, put down the phone, turned fully toward me with a broad smile, and said, "So how is life in New Mexico these days?" and for three or four minutes engaged me in conversation that showed a lively knowledge of various parts of the United States. This was ended by the arrival of Father Peter Kowalski, S.J.—a tall, slender, black-and-white priest— pallid in face and hands, black in hair and cassock.

The Cardinal introduced us, saying that Father Kowalski was superintendent of documents. He then took up a pen and wrote a word and initialled it on my last page. He handed it to Father Kowalski, and said, "Mr. Horgan is here for research. He is to have everything he asks for."

Struck by the bolt of this, I yet was able to hear the superintendent say, "Yes, Your Eminence—everything, of course, except materials sealed under the hundred-year rule . . ."

With a shade of asperity, the Cardinal replied, *"I said everything. Please conduct him to the shelves for a first look."*

Whiter still under astonishment and reproof, Father Kowalski bowed to me to follow him. I began to stammer my overwelling thanks to the Cardinal, but he halted me, shook hands to prevent my kissing his ring again, made the sign of his blessing over me, and said, "God bless your work, Mr. Horgan. Good morning."

Within fifteen minutes I held the first of the proscribed Lamy papers in my hand on that morning of November 2, 1959.

v

Father Kowalski gave me into the care of Mr. Anton Debeveč, a Yugoslav curator, who had a passive but not unfriendly Balkan temperament. He heard without emotion that I was to have access to "everything" and calmly set up a work table and chair for me in the stacks. After a few questions—he was fluent in English—he took me to the many shelves of my subject, with their thick, hinged boxes of papers. (Eventually my catalogue of papers consulted listed over eight hundred.)

But on that morning all I could do was make a symbolic gesture. I drew out a handful of papers at random, sat down at my table, and began to copy them by hand, in a sense "taking possession," still marvelling at the strike of fortune.

At a quarter before one o'clock, Mr. Debeveč came to me and politely said that the archives closed every day at one o'clock. I must pack up to leave. Also, the Propaganda would be closed all the following day to honor a papal anniversary, but I could return the day after, and every day as I chose. My table would be waiting. His announcement brought me out of my state of shock. I hurried to my hotel and telephoned Father Heinzmann. Before I could say a word, he cried jubilantly, "Congratulations! Extraordinary! I am delighted for you!"

"But how did you know?"

"But this is Rome!"—with a smile in his voice.

"I know, but—"

I was starving to know, too, what had happened to my cause between the time I left him on the previous evening and the time of the Cardinal's audience with Pope John XXIII this morning. When I risked a question about this, Father Heinzmann gave the effect of a shrug on the phone and said that sometimes things worked out unexpectedly. He then said that tickets of admission to two papal events of the next day would shortly be delivered to me at my hotel. He thought these would be of interest. He instructed me to call him if I needed any further assistance, wished me well, and hung up.

vi

As I began to inhabit my good fortune realistically, I was confronted with increasingly formidable aspects of it. How long must it take for me to copy by hand all the papers that I would need? How many mornings, weeks, months, even years? Had I come to Rome prepared to take up residence? How could I afford the cost? I had duties and on-running expenses at home. Yet to abandon my privilege and the archive itself was unthinkable. Could I engage an amanuensis to do my copying while I returned to the United States? But how could he decide what to extract? All circles of the superb dilemma went around in my thoughts for the next twenty-four hours. In the meantime, using Father Heinzmann's tickets, I went twice to the Vatican on the next day.

The first event was a *Missa da gloriam* celebrated in St. Peter's to commemorate the first anniversary of the ascension of John XXIII to the papacy. The incomparable basilica was thronged to the limit. My ticket seated me in a tribune high up between two arches overlooking the apse and the altar under Bernini's Chair of St. Peter. There was a long wait in the half-lit spaces which the vast crowd filled with the echoing surf of their endless talk. Every now and then in some cove of the crowd someone started applause which caught on and became rhythmic, rudely telling the authorities to get on with it, and then died off. When least expected, with the equivalent effect of a crash of cymbals, all the electric lights on columns and arches surged on, to be greeted by total applause. Trumpets sounded from the great central doors. The long procession slowly materialized—master of ceremony, Swiss Guards, acolytes, choir, priests, lower prelates, bishops, cardinals, the celebrant Cardinal Giovanni Batista Montini of Milan, later to be Pope Paul VI, and finally, in the *sedia gestatoria*, Pope John XXIII. Borne at the rhythm of walking bearers, his chair ambled through the air like a howdah, and he rode it in amiable adjustment to its elephantine sway. Constantly he gave his blessing, smiling right and left. His little eyes gleamed with sleepy benevolence. He wore the triumphant triple tiara. Half an hour later he was enthroned, the Mass began and continued for nearly two hours. The Pope himself read the homily from the throne. Cardinal Montini officiated with slim, aristocratic bearing. The recessional took as long as the entry. Like any Roman, I partook of the glory, the power, and the inner significance of the event, and some of it came away with me.

In the early evening of the same day, my other ticket brought me to the Vatican palace, up the Scala di Reggia, to the *stanzae* and a painted chamber where John XXIII gave a mass audience to a thousand or so pilgrims from Poland. Many hundreds more attended. It happened that I was on the inner edge of the crowd along the pathway to be taken by the Pope as he made his exit, again in the *sedia gestatoria*. The moment was memorable for me as he was borne slowly by, for in one of his turns of blessing, facing my side of the crowd, he peered directly at me in the shaft of his general benevolence, which I took to myself with a high smile. I think to this day that some gleam of communion passed between us.

I returned to my table in the archives the next morning, and the next. My problems of organization were no nearer solution; but a vagrant question lingered until it became an imperative. Finally, with apologetic diffidence, I asked Mr. Debeveč, "Do you ever make microfilms of papers here?"

"Yes. Would you want some?"

"Oh? Yes, I would, I would. —Could they be sent to me?"

"Yes. How much would you want?"

"Well, then, everything relating to Lamy, and the American Southwest, and northern Mexico, and the missionary church in the Middle West—" and for the next half hour we made a list together, defining the boundaries of my subject. My sense of relief was overwhelming. My problems of study were instantly resolved. I could work with the papers at home. I could travel at will to places there cited as significant to Lamy. A fine, long vista of planned work on my own terms reached out ahead of me. Mr. Debeveč for the first time smiled at my preoccupations. I gave him my address, even my telephone number at home, and thanked him with all my heart. We shook hands. I returned to the Hotel de la Ville, wrote a note explaining the turn of events to Father Heinzmann, reserved air passage for the following day, Saturday, and on that Saturday evening, November 7, 1959, joined friends in London for a time of reunions, concerts, exhibitions, theatre, and, in various forms, the giving of thanks for my mysterious Roman outcome. Three months later, my Vatican microfilms reached me in New Mexico.

vii

Once again in Santa Fe, I made my report to Archbishop Byrne. His satisfaction was almost equal to mine. Later, I met with an old friend and colleague, Fray Angelico Chavez, O.F.M., the New Mexico historian and archdiocesan archivist, and told him my story. He heard me out in Franciscan good cheer which broke down into scoffing as I went on to say that I had finally come to an explanation of Cardinal Agagianian's decision in my behalf. I said, "Remember that he asked me to confirm my statement that I was a Knight of St. Gregory?"

"Yes?"

"Well: do you know that his middle name is Gregory? He is Peter Gregory Cardinal Agagianian. The name Gregory might well have seemed a sign . . ."

Fray Angelico gave a little note of scornful laughter. In effect, he replied, "What superstitious nonsense! He is probably one of the most sophisticated men in Rome. Why would your parochial school clue mean anything to him? No. Tell me this: where had he just been before you saw him?"

"At the Vatican."

"Whom had he just been with there?"

"Pope John XXIII."

"Who had already proclaimed an era of new openness in the Church? Who else could give permission with one word to break the hundred-year rule, given cause?"

"Pope John."

"There you are."

1962

At Mrs. Longworth's

i

WASHINGTON IS A CITY of transient persons, fugitive ideas, and enduring monuments. Of this third category, the most enlivening through many years was the Dowager Patroness of the United States, Alice Roosevelt Longworth. Administrations came and went, political philosophies clashed and changed, but Mrs. Longworth for seven decades provided that continuity which stood for more than itself, in a historical sense; for, coming to brilliant visibility as a girl, during and after the tenure of her father, Theodore Roosevelt, as President, she had three great phases of effect in the capital, each with its special character.

The first of these was her young womanhood, during her White House years, when she was known around the world as Princess Alice; gave the energy of her style to a shade of blue; established her high originality in public as a lifelong attribute; released her great share of the Roosevelt vitality into the national character; and without working for what other ladies—opera prima donnas, theatre stars, British suffragettes—had to seek professionally, she became the embodiment of the sort of glamour that demands imitation—though her particular graces of wit and intelligence, both often reckless as she expressed them, remained unique.

The second phase came when, as wife to Speaker of the House Nicholas Longworth, she spent her middle years in active politics, whether making campaign speeches from the brass-balustraded platforms of private railroad cars or, in evening drawing rooms, bringing legislators into line with deadly banter. She campaigned for her father against William Howard Taft; she campaigned for her husband in his biennial suits for his seat in the House; she gave loud and merry aid and comfort to the opponents of Woodrow Wilson; she twice, in famous verbal cartoons, did hilarious damage to a Presidential nominee—it was Thomas E. Dewey—helping him to lose his two runs for the White House by describing him, in his first, as "the little man on the wedding cake," and, in his second, by declaring that he could not win even then, since "a soufflé never rises twice." With her closest friend and political ally of the old days, Ruth Hanna McCormick (Simms), she worked in every sort of job of participatory democracy except that of seeking office herself. Her names, Roosevelt and Longworth, were of value in these undertakings; but they would not have worked in and of themselves. It took her spirited character, her civilized gaiety, and her all-out convictions to make her a figure of political consequence—one of the first American women to achieve this position.

As the years drew on, she knew personal sorrows—the loss of her father, her husband, her daughter, her son-in-law, her best friend. The third style of her life seemed to emerge in her sensitive and sensible survival of such changes. Her life became symbolic, as it remained to her dying day—a matter of presiding socially, rather than of acting politically. Her unsparing realism—in which she spared herself least of all—continued to see life as an affair deserving of serious judgment delivered with the lightest, most precise of witticisms. In these, the great range of her mind was marvelously evident. Her originality of thought and statement was supported by a fine tangle of reference and style coming out of her acquaintance with the world's interesting persons and her appetite for reading. All the new books poured in upon her. It was said she read all night, consenting to take a nap from daybreak until noon. It was then that the morning's letters, telegrams, and phone messages had their turn, and the liveliest personal life in Washington its daily send-off.

For many of her friends, it reached its peak late in the afternoon, when Mrs. Longworth received in her upstairs drawing room. Her house was obscured by heavy, deliberately unpruned vines—a miniature jungle over the recessed approach to her door, masking it from the incessant traffic of Massachusetts Avenue.

ii

The door is opened for you by a uniformed maid. You say your name as if it were Strether or Selden, and give her your hat, gloves, and stick (these accessories are often more ideal than real, but they suggest the atmosphere of a house out of pages in Henry James or Edith Wharton). The light is dim as you mount stairs to the next floor. At the turn of the stair you pass by a great pelt of a grizzly bear, hanging in reference to the trophied life of T.R., the Rocky Mountain hunter. From the stairwell you enter a first drawing room facing the avenue. Here, between the windows, is Peter Hurd's coolly elegant portrait of Mrs. Longworth, painted when she was eighty-one years of age. Against an abstract background of pearl gray, she is shown wearing a heather tweed jacket, a short string of pearls, and a model of that famous black hat, with its round crown and wide, down-turned brim, which she has adopted as her hat for occasions. Her eyes are gray-blue. Her hair, swept lightly past her ears, is silvery. Her face is pale, with a remote coral glow. In repose, her expression is faintly melancholy, even in the hint of the smile lifting her cheeks. The portrait is a lovely first glimpse of her, and of the depth of feeling rarely otherwise seen in the high spirits that play across her face in conversation.

You turn to the left, perhaps hearing voices already there before you, including her own, the strongest, in words spoken at high speed to keep pace with her flow of ideas, accompanied by hoots of Rooseveltian laughter, and you enter the second drawing room, where, near a superb portrait of her granddaughter Joanna Sturm by Henriette Wyeth, Mrs. Longworth presides at the tea tray set before her at her small, low settee. She may, or may not, be wearing the black hat. She hails you, as she does every guest, in a burst of gaiety; you are introduced around, told what is being talked about as you arrive, given your tea and the thinnest-known buttered slices of a particular white bread, of which there is a generous pyramid on a silver dish amid all the other apparatus of the tea ceremony. The company— it is never large for tea—is ranged on low chairs or ottomans, facing the hostess.

The first element of the room is comfort, with no attempt to state a style except that most genuine of all styles: the expression, here the profusion, of diverse objects adhering to a biography. Small standing photographs, most of them presenting recognizable personages, on cloth-covered surfaces; a grand piano; some old shadowy paintings, probably "good," in dim gold frames; lamps with pleated silk shades; a Chinese painting, almost wall-high, of a glaring tiger; flowers on several tables; dark, rich rugs; a mild golden light; nothing "matching"; everything well used; the chairs and sofas so placed that even when empty they suggest continuing conversation, for this is a house of talk. The temperature cool. On a small table to Mrs. Longworth's left is a telephone. This may ring several times during tea and be dealt with briskly, in a manner that may even include for the invisible caller a description of who's here and what is being talked about. Mrs. Longworth's telephone "presence" is strong, her voice vibrant, her laugh caught up in her words. Telephone calls are not protracted; end abruptly, with no tapering off in any word of conclusion. Back to the tea circle, and the drawn curtains, which have established evening within, though late afternoon may still be rushing by in the avenue traffic outside. Out of separate occasions a composite hour, its scandals and credulities, its romping dialogue, come into memory's compass.

iii

To suggest her grasp on life itself, you have only to note that, in her late eighties, Mrs. Longworth is delightfully pretty. People always speak of "good bones" as the great lasting ingredient of beauty in age; and the item has its place here. But there is more. It is her whole bearing, which carries dashing comeliness. She sits erect on her sofa against the wall, looking very small, and, but for the energy of her every word and gesture, she might appear frail—which taken objectively she surely must be. Yet the animation in her pale eyes, full of the light of her darting intelligence, and the quick turn of her small, neat, finely shaped head, and the onrush of her speech, with its hilariously precise vocabulary, delivered in an accent comfortably placeless though unmistakably aristocratic, and in a strong, finely placed voice, get rid at once of the notion that age, apart from matters of long experience of people and style, has anything to do with how you regard her. She is a master of the art of dialogue, in the high tradition of drawing-room comedy, though you sometimes hope she will go in for the monologue, and, yes, at times she creates a sort of aria or, in the classical French dramatic sense, a *tirade*, in which, by lightning-quick association of ideas, she spins out an anecdote, a characterization, a judgment, which unhappily lacks its Boswell. All this is far from artless. She knows her powers, plays them according to her audience, and carries off her effects through astute improvisation. "As good as a play," in the old Briticism; and all too often, her callers have come for a show, though the most frequent ones are those who love her beyond all the rhetoric and her status as an institution. It is a measure of her absolute self-awareness that she once said, after some reported exchange that made the tears roll down her listener's cheeks in laughter, "You know, *I sell myself . . .*" So she shares in the sense of a performance that attends her.

At her gatherings, her granddaughter is often present. Joanna Sturm, in her twenties, is the closest "family" left to Mrs. Longworth, and has lived with her grandmother for a number of years. There is no sense of one "taking care" of the other, but on the part of the elder, there is now and then a mock challenge of the young woman's presence. Joanna often knows what is coming, sits a little removed, saying little, gazing steadily with her clear gray eyes, sometimes prompting her grandmother to say, with a small howl of drollery, "Joanna disapproves of me when I say" whatever it is. Joanna makes no move to contradict this. When she does speak, it is as rapidly as her grandmother, with as much crisp sense and charm. She reads as voraciously as Mrs. Longworth, is a frequent traveler to far places— the American West, the Arabian Near East—and at large parties in the house, when several groups necessarily form, one such always gathers around her for her calm beauty and quickness of mind. She bears a strong resemblance to an early photograph of Alice Roosevelt.

It is never long until the subject of the other Roosevelts comes up —the F.D.R.s. Here there is always matter for damage. In her autobiography, *Crowded Hours,* published in 1933, Mrs. Longworth remarked that she had "a proclivity toward malice that occasionally comes over me"—a simple acceptance of a trait that, reported secondhand, sometimes seems cruel, but that, received direct, with all the lively airs of zestful comedy, finds itself invested with skill and charm, and what remains is not always wounding, but only amusing, with nothing of the serious attack about it, or the attempt to missionize opinions. In her many references to the non-Oyster Bay branch of the family, there does remain, though, a strong flavor of old partisan loyalties to her father's first political home, the Republican Party. In her response to the fact that her cousin Franklin won his way as a Democrat to what Mrs. Longworth always refers to as "The House" (and we know she means her childhood home of seven years at 1600 Pennsylvania Avenue), there is a chaffing mockery of what must always have struck her as a wild aberration of politics. She and Franklin and Eleanor were close in their youth. Perhaps she once admired him; perhaps she once felt sorry for her plain female cousin. These days, giving a scene on her sofa, Mrs. Longworth says, after the Lucy Mercer story became public:

"Oh! I was so glad for Franklin. Poor creature. It was time he had a little fun."

That this fun was what broke the heart and changed the life of the President's wife makes no change in a lifelong opinion. Eleanor was *always* earnest. She was *"oh, so good."* She was *"worthy"*—an inflection on this, which mocked the whole idea. There is a little hint of never-lost wonder that so handsome, amusing, lighthearted, if not too bright, a cousin should have married Eleanor.

"Have I ever done you my Eleanor face?"

"Oh, no. Would you?"

An immediate transformation, hard to credit. The exquisite small head, with its finely proportioned features, turns into a caricature of her cousin Eleanor—teeth prominent, eyes soberly searching, body slumping, head thrust forward from hunched shoulders as if in search of worthiness itself. It is a scandal, and when in a few seconds the pose is dropped, the general laughter includes none merrier than that of the actress.

"I do a number of others. Remind me one day."

Various Presidencies play a large part in Mrs. Longworth's life and talk. She accepts them all, not entirely impartially, but with a sense that since they come and go, and since she remains on stage and who she always has been, it is a sort of obligation for her to be nonpartisan and grant due attention to the incumbent. Her judgment, of course, goes further in personal terms. The Lyndon Johnsons are mentioned.

"I like them both," she says. "I've known them, of course, forever. He's an enormously effective man. It is amazing how many people who think they have judgment miss the fact that he is highly intelligent . . . *She* is an extraordinary woman. I do like her so much. She does ring true."

The Kennedys?

"Of course, they all delight me. Jack was a *charmeur.* Some people can impersonate intelligence and then wake up to find they possess it. I did love what Mrs. K. did to The House. And there was always what was so often lacking in other regimes."

"?"

"Good talk." A gust of amusement. "Did I ever tell you about Bobby and the mountain? . . . You of course remember that preposterous affair of the Canadian mountain which the brothers and some of the rest went out to climb after Jack's death, and how they took along a flag specially run up for the purpose, and unfurled it at the top—a Kennedy flag, something no one had ever heard of before, with a device—I suppose a fantasy of heraldry run up by loving hands at home. Soon after the conquest of the mountain, and the planting of the flag, when they bestowed the name Mount Kennedy on the helpless rock, I saw Bobby; he was here at a party. I attacked him." Her eyes dance with merriment. "I said to him: 'Very well for naming the mountain, I suppose, but really: the flag is too much of a muchness.' " She always loved provoking a response, and had one then. "Bobby was instantly in a rage with me; all blue glares and an Irish flush. He was speechless for a moment, looking for some way to come back at me. Then he found it. I could see his thoughts on his face. He was talking to a very old woman, and this gave him the clue. He said in a fury, 'Alice, have you made plans and given instructions for your funeral?' For he thought the best way to wound me was to make me think of my own death. 'Don't be an idiot,' I said; 'of course I have, even down to the pallbearers.' He glared at me, and I said, 'It is all arranged for you to be one, and I've given you a partner, and you'll both sit side by side in the front pew, the two of you, you and Dick Nixon!' " She laughs briefly at the high ceiling. "Ah, how furious that made him! . . . I love Bobby; we are the best of friends." This is before the second tragedy of the brothers.

A snub of a more lethal kind is described with joy. During the Eisenhower Administration she was invited to a state dinner at The House, and the White House arranged for Senator Joseph R. McCarthy to escort her that evening—a masterpiece of obtuse ineptitude. Bringing a senior-prom nosegay in cellophane, the luckless man, then at the height of his obscene antics in the Senate, came to call for her.

"He wore white tie, carried a tall silk hat, and bore up under an opera cape with white satin lining thrown back on his shoulder: an elderly chorus boy with a blue jaw. When I came down the long stairway, he greeted me by my first name. I paused on the lowest step. Could I believe my ears!" She smiles in delight at what is to come. " 'Senator McCarthy,' I said, 'my secretary calls me by my first name. My hairdresser may do so if he likes. My father's chauffeur used to do so. To you, I am Mrs. Longworth. Come along.' "

As to Presidents, her own father was not immune from her analytical strikes. She once said of T.R. that he always had to be the corpse at every funeral and the bride at every wedding. In her book of the thirties, she described how cronies from the Congress came to play poker with Nicholas Longworth, one of whom was Senator Warren G. Harding, who as President held for some time the championship for presiding over a corrupt Administration. She didn't find him personally culpable. He was, in her judgment, not a bad man—"he was just a slob." His wife, who got herself up like a walking floor lamp in the period of tassels and fringe, was a relentless shrew. She pronounced her husband's name most remarkably. It went, says Mrs. Longworth, something like this—"Wurr-rran. Wurr-rran." And the impersonation actually evokes that unlucky woman, with her fussiness of dress, her pince-nez, which, gathering a pinch of flesh at the low center of her brow, gave her a look of permanent headache, and her black band, which held her neck together. Another Presidential wife—Mrs. Taft—comes in for a performance, too—Mrs. Longworth's face disappears; in its place, the dropped eyelids, the mindless adoption of whatever might be occurring, the thick loose outthrust lower lip, together with a slow, mechanical turning of the head from right to left, back and forth, conjures up, absolutely, the look of a passive camel.

"How on earth can you do it?" people ask at such transformations when she resumes herself. She shrugs. She supposes it is some knack of not only looking like but *feeling* like her victims, for an instant or two. This kind of skilled farcing stands for more than japery; it is proof of a gift for knowing very sharply the essential life in anyone else. She could describe it in words, she could enact it in being.

iv

This sort of hilarious communication played a large part in an audience she gave to a British journalist, a young man named Aitken, a grandnephew of Lord Beaverbrook. He came to Washington with a CBS crew to tape a television interview with her. It was a virtuoso performance by both participants. She filmed very handsomely. Her spontaneous remarks, spoken at her usual lightning speed, sparkled and danced right off the screen. She had moments when she would speak seriously, looking earnestly at her visitor, leaning forward a trifle, her brows raised, her eyes luminous and sober; and in another moment, the old mischief was back, and the style once again was epigrammatic, irreverent, the very essence of civilized badinage. She talked politics, and about the life in Washington; she candidly weighed Presidents, and their wives, and public characters, and policies. Aitken asked her if she thought her father was a Great Man, and she replied that she didn't know; nobody knew; it was too soon to know for another hundred years; perhaps he was, perhaps not; but she did know that he gave his best. It was a startling objectivity to come from a Presidential daughter, and it gave a sudden insight into her character, capable as it was of a pragmatic realism, which, beyond comedy or malice, explained, if it might not always excuse, the mockeries, funny or harsh, in her inexhaustible repertoire of social commentary. (Sample: those who "talked" a cause that others enacted were "echo-activists.")

When the television episode was over, I telephoned her from Connecticut, saying among other things that she was the last great actress of drawing-room comedy. I was referring to how such comedy had to rely mostly on manner. Manner, above all, carried the text. Without manner even the most brilliant scene fell flat. With it even the poorest scene went along with sustained energy and wit. When manner and text were equal to each other, as they always were for Mrs. Longworth, high style was the result. I had in mind such artists as Mrs. Fiske, Ethel Barrymore, Gladys Cooper, Edith Evans, Katharine Hepburn. Mrs. Longworth never acknowledged a compliment directly, but there was a sense that all this pleased her, and she turned it aside by asking,

"Don't you think young Aitken altogether good at it?" (I.e., his job.) "Most of those inquisitors are so banal. Asking the right question has everything to do with it."

"Your answers were marvellous."

"But you've no idea," she said, "how much they cut out of the tape! All the best parts, by which I mean the wicked parts. I said whatever came into my head, and I did some of my faces, but they thought much of it too dangerous"—she laughed—"and the twenty minutes you saw was a much edited version. Too bad. Still, I suppose."

Within two weeks, I received a telegram inviting me to dinner at her house, black tie, eight o'clock, and when I telephoned to accept, she told me with glee that CBS had given her a tape of the full, uncut interview, and she would have it run off after dinner "and we will all howl."

There must have been twenty-four for dinner. She received everybody in the first upstairs drawing room. She was resplendent in the evening dress she had settled upon as her permanent model, always the same design, if in many varying color schemes. It was a high-necked, long-sleeved, floor-length dress of metallic brocade. It had pockets along the side, and she often stood with her hands thrust into them, her feet stanced apart, a figure of happy authority and strength. She took care that people met, if they didn't know each other already. Joanna was there, and some vital young Roosevelt men cousins. Mrs. Longworth moved about the two drawing rooms while the cocktails went around, and then when guests began to sit down in clusters she took to her little sofa with Henriette and Peter Hurd, for all they had to talk about since they'd last met.

Dinner arrangements were on the grand side, rather like an intimate version of the banquet gear displayed in Apsley House—much bossed silver and gold, which spoke of family, and The House; the wines in heavy crystal; footmen working along in back of the chairs. Best of all, talk went on at normal voice levels but nonetheless animated for that. As for animation, the hostess, with Andrew Wyeth beside her, was enjoying the event more visibly and volubly than anyone else.

During dinner, matters were going forward in the front rooms— a movie projector was set up, chairs were turned to face an unrolled screen, and cushions thrown down for those who would have to sit on the floor to see the uncut CBS interview. When everyone was settled for the show, Mrs. Longworth called out to one of her young great-nephews, at his post of operator, to start the reel. She stood, she wandered in the little spaces among the chairs and cushions, and delighting in the film as much as anyone there, she cried out from time to time, "Oh! This was cut! You'll see why" or "Watch for this, now!" or "I could have said more at that point," and, in general, providing a running commentary to supplement the entertainment, and leading the laughter, which time and again erupted from the audience. It is almost useless to try to describe live *performance,* and a synopsis of the epigrams, impersonations, subject matter would take as much space as this whole piece. One sample on the film characteristic of the outspoken, self-unsparing play of her memory was this: when, vacationing in the Adirondacks, Vice President Theodore Roosevelt and his family received word that President William McKinley had been shot and was on his deathbed, the young Alice (she was seventeen years old), exclaimed, "Oh! Hurrah! We're going to be President!"

Put simply, the screen gave us a recorded personality at its fullest play; and alive in our midst, enjoying it as much, if not more, than anyone else, was the original personality itself, embodied in a being of immense style who had no truck with either hollow vanity or false modesty. That was the point of the affair: she was beyond caring about the terms of her effect, so long as it amused her to animate it for the amusement of others.

Conversation followed the film. Everyone had seen and heard much to set it going. She had done a sequence about the Hardings which reminded her that recently she had received a new biography of President Harding, which, by a court injunction in favor of the Harding heirs, had had to be published with many excisions. The publisher dramatized this censorship by leaving large blank spaces in the book to show where the forced cuts had been made. But never mind: she knew what was left out: come along—and she led a couple of other guests and me up to her bedroom on the next floor. There, in a profusion of books on a wide table, was the Harding book, and, with it, she had a set of proofs sent her by the author.

"These are the uncut proofs," she said gleefully. "I've had a wildly good time collating the two texts. Look here!" And she found a blank half-page in the book, and the exiled paragraph in the proofs, and showed them together. On any level, to any degree, the passion to know exhilarated her; and so did any opportunity to subvert pompousness, flout repressiveness, or deflate pretension. I looked around. The room was crowded with books and memorabilia. It was otherwise unremarkable in its old, simple, not even "good," furniture. It had the air of being undisturbed for decades. Books stood in rows or lay in piles wherever possible. I remembered with amusement that it was my habit to send an occasional bundle of books to Mrs. Longworth and Joanna, to share copies of some I had particularly liked. One time, after something of an interval, came a note from Mrs. Longworth saying, "I grovel—for never telling you my enjoyment and gratitude for BOOKS." Someone in Washington once repeated to me how Mrs. Longworth had declared with light irony, "Paul Horgan is educating me." Ha.

v

Dining one night in Washington at the Douglass Caters', I was amazed to hear that Mrs. Longworth was coming, though she had only three weeks earlier endured surgery for breast cancer—a double mastectomy. When the guest of honor arrived, she was established by Libby Cater on a sofa near the fireplace, and Libby took me to her, saying, "You won't be sitting with Mrs. L. at dinner, so I want you to have a chance to talk with her now." Mrs. L. looked splendid, not at all like a convalescent patient.

She said to me, "I must give you my outrageous remark for the evening immediately and have it done with. The subject is surgical."

"I'm all ears."

"Well, then," she said, bracing her diminutive figure in its long metallic folds, "I claim to be the only topless octogenarian in Washington."

If there was any vanity here, it lay only in the extremity of the wit. Her indifference to ailments, or perhaps her power of discipline, showed strikingly on the occasion of another evening. Vera—Madame Igor—Stravinsky was to have an exhibition of her paintings in Washington. I was going there with her and Robert Craft for the opening. I telephoned Mrs. Longworth to ask if I might bring them to tea.

"No! I'll give you a dinner party!"

A date was fixed; the event took place as planned. It was another evening for a couple of dozen particularly interesting people. Madame and the hostess hit it off splendidly from the first moment. Mrs. Longworth came downstairs a little late, after my party arrived. She was in tearing spirits throughout the evening. All the more, then, was I astonished to hear from my dinner partner how she had been told on the telephone earlier the same day by Mrs. Longworth that the dinner would have to go on without her, for she felt too ill to leave her bed—because of a chronic ailment, which was unpredictable but which sometimes forced her to cancel engagements. Joanna would take over.

"I never expected to see Alice this evening," said the lady.

"But look at her!" I said. "Listen to her!" For I sat at her side, and she was at that moment having a swift bout of verbal cross-fire with her other neighbor—I think it was William Walton—which had them both laughing. And so it went all evening. Her vitality flowed through the whole gathering, and the effect—not imposed or intended—was to lift spirits, let others sound at their best, create an airy fabric of dialogue and sense, which some few can do, and most cannot, of themselves. Toward midnight, when people began to drift away, as Madame and Craft and I went to her to say good night, Mrs. Longworth stood in the wide doorway between the two drawing rooms and, as if reluctant to see us go, gave a little supplementary show, saying:

"Have you ever seen my gorilla?"

When we said we had not, she, in her subdued robe of gold-and-silver threads, did a face, and made a lumbering parentheses of arms and a hulking of her tiny shoulders that, like all artful dramatic transformations, abolished for the observer the original scale or proportion of the performer, so that only an astonishing view of the representation remained. I suppose it was in something of this sense that Maurice Baring said of Sarah Bernhardt—who was plain and unremarkable offstage—that "she could act beauty. Great beauty." So we saw a most convincing gorilla for seconds, in our moment of leaving. Mrs. Longworth seemed not to want the party to be over. How to let go any moment of amusement or response? She glanced about. Her eye fell on the long Chinese painting of the tiger, with its fierce eye and swept mustache.

"Oh: see that," she cried. "That is my portrait of Dean Acheson" —and in truth the likeness, the caricature, was more than fanciful. But, alas, good night, good night.

vi

With cavalier grace, she managed any absurdities visited upon her from forces of the times, such as commercial restlessness in her neighborhood on Massachusetts Avenue. Some old houses adjoining hers were torn down to make way for a new hotel. During occasional visits to Washington, I would see the hotel going up, and marvel how they could build it actually adjoining her north wall without inflicting every sort of inconvenience. But nobody imagined the one that actually occurred. The builders, about their enthusiastic work, knocked a great hole through her bedroom wall.

What on earth!

Yes, but they were most chagrined. Shambled becomingly. Made offers.

Offers? Repairs?

Yes, of course, to close up the hole, which seemed the minimum. But they went further and proposed to paint not only the new plaster but all the rooms on that floor, to match.

And they did?

No. Too much bother. Think of moving everything; it was not worth the trouble. It would, perhaps, even have led to repainting the entire house, which would be unendurable.

There it rested—though not forever. The hotel people, perhaps feeling that something promising had been struck up through the mishap, came around when the building was finished and declared that they intended to have a Grand Opening, and they thought it would be fine if their distinguished neighbor would agree to be present at the dedication, and cut the ribbon.

It struck her as highly amusing.

Did she do it?

Oh, yes, certainly. How pompous not to have! But a while later, they were back with another idea, and she wasn't sure about this one.

"What was that?"

"You see, they are going to have a new dining room in the hotel, and they want to name it Alice's Restaurant, and have me cut the ribbon there, too. What do you think?"

"Good God, no." There was at the time a hit movie called *Alice's Restaurant,* which was a film that traded on all the dejected and sometimes ruinous hang-ups of the youth counterculture, including drugs. "You can get anything you want / At Alice's Restaurant," ran the nudging refrain of the musically illiterate title song of the piece. "Do you know about the movie?" I asked.

"No, I haven't seen it. Of course I have heard of it," she said.

Having seen it, I explained what it was, what it stood for.

"At best," I added, "the hotel is again exploiting your good nature, and at worst, in this case, making a vulgar joke. Since you've asked, I'd strongly advise against doing it."

I believe that was the end of the matter; though not of Mrs. Longworth's encounter with the youth culture. Some time afterward, in a long-distance conversation, she asked if I had ever seen the rock musical called *Hair?*

"No."

"But you must. I saw it last night," she cried. "There is a road company now playing in Washington. It is ravishing. They really *are* flower children! I quite fell in love with all of them. Why haven't you seen it?"

"I am sure it is too loud for me."

"Yes, true, it is deafening. I kept closing my eyes and falling asleep to get away from the noise. Though I did wake up in time for the nude scene. Yes, I found them all utterly beguiling, and after the play I went back to see all the young people, and I asked the whole company to tea with me, and they came yesterday. It was enchanting . . . Why don't you come down and see it with me again, and I'll ask them all to tea for *you?*"

This happened not to be possible. There is no doubt that it was sad to miss an opportunity to see Mrs. Longworth casting her spell over a group four generations removed from herself. But I did not marvel, any longer, over her brisk and familiar watch upon the world as it ran along before her. In the late spring of 1973, I was in Washington again, and was asked to come round late in the afternoon. As I came in, she heard me, and before any other word, she declaimed in delight, with no hint of sentiment for or against, but only with zest for the spectacle itself,

"Aren't you absolutely loving it all?" She meant Watergate.

vii

On her eighty-ninth birthday, after everyone's fond marvellings, she disposed of these, and looked ahead, like a presiding lady in her own city, leading its public antics.

"On my ninetieth," she said in ringing tones, "we're going to put a tent over Dupont Circle and dance in the streets!"

The spirited plan did not come off, why, I never heard. She died in her sleep on February 20, 1980, at ninety-six.

But well before that, wondering about her increasing frailty, I telephoned late one Sunday evening. It was reassuring when she herself answered.

"Oh," I said. "It is you!"

"Yes. I'm in the kitchen."

"The kitchen?"

"Yes. I sent them all off for the evening. I said to leave just a bite for me. I'm after it now—meat for the cat." Laughter.

1 9 6 3

Roma Barocca

i

IN ROME ONE looked for definitions—an impulse perhaps brought about by the contrast and combination of the incorruptible antique with the decaying modern. Somewhere between those two orders of historical effect abided the baroque; and it was the baroque that spoke to me most persuasively on my arrival in Rome on Monday, September 23, 1963, and throughout the week following. It occurred to me that any act of the arts, philosophy, or human relations which, on its way to completion, developed an appropriate flourish was an expression of the baroque. Itself, my presence and purpose in Rome could have been thought of as an expression of the baroque, when seen against the terms of my life at home in New England, where I divided my days between my office as director of the Center for Advanced Studies at Wesleyan University and my work as a writer in my own silent library. The only flourish of presence there came from the cat, generically a master of the baroque style in pose and behavior, style and impulse.

ii

On the following Sunday, September 29, 1963, at eight o'clock in the morning, the inaugural assembly of the second session of the Second Vatican Council would convene in St. Peter's Basilica. It was my flourish—a serious one—that I expected to be present. I was still working on preparatory studies for a biography of the first Archbishop of Santa Fe, Jean Baptiste Lamy. I had already visited many of the backgrounds of his life in Europe and the United States. It was now important to my sense of his place in the Church that I experience the atmosphere, the legislative earnestness, the power, and the grandeur of a world council of the hierarchy, in St. Peter's, where in 1870 Archbishop Lamy had attended the first Vatican Council. If I was to place him at the 1870 Council, I felt I must see for myself the setting of such a convocation, with its ceremony and protocol of disputation, and the moral force represented by hundreds of bishops gathered at the tomb of St. Peter to reaffirm his teachings and—the touch of the late Pope John XXIII—to test them for nuances of change in the modern world. Letters of appeal on my behalf had preceded me to Rome and I must now find my way to activate them. My ticket of admission to the Council had not yet come to hand.

But I had other urgent commissions in Rome: to meet and interview certain candidates proposed for the Fellowship at the Wesleyan Center.

Lunching in New York earlier on with Dr. Henry Allen Moe, a Wesleyan trustee and my principal advisor on appointments to the Center, I told him of my travel plans—visits to Rome, France, and England to meet Fellowship candidates—and my personal pursuit of Lamy at the Vatican Council. Henry Moe, as founding president of the Guggenheim Foundation during forty years, had a rich mental file of distinguished people in all the scholarly fields. At mention of Rome, he became thoughtful, with that glistening energy in his eye which was persuasive. After a pause to order up a charming smile— another of his administrative weapons—he asked, "How long will you be in Rome?"

"Just under one week."

"Would you have time there to seek out a candidate I will propose to you here and now?"

"Of course." I give only the gist of what followed, but it is enough.

"What would you think of having a cardinal of the Roman Catholic Church in residence as a Fellow of the Center?"

I could only sit back and try to see the idea in mid-air. It delighted me for its daring, but a cautionary note sounded. Wesleyan was famous as a small, highly liberal university, with a faculty whose members had been granted great collective power. What would certain ones think—our theoretical Marxist, our historical determinist, our loyal Freudian? But I must give an answer to my smiling host.

"Yes, well, I suppose everything would depend upon the nature of his qualifications, beyond princely rank *in ecclesiam*"—I smiled back —"as a scholar or productive thinker."

"Rest easy." Henry Moe gave me a succinct sketch of his candidate. He was a Spanish Benedictine, by name Anselmo Cardinal Albareda, who now lived in Rome to pursue the writing of his magnum opus—a life of St. Charles Borromeo, to be complete in four volumes. He was said to be at work on the last volume at the moment. At one time he had been sub-prefect of the Vatican Library, actively in charge of its program of technical modernization. It was in that capacity that he had met Henry Moe, who then was involved in the building, equipping, and technical functioning of the new Firestone Library at Princeton University. At Moe's suggestion, Cardinal Albareda came to the United States as a consultant on the affairs of the Princeton library. They became close friends. Both men delighted in original notions in the intellectual life. Both, to Moe's charmed relief, were connoisseurs of recondite humor as it might appear in matters of history, literature, politics, or human character. Moe had rarely met a man more delicately sophisticated in worldly matters; yet he was one who in his religious and scholarly vocation spoke through refined sensibilities. They enjoyed talking all kinds of shop. They were both great administrators. They both had read everything. With resonances out of history, they retained their composure as they saw the daily world go by. What was more, Henry Moe, without undue weight upon the word, was glad that Cardinal Albareda was a gentleman, like the subject of the great book he was working to complete.

"I have seen him amidst other scholars. There would be no risk." Henry Moe, a nonconformist, felt that it was his affectionate respect for the man which relieved him of undue sectarian reverence for the Cardinal. "In any case, Father Albareda's great work on Charles Borromeo deserves to be completed and I urge you to think about his appointment as a proper means to that end. —Shall I write to him, asking him to receive you in Rome?"

"Well. Yes. Let's try it."

iii

In my notes I had the name of another resident of Rome on whom I intended to call. This was Luigi Barzini, Jr., a distinguished journalist and legislator. He was the son of the man who for generations had made the *Corriere della Sera* of Milan a world newspaper with his coverage of the diplomatic scene. Luigi the younger was nominated to the Center by a Fellow already in residence—John Lackey Brown. I had a particular regard for Brown because of his animated omniscience in several literatures—French, Italian, British, Spanish/Mexican, American. Until recently he had been high in the secretariat of the American Embassy in Rome, and had come to know Barzini well. He assured me that as a man of letters, a scholar in public affairs, Barzini would make a proper Fellow—he was a prodigious worker, a restless inquirer, and by temperament was a contributor to "the gaiety of nations." It was not known to me whether he was in Rome at the moment, but I would try to seek him out in his turn.

My first order was to secure my admission to the Council. Advance instructions at home told me to present myself at the North American College at number 30 Via Umiltà and ask for Father Raymond Lessard, a young American priest who could offer guidance and consolation to visitors astray in the Vatican bureaucracy. The North American College was an elite institution whose American seminary residents, it was widely believed, were on an early path to the mitre; and in point of fact Father Lessard himself was eventually appointed Bishop of Savannah.

On my way into the entrance of the College, I recognized someone who as she scurried past me to the street paused for a fraction of a second as though to identify me, thought better of it, and went on. But though time had not stopped for me, it had for her. I had not seen her for many years, but like many women widowed in middle life she became fixed in character and appearance; where I, much younger, showed the changes worked on me by the years. She was an old friend of my mother's, whom she kept informed of her lonely life, or so she thought of it.

"Mrs. O'Shea!" I called out after her, using here the name I gave her in one of my novels. She paused. I spoke my name, and she became all charm, like any busy person who had time for anyone.

"Great heaven, what are you doing in Rome?" she asked.

I knew that as a devout and imaginative widow with an eye to her personal salvation she had decided to live out her years in Rome. Her lonely life was in fact one of abounding busyness. She lived on the delights of burrowing helpfully in the Roman tunnels of unofficial ecclesiastical politics and society. In due course she made for herself a formidable position whose obscurity was its strength. True, she had arrived with helpful credentials: her younger brother was an auxiliary bishop back home, her older a powerful financial advisor to the Holy See on its American portfolio; she kept up an active correspondence with two papal countesses who reigned in their respective parishes on the North Shore of Long Island. Keeping only a small living allowance for herself, she had donated the considerable bulk of her husband's estate to the Church. In consequence, she wore the yellow-and-white ribbon of the Cross of Honor *Pro Ecclesia et Pontifice.*

"I am here to attend the opening session of the Council next Sunday."

"Great heaven! How did *you* ever get in?"

"I am not in, yet. I am just on my way to ask for my ticket."

"Father Lessard, I suppose?"

"Yes."

"Are you going to have any trouble?"

"I don't know."

"Where are you staying?"

"Hotel de la Ville."

"How*ever* did *you* get a reservation? —These crowds and crowds arriving daily for the Council!"

"It was arranged in Washington."

"Oh: the Nunciatoriate? —Are you a delegate?" she asked enviously. "Go early if you expect to get in!"

"No, no, only an observer for research purposes—a book I am working on."

"Then *that's* all right. Well, it is nice to see you after all these years. How is Rose? She is an angel, writes to me now and then. —Do you know Rome?"

"Not well. —I have other work here, too, candidates to interview for Fellowships at my university."

"Who are they? Do I know them?"

"Cardinal Albareda and Luigi Barzini."

"Of course I do. —I doubt if you will see His Eminence. He is not too well, and he is very busy with the Council. —Barzini is out of town."

"Well, I'll be looking them up."

"If I can help—" She burrowed in her handbag and produced a card. "Ring me, preferably before nine, I am often gone for the day after that. Be careful at the Hotel de la Ville. There have been episodes. I must run now. My love to Rose. —You do look different, quite successful."

I watched her away. Her rapid steps seemed to convey her thick little figure on casters, leaning her this way or that to scoot through hazardous openings in the sidewalk crowd.

iv

A few minutes later I emerged from the North American College with my admission ticket to the Council in hand. Returning to the Hotel de la Ville, I found evidence in my room of what Mrs. O'Shea might have regarded as an "episode." My luggage had been rifled. The contents of my working briefcase were spread out on my bed. My suitcases were open on the floor beside their spilled travel necessities. Other clothing hanging in my closet had their pockets turned inside out. Nothing was missing. What had "they" been looking for? Money? But I left no cash in my bags. If I was a spy, what evidence was searched for? If the intrusion was part of the security arrangements for the Council, why had I been given a ticket of admission? I rang the manager of the hotel, demanding an inspection of the disarray in my room before I put it right. It was courteously granted within half an hour, embellished with infinite apologies, graceful shrugs, and subtle hints that it was only persons of consequence who were treated to such barbaric incursions . . . All inquiries would be made and the police informed. *Per piacere, signore* . . .

My telephone rang.

"Cornelia O'Shea. Cardinal Albareda has heard about you from someone in New York. He will see you for a few minutes. Please telephone—here is the number. His secretary has all the information. His address is difficult to find; tell your driver it is in the vicinity of the Castel Sant'Angelo. He'll have to look up and down the byways there. Perhaps you will let me know how it all works out." A perfect example of how Mrs. O'Shea conducted her incessant quest for whatever was happening in Rome.

After some forty minutes I found the doorbell to press for the second-floor apartment of Cardinal Albareda and was admitted by his secretary-chaplain, a small, swarthy Spaniard, who silently gestured toward a sitting room with tall windows, and disappeared to announce me. I passed through the foyer where a tall mirror rose above a narrow table. On the table was a red velvet cushion braided in gold with gold tassels. On the cushion in front of the mirror sat the Cardinal's scarlet biretta, like a treasure of regalia and a signal of rank.

The sitting room was divided into two spaces, separated by scarlet draperies swept up and apart by loops of gold cord. In the farther half of the room, against a tapestry-hung wall, was a low tribune on which a throne of gold and scarlet sat under a cloth of honor. There, obviously, the Cardinal received visitors on stately matters. I could not see myself in that category, and I took a chair near the windows. A more comfortably empty chair faced me. In a few moments His Eminence entered, striding rapidly, smiling broadly.

In heavily accented English he said, "Welcome, a welcome to the friend and emissary of the famous Dr. Moe!"

I stood; he held me to a simple handshake and seated us both with a broad gesture. He sat leaning forward, his hands clasped and set upon his knees. He was not a large man, but his focused energy and forwarded goodwill gave him dimension. He was dressed in a simple black cassock piped in scarlet, and he wore his scarlet zucchetto. His smile was kind, his dark eyes were intently serious, as he said, "Now tell me:"

With many little nods and side glances of estimate and understanding he listened as I stated my mission—to enlist him as a Fellow of the Center for Advanced Studies. I described the terms of the appointment of Fellows and the circumstances of their residency. Our small group of about twelve Fellows for the academic year was designed to represent highly varied fields of advanced creative work, such as philosophy, the fine arts, public affairs and diplomacy, the sciences, literature, social studies, and religion. It was our belief that Fellows appointed from such contrasting realms of study would bring much of interest to each other and, by their working presence and informal interchanges with faculty and students, would enrich the broader life of the university. I cited as typical the appointments of such eminent members as Erik Holmberg, from Upsala; Sir Ronald Syme, classicist; Hannah Arendt, sociologist; the novelist C. P. Snow; Mircea Eliade and Father Martin C. D'Arcy, S.J., theologians; Michael Polanyi, philosopher of science; Lewis Mumford, historian and critic of technology; Richard Wilbur, poet; and Sergio Gutierrez Olivos, ambassador. Each was provided with travel expenses, a uniform stipend, a university house or apartment, a private study at the Center, and such access to the life of the university as his ongoing work allowed.

As for His Eminence, he was, I knew from conversations with Dr. Moe, engaged on a master work on the life of St. Charles Borromeo, of which the concluding volume remained to be written. It was our hope that a year of our Fellowship would afford opportunity for further work on it. For the rest, life at the Center was simple; no obligations beyond those defined by the Fellows would intrude upon their work at the Center.

There followed a few questions, framed with exquisite politeness, but clearly of importance. The university—was it a religious institution, as its name suggested? True, it had been founded in 1832 by the

Wesleyan sect, but since 1910 was administered as an independent liberal-arts institution of higher learning.

And how were Roman Catholics—particularly clergy—regarded there? The Department of Religion itself had nominated eminent Catholic scholars and clergy to the Center; for example, Father George Tavard, Father Walter J. Ong, S.J., and Father D'Arcy, already cited. A Catholic chaplain served also as a member of the faculty.

It had to be raised—the curious, he would even say exotic, matter of a prince of the Church suddenly arriving to take up residence in a secular university where surely the customary ecclesiastical protocol could induce awkward public or social situations? Yes. But these would largely be under the control of His Eminence himself, and every protection of whatever status His Eminence chose to elect would be undertaken by his hosts.

Followed then a long, reflective, and smiling silence. I felt I should neutralize my presence and my purpose of persuasion as far as possible, and I gazed out the window into the white Roman sunlight over the Castel Sant'Angelo. The scene, the depth of history immured in Hadrian's tomb, at its summit the Archangel Gabriel's upraised sword, the fantasy of establishing a cardinalitial scholar on the banks of the Connecticut River, combined to enfold me in a swirling gesture of the implausible baroque. Despite the sincerity of my undertaking that morning, what now followed so readily still came as a surprise.

"So I will tell you," said Cardinal Albareda, lightly patting his hands together once or twice, and went on to state his case. He was prepared to accept our invitation to come to us as a Fellow to continue his work on St. Charles Borromeo, but only at a deferred time. He was much occupied with the work of the Second Vatican Council, now in session, and would continue to be for the next three years, when the Council should have closed and its summary works completed. He would thus be unable to come to us until after that time. But if there should still be a place for him, then yes, he would come. But there were details to be found acceptable by both parties to the arrangement. He would come incognito, as it were, as a simple scholar-priest. He would be accompanied only by his secretary, whom I had met. He would not expect or accept ecclesiastical honors, even those extended by his fellow-prelates of my country, and he would be grateful if his colleagues at the university would think of him simply as Father Albareda, O.S.B. Could we therefore expect to resume our plans, under these terms, after the adjournment of the Council, and meanwhile to preserve on both our parts in *strictest confidence* any word of our congenial arrangements?

In principle, then, my first mission of recruitment was accomplished. Its tentative success surely was the result of the earlier friendship and representations of Henry Moe. In observance of the Cardinal's requirement of confidentiality, I made no written account of the morning's work, reserving the news for a spoken report to President Victor L. Butterfield and Dr. Moe on my return home. (They received it with approval and varying measures of enthusiasm. Like any head of a university, the president took a double view—one focused on the factional character of his faculty, the other on a future good, however bizarre, to be pursued for its own sake; the other gazing with an almost mischievous satisfaction on yet one more blow on behalf of world scholarship, trust in enlightened comradeship, and delight in the originality of the affair.)

My leave-taking in the shadow of the Castel Sant'Angelo was warm. I left with the Cardinal's blessing, a hearty handshake, and a sense of simple friendship newly established and open to later days.

I returned in some elation to the Hotel de la Ville, where the hall porter with ceremony handed me a message to say that Luigi Barzini, Jr., had arrived in Rome from Cività Vecchia, where he landed from his yacht yesterday, and was now in residence on the Via Cassia—Cornelia O'Shea at work.

It was like a call to action from a stern daughter of duty, whose omniscience was becoming a trifle menacing. Nevertheless, I telephoned to the Via Cassia and was informed in a rich voice that the Signore was occupied at the moment but if I would state my purpose? It was recalled in the same voice at the Via Cassia after a moment's rummage through recent correspondence, "Ah, yes, of course, Misser Horgan, it is here, your letter. —Should we say tomorrow morning at eleven o'clock, here?"

v

Once free of the knotted traffic of central Rome, my driver had us headed north into the country on the Via Cassia. I had explicit directions from John Brown. After about half an hour I should begin to watch for "a marble farmhouse" set in fields and trees but visible to the left of the ancient highway. It would come as no surprise for its appearance, after our drive past Roman ruins along the way—tombs, villas, monuments. I remember hazy blue hills to the north and nearer cypresses and motor stations proper to Highway number 2, as the Via Cassia had become.

And there it was, a classical set of cubes in pale stone, in its Arcadian grove. I was admitted by a manservant in a white coat, and taken to an ample library walled in books to the ceiling, with a grand central desk fitted out elegantly for both correspondence and literary composition. As I waited I roved the shelves. In ordered profusion, there were sections of books in German, Italian, French, and English. I read highlights along the English titles: the important historians, Gibbon, Macaulay, Trevelyan, Butterfield, Churchill, and the lot; the grand roster of poets from Chaucer to Yeats and Eliot; the biographers and social observers, including Aubrey, Boswell, Burney, Lockhart, Forster, Greville, Creevey, Strachey, Guedalla; essayists and belles-lettrists from Sydney Smith to Beerbohm, Hazlitt to Woolf, Isaac D'Israeli to Gosse; theatre from Shakespeare to Shaw; the grand line of novelists from Defoe to Thackeray, Dickens, and Trollope, to Meredith, Hardy, Bennett, Wells, and Aldous Huxley . . . A well-rounded man, I said to myself, and turned to see him as he came in, greeting me with a smile and a hearty, broad-grained voice that spoke of good living and self-content.

A tall, shapely man, he bore himself in sculpturesque elegance. His head was large, his eyes dark, his facial features broadly modelled. A habitual smile lifted his cheeks and nostrils in a suggestion of tolerant amusement. As I came to know, he combined a keen urbane interest with amused skepticism as he surveyed persons and conditions, great or small.

He greeted me heartily. We went to sit down near windows where a small table was soon equipped with coffee and cups by the manservant. A genial inquisition followed which I answered with persuasive

descriptions of our institution and purpose, ending with an impro-
vised aria of praises reflected from John Brown. He repaid Brown
with compliments on his own part. He wondered how otherwise I
had selected him for nomination. Did I know his writings? His
record, even his scandals of liberalism, as a Deputy in the Italian
parliament? His record as an occasional lecturer at home and
abroad? Would he be required to teach if he came to us? Actually,
he was planning a large work and would prefer to be undisturbed by
other scheduled commitments . . .

I must have given satisfactory, if transparently imprecise, answers
to most of his questions. He was skilled in the art of being interviewed
—he knew just when to shift the emphasis and take control, inter-
viewing me instead. Why had I not published my work in Italy, so
that he would have had a more courteous awareness with which to
receive me? He had seen books of mine in England. He was passionately devoted to English literature. I waved at his shelves and said
they were eloquent witnesses to that. He wondered if at the Center
he might expect the company of literary men and women at high
table—an experience he had much enjoyed across the range of
European universities. I replied that high table did not figure in our
scheme, but that Fellows dined every Monday evening together with
faculty colleagues, often including the president, and on that occasion a paper was read by one of the company and discussed by all.

"Capital!" he exclaimed; just the sort of event that he enjoyed
most in life—and here I had my first recognition of his endearing
trait of scattering wild compliments. With his urbanity of manner
and breadth of interests he blessed whatever seemed to concern
anyone he happened to be with. In an almost casual word of assent,
he declared that *of course* he would join us in a later season for a few
weeks—a full semester or academic year or even a single semester
were not "in the cards," as he had regular duties in the Chamber,
not to mention the "receipts" he continued to cook up as essays and
articles on his "stove" over there—indicating his great desk. We
would correspond about his proper dates, duties, stipend, and the
rest, in due time. Meanwhile, surely, I had not come to Rome
expressly to meet him?

But yes, I had, though I had to confess that other concerns drew me also.

These were?

Well, the hope of enlisting another Fellow who, having accepted provisionally, desired that his appointment be kept confidential; and too, there was my historical interest in the proceedings and the atmosphere of the Second Ecumenical Council, set to convene in a few days, when I planned to be present.

Ah: the first he must respect; but the second he found merely fascinating—though not precisely in the way I did. With raised eyebrows and an elaborately tactful smile, he seemed to suggest silently that perhaps one might cope with one or two bishops, but nearly three thousand . . . ?

On that genial note of secular Roman skepticism I took my leave, looking forward to welcoming Luigi Barzini in Middletown whenever his enterprises should allow.

vi

Cornelia O'Shea knew what she was talking about. At half past six in the morning of September 29, 1963, I arrived at a portico of St. Peter's—the entrance of St. Helena, whose statue holding the Holy Cross stood in an immense niche in the mighty northwest pier of the crossing. There I found a throng slowly inching its way forward into the basilica. It took me perhaps forty minutes to come into the illuminated shadows of the vast interior, where my vision and imagination seemed to become as one. So lofty that it seemed afloat as part of the sky, the dome was a source of light. Reaching away to the left, the coffered vault dwelled in its own distance of veiled blue. Closer to earth, towering pale pilasters and arches showed more substantially in their jewelled effects of white and gold, and white and gold became the prevailing tones of both the place and the ceremony as the hours advanced.

In amiable but unflinching determination the secular bodies of Rome in one mass moved into the vestibule and then to the floor of the north transept. There awaited ranks of common board bleachers set up facing the left side of the high altar under the baldachino of Bernini. With a clapping of boards under climbing and competing spectators, the bleachers were rapidly filled up. The tickets marked only the number of the rows. You had to fight for your row and then for your haphazard place in it. Much dispute, some in the good cheer of carnival, other in the rage deserved by any preemptor. When I settled into my narrow enough plankage, I saw down in front that several other rows of bleachers were reserved for accredited observers of other faiths, who were supplied with cushions and railings.

Golden light, almost palpably defined by motes of gold air, shone down upon the high altar from within the canopy high above. The altar, save for its six lofting golden candelabra, was undressed. Its vacancy was eloquent—the celebrant was not yet present. But on the altar, with a significance that seemed to me hypnotic in its power, was a supreme object that had for centuries defined the papal authority to the world. It was a triple tiara of severe modern design, standing upon a low pedestal of wood. Its cone shape of spun silver was encircled at equal distances from top to bottom by three golden crowns, unjewelled and pure with their plain shallow points.

The world did not yet know it, but the tiara standing upon the empty altar instead of rising from the papal brow was finished with its personal assertions of history. The very fact was soon made plain in the most dramatic way; but as the immense *aula* of the church was filling up with bishops arriving not in procession but at random and carrying their white mitres, a new era of the papacy and its world protocol took place. Pope Paul VI arrived at the entrance from the Vatican palace in the *sedia gestatoria;* but there his bearers set him down. He stepped forth on to the pavement. He, like all the other bishops, wore not the tiara but his common white mitre. Proceeding on foot through a great aisle of applause, he went to the high altar. There he was ceremoniously vested for the solemn Pontifical High Mass that would formally open the second session of the Second Vatican Council.

Facing the throng of twenty-three hundred Council Fathers from their dioceses in every quarter of the globe, the Pope, tall, slender, encased in white-and-gold vestments of incomparable splendor that enlarged the solemn elegance of his gestures, was the focus of an emotion that had the force of weather.

This had many sources. First, there was the power behind the purposes of the assembly, conjoined to belief in the tenets of that power. Believing in these, the assembled Council Fathers, praying to their founder St. Peter before whose tomb they were gathered, declared that they were there by the sanction of the Holy Ghost, under the will of the Christ Himself; and thus, tremendously, in the unity of the Holy Trinity, under the will of God Almighty Himself. Second, anyone gathered within the vast and magnificent fabric of the basilica would never resist the shock of astonishment, admiration, and wonder at how much manpower, treasure, and popular strain must have gone into its creation. Third, it was the most rare of individuals who putting himself within the reach of the greatest of shrines did not respond to it as an incomparable masterpiece of the assembled arts of architecture, sculpture, painting, and enacted ritual drama, and, on occasion, music. And finally, sensation was complete when the grand nave, side aisles, transepts, *aula*, sanctuary, and arched balconies were all filled to their limits by the Romans who owned both place and spectacle. They had admitted their guests, the crowded lives of more than twenty thousand bodies, ardent with the occasion, creating extreme power that generated a positively thermal excitement.

I felt it. To share excitement, I turned to my neighbor on the right —an experienced Italian who was mechanically eating a long roll stuffed with oil and greens. In response he lowered his shining eyelids halfway and quietly went on with breakfast. I turned to my left, where sat a ruddy, middle-aged priest holding a pocket missal and a sheaf of papers against his ample waistline. Before I managed a word, he said in a light convivial voice, "Isn't it something!"

I took his proferred hand and answered, "It certainly is!"

"You are American? —I am Father Horgan, from Melbourne."

When I told him my last name, we both laughed, feeling like allies and seatmates specially chosen. In no time we were off on outlines of personal history, speculations about the future intentions behind the summoning of the Council, the exalting distractions of Rome with its laminations of history.

Before us in the shower of light falling from within the lappets of the baldachino, the shift and weave, the unfolding of the Pontifical High Mass was beginning as Paul VI, attended by prelates who managed the folds of his huge white-and-gold cope, censed the altar at all its dimensions; for it stood there as an image of the body of Christ upon which the holy sacrifice itself would once again be enacted.

Father Horgan and I opened our missals and followed the liturgy to the end. The intonings from the altar were slow, in consonance with the great space where they were enclosed; the responses were slow as chanted by the assembled bishops; and the musical interventions were slower than all—the great communal prayer would have been better without them. The several choirs were involved by turns, all equally strident, faithless to pitch, indifferent to rhythm, tempo, and ensemble. Female voices were heard, sounding like matronly crows answering the quavering gobbles of their male kind. But like redemption, a white blade of pure tone from a boy cut through to the vault. The Sistine Choir had once been incomparable, according to eighteenth-century travellers who wrote to say so. The child Mozart went ravening away to write down what he had heard.

vii

At the conclusion of the Mass, Paul VI descended to kneel at the threshold of Peter's grave, there to make his confession of faith. All Cardinals then came forward to pledge homage and fealty. As by turn they knelt before him with hands praying, Paul pressed their hands between his in fraternity. The Cardinals then together offered their own confessions of faith to their primal father.

On the tribune before the altar, facing the long nave, a throne was set to receive the Pope. There he would deliver his homily to open the second session of the Council. I had a perfect profile view of him. As he sat, he was framed in front by Bernini's columns of spiralled bronze, climbing with their grooves and bronze leafage. At his sides were the Cardinals Ottaviani, Secretary of the Holy Office, and di

Jorio, Pro-President of the Pontifical Commission for the Vatican City. On the left a papal chamberlain was on guard in Renaissance costume, including ruff, stars and orders, and drawn rapier.

I took out my small watercolor block and my India ink fountain pen and furtively drew a fast outline sketch of the sumptuous scene. Later, under less constricted conditions, I would add watercolor and "atmosphere." Lord only knew what I could do with backgrounds and soaring ceilings in their blue-and-gold firmaments. My drawing was a highly inadequate translation of a vision; but it had its value for me: later it would bring me not what I had seen but what I had felt as I drew it—the general purpose of all my field-research drawings through the years.

Politely, Father Horgan paid no attention to my effort at drawing; instead, lifting his sheaf of papers he said that here was the Pope's address in Latin, as it would be given, and also in an English copy, which I might prefer to follow.

The address took well on to two hours. Though for the most part the head of Paul VI was hidden from me by the mitre of Cardinal di Jorio on his left, I had a vivid sense of the Pope's energetic delivery of his words, for his left hand, gloved in white and gold, was in constant motion, conducting, shaping, underlining, the text held by his right hand.

Papal prose necessarily permits itself amplitudes. The Council was assembled out of far, undefined areas "from the East and West; from the regions of the South and North." It was both a "human and divine phenomenon" that the bishops were creating by their coming together—their *"ecclesia."* They were in pursuit of a goal "that was beyond the earth and beyond the ages . . ." It was, then, the main purpose of the Council "not to discuss one article or another of the fundamental doctrines of the Church" but "to consider how to expound Church teaching *in a manner demanded by the times."* [Italics added.] His Holiness came no closer to particulars about how to accomplish the heart of the matter, but he did clarify specific fields for work: "The knowledge—or if you prefer—the awareness of the Church; its reform, in bringing together of all Christians in unity; the dialogue of the Church with the contemporary world."

Temblors at the roots of belief and structure were not defined in

Paul's speech from the throne, but the machinery for their discussion was put in place within the abstract definitions of the Council's purposes. Meanwhile, the urgent pontifical voice fell silent after giving the pontifical blessing worldwide, followed by adjournment.

My historical mission in Rome was now fulfilled.

viii

It was during the third session of the Second Vatican Council a year later that another of my Roman missions came to its end. Ambrosio Cardinal Albareda was dead in Rome. Henry Moe and I commiserated, for we both knew, as no one else at Wesleyan did, what a benign presence was lost to us—a fount of scholarly gaiety, serious learning, and simple courtesy.

But Luigi Barzini came. He came, and he bestowed. What you received from him was one of civility's highest graces—an ingratiating manner which, while obviously managed, was true to the nature that begot it. His smile could stand analysis alone. It started in a slight lift of the nostrils. A second later—all these minute actions in rapid sequence—the upper lip was raised to show a scalloped row of white enamel. Now eyelids were not raised, as might be expected, but were dropped perhaps a third of their ample folds. With these little announcements complete, the whole smile came brimming upon every feature of the receiving person, day, and world. Supported by a Milanese heartiness of voice, his presence could not have been more encompassing.

He was able to give us only a few weeks, as we discovered upon his arrival. The secretary assigned to him became expert at arranging his appointments everywhere—he had his clubs and drawing rooms in New York, his embassies and lectures in Washington, his exhibitions and conferences to open, say, in Boston, Chicago, San Francisco, Aspen . . . For he was newly and suddenly world-famous, and perfectly delighted to be. What was left of the between-times had its charm. He would remain through Christmas. His wife would join us from Rome.

What happened was that between the time of our meeting in Rome and the ripening of his Fellowship toward his term he had written a book which on publication had become a world best seller. It was called *The Italians*. Initially it appeared only in English—he explained that he wanted to have a foreign response before giving the text to his compatriots in Italian. The response was all he could have asked for. By its candor, skilled eye, tolerant courtesy, political sophistication, healthy gaiety, and downright skill in writing, the book earned an immediate success with serious critics and pleasure readers alike. So it was that on his arrival in America he was taken up in a forward rush of celebrity, and engagements across America.

But once in his office at the Center or at work with students or professors, or in the Fellows' lounge for a cup of coffee and a hearty gossip, or at one of the Monday evening dinners when the Fellows met to hear a paper by one of their number or a colleague from the faculty, Luigi Barzini had a rewarding voice in the proceedings. I remember one informal moment with a roomful of associates when he loudly said, pointing at me and smiling the achieved smile, "He *knew!*"

Everyone looked at me and I stared back. What on earth was he talking about?

"Before!" cried Luigi.

Before? was written on every brow.

"Yes, before I even wrote *The Italians,* he *knew.* He came to me in Roma, with my election to this Body, and now I am here, and the book is a monster, it all seems quite according to *his* plan!"

So he made his own accomplishment seem to be mine; and so, too, he indicated with the lightest urbanity how, if a material achievement had its interest as a process, it was in the end only something to give away in a convivial conversation—social plumage; a flourish; the baroque, once again.

Signora Barzini did arrive for Christmas. She was darkly handsome, and her toilettes were pronounced magnificent—Rome, Milan, Paris, on show by turns. With Fellows, guests, the Christmas dinner seated sixty. No program was arranged. It seemed only natural when with the pouring of the dessert wine Luigi Barzini rose to the occasion, making the original phrase seem like one of the happiest discoveries in English rhetoric. He spoke for perhaps twenty minutes. Contented impressions of his current visit to the United

States (perhaps the twentieth or so of his life, beginning in his youth as a stringer in New York for the *Corriere della Sera*). But this time it was a climax you could feel building along the way with increasingly enthusiastic allusions to affairs in the United States. And then he ended his survey flight, came in for an elegant landing, and greeted us all in the name of where we were, and the festal day, and the amenity of purpose that brought us together to lift our glasses to each other and our various muses, philosophical, political, scientific, literary, historical. In fact, he said, "I feel I am in attendance at the court of Louis Quatorze!"

This was too much for Wesleyan to swallow. The response was not quite what he expected. Heels thundered on our carpeted floor, coarse laughter shook the chaste crystals of our stark nineteenth-century chandeliers, a few vulgar whistles repudiated an obviously overdone compliment. A veteran of the Italian parliament, Luigi was, in all things, a connoisseur, including defeat. With radiant good cheer, he bowed deeply, arms opened far back, and sat down. The applause instantly changed to affection and approval of his presence among us. A toast, joined by all, was even proposed to him by our acerb Marxi-Freudian critic of society. *"Tanti grazie, Caro Maestro!"* cried Luigi. The candles guttered in their cups before we rose. The next day, he and his wife were aboard Alitalia for home.

My last encounter with him was most extravagantly true to his pleasure principle and to my joy in any completion of character.

One day in 1972 I landed in New York from the R.M.S. *Queen Mary*. In a five-day passage, the last three were spent in boiling through the outermost skirts of Hurricane Flora. The wonderfully designed old ship—the greatest sailor I ever knew in a dozen or so crossings—never left even keel in the oceanic turmoil beneath us (Denny-Brown stabilizers). Over and over she was pulled down against buoyancy demanded by her huge hull; and each time she had to struggle her way up to waterline. It was a new sensation at sea for me, and ominous, until I had enough hours of it to give me reassurance as I worked without interruption in my cabin.

But three days and two nights of being tugged at by Neptune in his depths had done something to my land legs, and once ashore, and free of taxi and luggage at my hotel, I took a turn of a few blocks to reset my knees. I was walking north on Fifth Avenue when a traffic light halted me at the curb. There was a sudden commotion across the street amid walkers coming my way. I heard a rich, beaded voice call out, "Paolo!" With great forensic focus the voice reached me. I saw an elegant hand in yellow chamois gloves remove a superb fedora hat in moss-green velours and sweep the air with it in a fan-like greeting. Ah! Luigi Barzini! I clothe him in his own style. I found that beaming countenance in the crowd and launched my own smile, and I watched as he pointed me out to a tall, sharply beautiful young woman on the right arm of his cinnamon-colored light top-coat with brown velvet collar. Held apart by the traffic light, we chafed within our unexpected gift of this stray meeting. And then the light changed, we were released, our crowds advanced, and in a moment we were in a pounding embrace, during which he managed to gasp, "This is my enchanting daughter, spending a few days with *papa* in spring!"

We were now safely halted in the shoal of the sidewalk. Luigi set out his hands and arms as if to hold a precious object. "Now," he cried, "let me tell you: when I awoke this morning in my St. Regis bed, I said to myself, *The one thing I want above all things today is to go out for a walk and to meet Paul Horgan coming toward me on Fifth Avenue!*"

It remains my favorite flourish of what might be called the personal baroque.

1964

Wilson at Wesleyan

i

I HAD DRIVEN FOR TWO HOURS through wet snow for my Sunday-evening dinner engagement at the Ritz in Boston. As though suspended in a box of still air, the lobby was all but empty. There were two armchairs. One was placed near the elevators; the other, far opposite, near the drugstore entrance. I came in past the elevators and in the dim light of Sunday evening I saw that the other chair thirty feet away was occupied by a bulky figure in a dark winter overcoat that was bunched upward about his neck and face—a great bird in a chill, swollen with its feathers. He seemed to be in some discomfort but he made no move toward easing his unwelcome situation. We had never met. I advanced upon him.

"Mr. Wilson?" I asked.

He had a little flick of speech, rapidly given, that often introduced what he had to say. (I needn't repeat it every time throughout these lines.)

"M'ym, do sit down. My wife is parking the car. She won't be long. I don't drive. —Horgan, is it?"

I sat down by the elevators and silence fell. After a few moments Mr. Wilson cleared his throat, as though to speak. But he said nothing, nor did I. What do you say to an unwelcoming stranger across thirty feet of hotel lobby?

He knew why I was there—to invite him to accept a Fellowship for the academic year of 1964–65 at the Center for Advanced Studies in the Liberal Arts, Professions and Sciences of Wesleyan University in Middletown, Connecticut. He could not agree by simple mail; he said he must know more of—of the styles of candidates, the seriousness of their study, the obligations expected of the Fellows—the—the (it had to be faced if not named)—degree of distinction attained by those elected for two semesters. In other words, who else was coming, and were they "anybody"?

Suddenly with remarkable agility he sprang forward out of his chair, for he heard before I did the sharp tap of rapid steps entering past the elevators. It was Elena Wilson, who was shaking snow off her great fur collar and murmuring apologies for taking so long about the parking lot.

"M'ym, yes, yes, never mind all that now, shall we go up?" he said.

The dining room was on the second floor. In my position as host I had reserved a distant table clear of neighbors. Both elevators were aloft. Mr. Wilson, dragging off his monstrous greatcoat, signalled that we would not wait, but would walk up to the second-floor lounge room for drinks before dinner. He started up ahead of us. By the time Mrs. Wilson and I had settled down in armchairs, half facing him on his sofa, Mr. Wilson had already sent for a double scotch whisky. Mrs. Wilson sighed. She patted her hair. Even from Cambridge, where they were spending the current academic year at Harvard, the drive into Boston on such a night, with a husband in a mood to destroy a reasonable (and much needed) year of employment, was no pleasure for her. But like most Europeans of a certain station in society—she was a daughter of the baronial Mumm family—she had a firm will and a light touch for social moments, including those darkened by her husband.

Now in the fuller light of the lounge room I could see Wilson more clearly. At sixty-nine, he had a full face dangerously near to mortal crimson. His eyes in their steady sidelong fix, as David Levine caricatured him, belonged to the reptile order—perhaps the landbound iguana of the Galapagos? His clothes were banker's dark gray. The rim of his belt rose above where his waist would have been, and when he coughed or exclaimed, the belt jumped farther toward his chest. His mouth was crowded by cheeks and jowls and he kept its corners turned down. He had a rolling gait, leaning back, to support the weight up front, and at every other step he pitched his tilt to the left, which slowed him slightly, and seemed to say, "resist!"—the impulse and the law within him.

Elena was taller than he; slim, with restrained elegance in what she wore, how she moved, spoke, and made her path upon the joys and troubles of her husband's crust.

Almost dismissively, Mr. Wilson now introduced me. "Elena, this is Mr. Paul Horgan."

"Oh, yes," she said. "How nice to meet you. Jean, Roger have spoken—"

Mr. Wilson crowded her out with his supporting batteries in the form of questions, fired close together. His thick voice became more clouded. Accusatively he said, "Well, then, wh-who's going to be there *next* year?"—that is to say, 1964–65.

I was pleased to answer. "Let me see: there's Herbert Butterfield from Oxford, the historian—"

"Yes, yes, I *know!*"

"And Willard Quine, philosopher; Moses Hadas, classicist; René Dubos, biologist; Father Martin D'Arcy, S.J., theologian; Sir Herbert Read, critic; Jean Stafford, the novelist. A few others pending—yourself, of course."

"We know Jean Stafford," said Elena Wilson mollifyingly.

"Will they have to teach a class?"

"Not unless they particularly want to, perhaps to polish some new work in progress."

"Where on earth would one live? What's Middletown like? Are there any good restaurants?"

"You see," said Elena Wilson, "I cannot be there all the time to manage house and meals."

"Yes," cried Wilson, "that's it, that's it, my wife can't be there throughout the whole time. The whole thing wouldn't work." He looked expectantly at her, a clear cue to rise and go.

"No," I said, "you'd not be too happy with the restaurants. But I should imagine faculty people would be dining and wining you."

"Y'you don't know much about university people, do you?" He seemed at a loss for further questions. "I don't know, I don't know," he murmured.

Elena Wilson knew better than to offer her countering opinion; but with a little play of charm—a smile rising to her high German cheekbones, a little rattle of bracelets, she kept things brighter. Her husband stirred before his next eruption. He had a nagging scrap of something to remember or, perhaps even better, to dispose of even if it should be true.

"Horgan," he said doubtfully, "are you a writer?"

"Oh, *Edmund!*" exclaimed Elena—for by then in my life I was reasonably well known as the author of a score of respectable books; moreover, both Mr. Wilson and myself had the same publishers— Farrar, Straus and Giroux.

"Yes, Mr. Wilson. Shall we go in to dinner?"

He brought further questions with him. "Climate? what about your winter. I have asthma, emphysema, bronchitis."

By now, I was pleased to answer that the Connecticut River Valley was famous for the great banks of polluted air that moved eastward during the winter months to stall for days over the beautiful Connecticut River on its way through a plague of sinusitis to Long Island Sound. However, I added, there was no record that the climate had ever put down either the Hartford Wits or the college faculties that thrived along its banks. Like a terrier, he could not loosen his jaws once fixed to shake and tease. If he was favorably moved by the sound of our reputable past company, he gave no sign. "I don't know," he said huskily, "there's always a risk, don't you know!"

Elena Wilson managed to convey a sense that nothing was yet final, and she said, "May we order? I am starved."

I was glad to have an interval that allowed me to brace myself for an hour of meaningless talk, for I believed my mission had ended, and I was done with persuasions in the face of Edmund Wilson's distaste for what we had to offer, including housing, stipend, perquisites, plausible associates, which had been set forth in earlier correspondence. Tonight's meeting had been arranged in tacit expectation of the agreement now in tatters.

But here we were, trapped at the dinner table, and I now scraped around in my head for something—anything—to say that might at least keep alive a social noise. An offstage reference, idly chosen, led me to say,

"One day last summer in Santa Fe at lunch with Igor Stravinsky, I brought him a present. He loves presents. It was a copy of *Patriotic Gore*. He said, 'Ah, thank you, I have been wanting it.' "

"He did?" Clear fresh rays of light seemed to descend through Mr. Wilson's acid rain. He mumbled, "Igor Stravinsky. How astonishing. Stravinsky? You really did?" His brow cleared. He sat forward. His profound respect for Stravinsky's place in the world was clear.

"What's more," I continued, "a week later, again at lunch, Stravinsky brought his copy with him. He was still reading it. He reads very slowly. He set the book on the table with edges even. He is a very neat man. He laid his long forefinger upon the cover and declared, 'This book is a masterpiece!' "

"He really did? How extraordinary," said Mr. Wilson with a glance at his wife. She clasped her hands under her chin and smiled wisely at him. She had outwaited many a mood. He turned back to me and said as though continuing an interrupted agreement, "I suppose there's a contract of some sort? You can send it on, Harvard till the middle of May."

Another Edmund Wilson now joined the party—jovial, solicitous, lightly gossipy. Had we heard the latest about Cal Lowell's mental condition? And recently at Harvard, where Leon Edel was a colleague, he, Edmund, had proposed a valuable James reference to him by page number in a book in the Widener Library. When Edel went to look and opened the page, a paper Japanese butterfly powered by a rubber band flew up. And there was the laughable but real possibility that his venomous little volume *The Cold War and the Income Tax* might lead to prosecution and jail for the author . . . The talk flowed on, the wine likewise. We emptied the Ritz dining-room, and saying good night, Edmund asked firmly, "So when shall we be expected at the Center in the fall?"

ii

In addition to Fellows cited to Edmund Wilson in our interview, others were expected to assume the Fellowships in the fall of 1964. These were Luigi Barzini, Jr., Italian world journalist and Member of the Chamber of Deputies; John Bartlow Martin, writer in contemporary affairs and ambassador to the Dominican Republic during its civil war; Wilson himself.

It was always interesting to discover how such a varied group of highly gifted and expressive people would take to each other. We gave Monday evening to a group gathering for dinner, to which interested faculty members were always invited, followed by the reading of a paper by one of the company and discussion of it afterward. The papers in general were superior, some of them brilliant in matter and manner. (Toward the end of the Center's brief history of ten years we published eighteen of these papers, with the editorial advice of Edmund Wilson. They appeared in a boxed set with beautiful typography by Will Lockwood, the director of the Wesleyan University Press at the time.) Fellows' wives were generally helpful in our small society, and one, Lady Read, wife of Sir Herbert, was a giver of light, tolerance, charm, and gaiety to us all. She accurately summed up our character for that year of 1964–65 as our *annus mirabilis.*

Of the remaining Fellows that year, three were immersed in their work, somewhat to the exclusion of close relations with colleagues. One was Willard Quine, the philosopher of linguistics from M.I.T., a large, brisk man with a ready laugh and a quick technique for exiting the door before a conversation took root. Another was the Columbia classics professor Moses Hadas, wreathed in the autumnal beauty of his white hair, rosy cheeks, and sympathetic eyes. A third was Hans Jonas, European-born philosopher of history. He was a deeply earnest man whose voluble wife was given to airs and fashions of the *belle époque.*

Of the members of the Society of Jesus none was better known and sought out for his intellectual gifts, social charm, and ease in the upper strata of worldly affairs than the Very Reverend Father Martin Cyril D'Arcy, S.J. He was a most arresting creature to look upon. He had a tiny body, reduced by God knows what discipline until he must have weighed less than a hundred pounds. He wore a Roman collar many sizes too large, from which his neck rose to support his great head. The head was kept in constant motion, nodding forward repeatedly, not in agreement or affirmation—it was a sort of tic, accompanied with a drone of breath from behind the great beak of a nose and the fierce eyebrows that gave him the look of an eagle off its crag—until you looked into his eyes, and found the strong light of his concerned humanity. Irregular teeth protruded in the classic British style—he was of course an Englishman all the way through —and he constantly extended his slender arms. His fingers were closed at their tips so they became little bundles of twigs, shaking out the answers he sought from within his enormous erudition. He was always dressed in immaculate clerical black. I had met him several times in the last high Catholic salon in New York. He always stayed at the Waldorf in apartments lent to him by wealthy communicants, or in their suburban houses that were kept fully staffed even in the absence of their owners. In great demand in secular society Father D'Arcy lightly exhibited the social skills of the upper class—privileged approach, bold address, unseriousness, ducal abruptness in abandoning bores. He was famous on several levels. For a brief time he had been the Provincial (that is, head) of his Order in Great Britain. As such, he easily made a great place for himself in the grandest country houses and the smartest life of the London world. Evidently his intention was to lodge the Society of Jesus firmly with the ruling levels and thus give it a secular respectability it had long been deprived of. But society played too distracting a part in the Very Reverend Provincial's administration, and Rome recalled him. With lovely ease he left office for priestly duties at home and abroad in guest professorships, individual lectures, quiet diplomacy when his Order could use his skills. A wide public delighted in his character as Father Rothschild, S.J., in Evelyn Waugh's novel *Vile Bodies*. Along the way his succession of books in history and theology sustained his reputation as a serious scholar. He celebrated Mass every morning. Anyone who ever attended him then had no doubt whatever of his profound spirituality, which left him exhausted after every Mass he celebrated.

iii

Our first Monday evening session each year was an early test of how the year would go. Welcoming each Fellow, I looked for every sign of harmony—and usually found it, beyond the conventions of company manners.

For a few minutes on this first evening of 1964, all was easy. But unaccustomed sounds were suddenly gathering at the far end of the room near the door. Fellows were edging away from a disturbance there. I went to see. I was too far away to hear all the words, but according to later reconstructions their tone was something of this order: "Pernicious nonsense . . . How can you . . . I suppose you were instructed!" It was Edmund Wilson, battering Father D'Arcy with angry disdain for some view or other that he had expressed. Nodding, nodding, Father D'Arcy seemed like a patriarch kindly enduring the tantrum of a child. "On the contrary, Mr. Wilson—my own conclusion." Something like "Sheer rot!" shouted Wilson, turning away with mottled cheeks and hacking breaths. Conversation rose in pitch, all about, the better—and kinder—to erase the quarrel. What could I do? I could hardly instruct Mr. Wilson in manners. Before I could hit upon a policy, Father D'Arcy hurried to me, wearing his fierce smile. He said suavely, "Paul, I gather Mr. Wilson does not take kindly to the clergy!"

His sportsmanship settled the ugly exchange at the doorway. I thanked him and we went on with the evening. A swift shifting of place cards put the disputants of the doorway far apart at dinner. They were not seen to speak to each other all week. At our next evening I watched the doorway. Father D'Arcy arrived first. He stood by the door, sipping his Harvey's Bristol Cream sherry. When

Edmund Wilson came rolling in, Father D'Arcy was upon him like a friendly hawk, greeting him with gaiety, and extending something in the form of printed matter to him.

"What's this, what's this?" stammered Edmund, thrown off his hostile guard. Father D'Arcy nodded his gift upon him, whatever it was, evidently made graceful remarks, perhaps a scholarly witticism at which Edmund, now taking comfort from his first martini just served, gave an unwilling burst of laughter, and the trick was done. The two took the nearest chairs and fell into lively conversation. A grateful ripple went through the company at the change of climate wrought by some magic in the repertoire of the Jesuit world states-man. It was an auspicious sign of a friendship which thereafter grew strong and easy. When Edmund was alone of an evening—Elena away, dinner in the hands of a part-time cook—he would telephone Father D'Arcy to come and dine with him; and dine they would, to conversation which would keep them at it till late. Edmund was a hearty host, and in the absence of irritants, such as voices too loud nearby, unwelcome intrusions, assumptions of personal intimacy on the basis of readership claims upon his work, he had all the signs and signals of the well-bred, comfortably-off squirearchy of Eastern sea-board society. He came from landowners, local town houses, Prince-ton diplomas, the medical, legal, and banking professions, collectors of books and paintings from nineteenth-century American painters, tailored wardrobes, good manners in formula unless disturbed; and somewhat more often than in other segments of American life, an underrunning melancholy managed, for the most part, with bravery and common sense. Now and then, as we have seen, such thought-lessly sustained decorum was split wide open by singular causes. Throughout his contrariness or combativeness, Edmund Wilson's bearing retained for the most part its well-bred style and accent.

Early in the autumn a wide jumble of faculty and Fellows were invited to a dinner party by an intellectual faculty couple, both of foreign birth. People were invited for seven o'clock. The Wilsons arrived promptly. Edmund was greeted with elaborate deference and presented with a double martini. For quite some time it was a thin party—few other guests were arriving. The martinis kept coming.

Wilson did not welcome an indiscriminate use of the given name on early acquaintance. Newly arrived guests addressed him as Edmund, at which he felt a twist of irritation. The more he drank and the longer he waited for his dinner, the greater his buildup of pressure at meeting loud, cheerful people who made him the star of the party by gathering around him. When his fast disappearing good manners required a blurt of response from him he clamped his lips the more tightly and gave a brief heaving response of laughter suppressed within. (When Rossini described for Wagner his visit to Beethoven in Vienna, he said that Beethoven's voice was "soft, and slightly fogged." It is a way to describe Wilson's voice. One could add that the voice grew foggier as events deteriorated.) He hated being conspicuous. Ordinary courtesies, little amenities recognizing his high position in the world of letters annoyed him. He became self-conscious. Intruded upon, he tended to become rude.

As the party went on without any sign of substantial food, he took on more and more to drink, blinked and nodded away overtures of common interest or incipient friendship, and at nine o'clock, hungry and drunk, he suddenly came out of his chair and demanded to know when dinner would be served. His host came running, profuse with promising explanations. Dinner was planned for ten o'clock, things were moving well in the kitchen, more people were expected, surely Mr. Wilson would have another drink meanwhile. . . .

"Certainly not!" he roared. "I've been here for three hours. I am already drunk and starving. Good evening! —Elena," he called, "take me home!"

The evening's centerpiece unsteadily made his way home to what we later heard was a supper of scrambled eggs, toast, coffee, and diatribes on the unspeakable social habits of academic barbarians.

A substantial body of faculty opinion concluded that its advance idea of Edmund Wilson was confirmed by his sense of himself. One instrument that he was judged by was the notorious postcard that he had had printed years before. It was amazing how many persons remembered it, with its list of the commonplaces of literary commerce. It read:

EDMUND WILSON REGRETS THAT IT IS IMPOSSIBLE FOR HIM TO:

READ MANUSCRIPTS,

WRITE ARTICLES OR BOOKS TO
ORDER,

WRITE FOREWORDS OR
INTRODUCTIONS,

MAKE STATEMENTS FOR PUBLICITY
PURPOSES,

DO ANY KIND OF EDITORIAL WORK,

JUDGE LITERARY CONTESTS,

GIVE INTERVIEWS,

CONDUCT EDUCATIONAL COURSES,

DELIVER LECTURES,

GIVE TALKS OR MAKE SPEECHES,

BROADCAST OR APPEAR ON
TELEVISION,

TAKE PART IN WRITERS' CONGRESSES,

ANSWER QUESTIONNAIRES,

CONTRIBUTE TO OR TAKE PART IN
SYMPOSIUMS OR "PANELS" OF
ANY KIND,

CONTRIBUTE MANUSCRIPTS FOR
SALES,

DONATE COPIES OF HIS BOOKS TO
LIBRARIES,

AUTOGRAPH BOOKS FOR STRANGERS,

ALLOW HIS NAME TO BE USED ON
LETTERHEADS,

SUPPLY PERSONAL INFORMATION
ABOUT HIMSELF,

SUPPLY PHOTOGRAPHS OF HIMSELF,

SUPPLY OPINIONS ON LITERARY OR
OTHER SUBJECTS.

For many people the image created by the postcard, which was widely reproduced in the literary press, was that of a personage indifferent to the wants of lesser mortals. Others found it cheeky and amusing. In any case, it established aspects of the image he brought with him to Wesleyan.

Rare attempts to pay court met with quick rejection. At one of the Monday dinners he was seated at my left, and next to him farther along was a professor who saw the world through the tunnel vision of Marx and Freud, and must have concluded that Edmund did not mean it when at the end of *To the Finland Station* he demolished the Marxist creed and deplored its effects. After we sat down the professor naïvely read the place cards on either side of him, and never before having seen Wilson, he was overcome by hero worship. I heard him say in awed tones,

"To think that I am actually sitting next to Edmund Wilson! That such a remarkable distinction should come to me! A critic without peer in our time! and I am dining with him!"

To which Edmund muttered, "E-eat your soup! It's getting cold!"

Sometimes I wondered whether he was fully aware of his fractious spells. Was it a philosophy? Perhaps like much philosophy, it was sometimes so, sometimes no. I hope I do not unduly emphasize his rudeness and irascibility, for he was capable also of real warmth, camaraderie, and generosity. Did undue emphasis give his outspokenness an unintentionally savage tone? Who could be sure—though at an elevated occasion later in the year I had a clear answer from the master himself that he knew what he was doing. . . .

A serious dinner party was given for Father D'Arcy on his seventy-fifth birthday. It was held upstairs at the restaurant "21" in New York. The hostesses were two ladies in society who were close friends and patronesses of Father D'Arcy. They asked him to provide a guest list. He led his roster with the Duke and Duchess of Windsor—it was believed that he still considered the Duke to be his king. I was glad to learn that he had included Edmund Wilson.

For an hour everyone passed along a reception line to be greeted by the hostesses and the guest of honor, and then stood about for cocktails. I saw Edmund across the room enduring admirers. The arrival of the royal couple was delayed. They had waited downstairs until notified that the guests had formed the royal circle in the foyer of the dining room to be greeted by them. They then came up to tour the company, shaking hands with everyone, receiving curtsies from the ladies, cleverly making recognition of friends, the Duke fingering his black bow tie, the Duchess clutching to her breast a gold reticule in the shape of a corgi, while everyone in mutual politeness sustained the fable of a royal court in rude New York. In a glimpse I saw that the exercise, along with martinis, had brought a dangerous flush to Edmund's face.

The party was finally settled at half a dozen or more tables for eight which were clustered before the high table where the guest of honor, the royal couple, and the hostesses were installed. At our table I was seated directly opposite Edmund, who at once detained a passing waiter long enough to order a cocktail. To his right was a woman whose credentials placed her high in the ranks of society—a dictator of fashion, former editor of *Vogue,* later curator at the

Metropolitan Museum, a famous wit whose charm was irresistible—
Diana Vreeland.

Between obligatory attentions to my own dinner partners I kept an
eye on Edmund, wondering when an emergency relief escort might
be needed, for without break he continued with his martinis and also
gave attention to the wines as they came. A number of times I saw
him suddenly drop his head forward and take a nap even as Mrs.
Vreeland animatedly beguiled him. With great management he
would come awake, rejoin the party for a while, only to lapse again.

Later, as I gave him a lift to the Princeton Club, I said something
like, "Were you making heavy weather, back there at the table?"

"I don't know if you noticed, but I faded out once or twice." He
chuckled. "After the first time, the lady said to me, 'Mr. Wilson,
either you are drunk or I'm boring you!' to which I rose with every
gallantry. I said, 'N'no, Mrs. Vreeland, I am not drunk, and you are
not boring me, delightful, quite charming,' and so on. But then I
went off again, and she *made the mistake of returning to the battle.* She
touched my arm and said, 'Well, Mr. Wilson, after all, I think you
are drunk and I *am* boring you!' So I squared upon her, and I said,
'Very well, Mrs. Vreeland, I *am* drunk, and you *are* boring me!' at
which she quite properly turned her back on me!"—accompanied by
a wheeze of wicked laughter. I had my answer.

iv

Wilson saw society in two serious modes: under his scholarly eye as
a pattern of intellectual abstractions and flexing social configurations;
again, as his personal encounter through which he felt the pleasures
of his life as well as its discomforts and its dangers to his independence and well-being. Through the first mode he created the magis-
terial body of his formally published work, so finely tuned and beautifully written. Through the second, he provided his self-portrait in
voluminous notebooks. Over the years these informal texts were
published in volumes separately devoted to the decades of *The Twenties* through the recently published *The Sixties*. Entries ranged through
autobiography, reflections of intellectual society, and records of a

large number of sexual partners, whose reciprocal practices he explicitly exposed. Also included were wry, sometimes malignant,* sketches of acquaintances, friends, and benefactors.

Like many people of uncommon energy and originality, he imposed his own parody of society upon the general one. On a Main Street corner of Middletown he discovered a typical commercial restaurant run by a family of Greeks with whom he conversed in their demotic speech. Behind the cash register there was a banquette and table more or less secure from public view. He took possession and named his corner the Ritz Bar—a comic mixture of reference to the expatriate crowd in 1920s Paris with the incongruous local restaurant where the menus were coated in limp yellowing plastic and the air was weighted by pungent grease. For a late-afternoon drink he would recruit a single friend with a command invitation: "Meet me at the Ritz Bar at five-thirty." It was there through idle talk that I came to know him for the hearty companion he was when at ease, off guard, in talk that ranged from literary subjects and gossip to corny jokes, to an occasional deeply felt emotion that required no comment. He never talked about his work or that of his guest. He delighted in mischief—the Widener Library butterfly—and fielded his share.

One of his successful outrages was his seduction of a beautiful King Charles spaniel who was under harsh command to spend his day under the desk of his mistress, an important secretary at the Center. Edmund used a pleasant custom of the Center to entice the dog down the hall to his office. Every day at eleven o'clock the staff passed out cookies and milk or coffee or tea to the Fellows in their offices. How, I never knew, but he told the dog that cookies awaited him down the hall if he could get away. The dog's skilled management of the slow, crouching, hazardous journey to Edmund and the cookie plate was a success more often than not. Out of sight of a jealous mistress, Edmund and the spaniel became secret friends. (There is a sequel to the cookie hour, as we shall see.)

*"I am always surprised when people writing about my books say . . . that I am a misanthrope. I see that the men I have written about—Duplessis, Mario Praz, the Marquis de Sade—have all been to a greater or lesser degree remarkable for a certain malignancy." — Edmund Wilson in *The Sixties*, p. 469

But he could be irascible if his comfort were invaded. One evening he and Elena invited Jean Stafford for dinner—a provincially early dinner, to Jean's disquiet, for she loved long, leisurely drinks and dinner on which to float her wonderfully constructed narratives of comedy, outrage, or delight, such as would take her out of loneliness and successfully abolish half the night away. Her monologues were fugitive works of art. Her measured pace cast a spell. On this evening, it worked in reverse. Dinner was early, hurried, and necessarily cut up by interruptions for service. Immediately it was over, Edmund abruptly said good night and went up to bed, leaving Elena and Jean alone for their coffee in the small sitting room at the foot of the stairs. Over the fireplace hung an Italian Renaissance portrait of a young man in the manner of Bronzino—was it a Mumm family treasure that travelled with the Wilsons to compensate for impersonal, sometimes seedy visitors' quarters in Faculty clubs or masters' houses?

The moment for coffee and the launching of a Jean Stafford chapter was suddenly faced by an apparition. It was Edmund halfway down the stairs in his bathrobe.

To his best friend among the Fellows, "Jean!" he called out in his fogged voice, "Jean! Go home! It's after nine!—I can't get to sleep. I can hear you talking but not what you're saying! It's intolerable! Good night, now!"

Elena could only shrug. Jean took her way back to her Center apartment and the company of her famous cat Elephi, about whom she wrote a beguiling little book. It was a monument to Elephi's cultivated manners—she did not lap her cream from the edge of the dish, but with delicacy took up a pawful at a time and licked it there. Friends were sometimes privileged to watch this, in the midst of Jean's hard-edged loneliness. She was frail—had suffered the loss of her adored husband, Joe Liebling, and a heart attack, and near-fatal pneumonia, all within the last two years. Her life was full of ironic satisfactions. She described examples to me now and then—Edmund's intense feeling for her even in his rudeness; her courageous pretense that *The New Yorker* would soon again accept her short stories as in younger and happier days; the venerable professor on our campus who had come several times after dark to scratch at the secluded outside glass doors of her apartment to plead his almost sickly hunger for her. Her most difficult response was to dismiss his tribute without laughing, yet the old longing touched her. It took several of his moth-like strivings at her door before he gave over his pathetic campaign.

In addition to Father D'Arcy and Jean there were other Fellows with whom Edmund became friendly. He was never drawn into the charmed circle created by Herbert and Ludo Read—their British character might have put him off. Barzini probably amused him; Dubos in his humanistic biology and intense workman-like habit in writing would surely earn his respect. For a warm relationship, it was the family of John Bartlow and Frances Martin, with their two appealing young sons, who tapped Edmund's feeling.

In mid-term John Bartlow Martin was called to Washington by President Johnson for consultation. Martin had written extensively about Latin American and Caribbean affairs. The Dominican Republic was consuming itself in a domestic war over possession of the presidency. In short order Martin was sent to Santo Domingo as ambassador to observe the conflict and attempt to put together negotiations for a peaceful settlement. It soon became clear through sporadic telegrams and phone calls from him that Ambassador Martin was in serious danger from the war flaming in the streets. For hours at a time he was obliged to remain prone on the floor of the American Embassy as bullets flew through windows and doors. He barely maintained communications with his family and Washington. The public reports of the disorder were lurid. Frances Martin and her sons were deeply troubled by them. The concern of everybody at the Center was acute. Edmund found occasion to show the worried family thoughtful little attentions that helped to keep up their spirits. This could amount to an almost paternal tenderness, as I had occasion to see.

One evening when he was unengaged I asked Edmund to have dinner with me. I rarely saw him alone for as much as a whole evening—there were all the other Fellows for me to entertain, and he was occasionally absent in town with friends or business at *The New Yorker*, for which he kept up his work as principal literary reviewer. We were hardly settled at the table, with a launch into promising conversation, when Frances Martin and her sons appeared forlornly in search of their supper.

"We must have them with us!" said Edmund, and he heaved himself forward to welcome the lonely intruders. He scraped extra chairs to the table, seated the family with murmurs of welcome, in which I now joined, and in a few moments of trivia he created a dinner party which went on for nearly two hours, during which he had the hearty, yet polite, young boys—eight, ten years old—laughing at his jokes and stories. He quizzed them about their hobbies, tastes in books and movies, games; with gratitude Frances Martin saw his devices for distracting her sons from the dread of the danger that had their father in its idiot grip. Edmund was a practiced amateur magician, and he promised to do his tricks at another time. The boys reciprocated his high-spirited sallies. In all his exhibitions of austere intellect, rudeness, or damaging raillery, he had never shown us his feeling for children. This had no hint of sentimentality —he spoke to the boys as to adults but within likely frames of their experience, and with breathy good manners they joined in his play. Frances Martin and I exchanged veiled glances of pleasure in his lovely tact that evening. When John Martin returned safely from his mission, it was to find a new family hero who at other moments as well had given his concerned friendship when it was most needed. Like Doctor Johnson, he would have scoffed at any notice of his kindness.

In fact, it was a key to his temperament and sometimes touchy behavior that he hated being in any way conspicuous ("E-eat your soup . . ."). One evening I dined with Roger and Dorothea Straus in New York. It was a large dinner party—perhaps eighteen guests, all of them very much to the fore of the best New York could offer in arts and ideas. Edmund was coming. He was late—in fact, the last to arrive, which put him through an ordeal. As he advanced into the company, everyone looked up from their conversations; some rose from the chairs arranged along the walls and under the great window at the upper end, halfway around the room, where I was seated. Being greeted by the first in line, Edmund was handed along to the next guest, and so to the next, until he was to his discomfiture trapped into making the royal circle, with a handshake and a necessary word to each person who greeted him. His color rose. Leaning back on his short steps of progress, he felt exposed. He was being "appreciated." In a hurry to get it over with, for he had the whole room to tour, he resorted to monosyllables or mere noises by way of "Good evening." When he rounded toward the window, he saw me and a blink of relief crossed his face. He shook my hand. His handshake was unique. In its habit it expressed not mere reluctance but distaste for the gesture. He pressed his arm close to his ribs, extended the forearm as little as possible, and offered his inert hand as it retreated within his cuff. In his distraction, he found my name, uttered it, and said to me,

"M'ym, you've shaved your mustache!"

"No," I said, "but I've got my glasses off."

"That's it, that's it!" he all but shouted, and continued his rounds.

v

His oddments and crotchets put some people off, and also invited caricature—as in some of my moments with him here. A Center secretary earned a sharp rebuke for referring to him as a "screwball." In the hallway of the *New Yorker* office in Forty-third Street, he appeared in the doorway of Brendan Gill's office and said, "I know why they hate us. We get cookies and they don't!" and disappeared, leaving Mr. Gill baffled. When later he asked Jean Stafford what Edmund could have been talking about, she was able to finish the story: in effect, Fellows of the Center received special attentions which, Edmund was sure, the faculty resented.

He went his own way. At one point in the year he was engaged in a battle of letters with Vladimir Nabokov, conducted through the columns of *The New York Review of Books*. The subject was their respective translations of Pushkin—whose was the better. In a certain essay-length letter, Edmund felt he had demolished his adversary, and he invited the poet F. D. Reeve, and former professor of Russian at Wesleyan, Helen Reeve, also a Russian scholar, and myself to his office to hear him read his crusher in the dispute. It was a memorable afternoon, as he marshalled all his big guns. I, knowing not enough about the essential matter, could not give points to him; but in the realm of style, organization, wit, clarity, and sheer weight of citation, Edmund's paper was a triumph.

But no surprise. As everybody had long known, at work he was a model professional and scholar. In addition to his lengthy essay-reviews for *The New Yorker,* he worked on three books while at the Center. His desk was always thick with galley proofs. One venture that occupied him, quite by coincidence, was a review for *The New Yorker* of my critical selection of the work of Maurice Baring. He read (or reread) almost all of Baring's great variety of work in fiction, literature, Russian history, drama, and parody. He gave me high marks and intended a compliment in the heading he gave to his essay: *How to Read Maurice Baring Without Being Bored.* My response to this was not quite satisfactory, since the title indicated that it was possible to regard Baring as a bore, a view that I could not accept. When after months of delay the review ran in the magazine it took up a dozen or so columns. When Edmund showed it to me I made no comment on the title; but for its exhaustive treatment and its fine-tuned critical summations, I felt confirmed in the most serious way, and so was our working relationship in that academic year.

He appeared twice as the contributor of papers to the Monday evening readings. The first was devoted to excerpts from the manuscript of his little book *O Canada;* the second was given to a startling essay on the Marquis de Sade, with illustrative quotations of Sade's writings from prison, many sexual details of which were enthusiastically degenerate. These were bluntly cited without inflection—presented only as of interest since they described aspects of human behavior, and as such were (or should be) of common interest. Listeners that evening were put in mind of certain passages in Edmund's published notebooks of the decades from *The Twenties* through *The Fifties,* when his candor concerning his own erotic tastes was as blandly put forth as Sade's—no matter to what extent of humiliation of the involved partners. Fullness of truth was all. To maintain it was the grounding duty of the critic of life, and without moral judgment, to give the critic's task its freedom.

Like many writers, Edmund entered upon his daily work through little acts of ritual. He once told Dorothy Mendenhall, his elderly

cousin, "I couldn't write without washing my hands"—a statement
of interest as both simple fact and symbol. He came promptly at nine
o'clock every morning to his office. At the cookie break for elevenses
he did not habitually join the other Fellows. While friendly enough
to his colleagues, he tended to establish his own terms of society—the
little dinners with Father D'Arcy, the occasional rendezvous at the
Ritz Bar, the frequent late afternoon at Jean Stafford's glass door
hidden from the street by bushes and trees. He once wrote to me
from Talcotville, in upstate New York, where he was spending a few
days at his old family house, inviting me to come one day for a visit.
His purpose, he said, was to see what I was like away from my job.
The implication that I might be of different characters on the job and
off seemed to me disreputable, and I stiffly replied that I was not
aware of any difference. He hastily replied that he intended no
discredit—only that it would be agreeable to come together beyond
the distractions and interruptions that my position forced on me. We
could talk. He could show me the fine eighteenth-century stone
house he had inherited. Upstate New York was full of interest . . .
When I read *Upstate,* which he published five or six years later, I was
sorry that I had not gone to stay with him there.

His work was all-consuming, and it left him lonely, for the most
part. Its sheer volume demanded almost all of his energies. His
preoccupation with it made him seem distant from other people;
many found it a formidable idea to approach him with anything like
ordinary spontaneity. His volatile responses, friendly or not, seemed
in obscure ways to suggest a turbulent emotional life hidden from
others—and perhaps from himself. Of all those at the Center, it was
Jean Stafford with whom he was most comfortable. They were alike
in their ironic pessimism, their use of liquor, their antic humor, and
the unrelenting realism they turned toward the world. When he
sought out her and her bottles at the end of the day's work he was
sure of his welcome—though in her own stern use of fact she told me
that he was costing her a fortune at the liquor store.

At another time, after some hesitation that had something fearful
about it, she said that late one evening when she was reading with
Elephi the cat on her shoulder, Edmund appeared at the glass door.
He stood outside, refusing to come in when she slid the door open.

In the light reflected from the street lamps high overhead she saw in his face an expression of anguish. Out of what chambered doubts and dreads had he come there?

"Jean," he said thickly, "don't die! don't die!" and walked away, leaving her shaken.

vi

In these pages my intention has been to suggest by anecdote and description what his presence was like. Critical discussion of his work belongs elsewhere. Long after our association ended—and toward the end it was reduced to the occasional letter or message relayed by friends—he remains vividly alive in my recollection. I heard from Roger Straus, his editor and publisher, how in his last days, even following a stroke, he worked at his defined task till he could no more —the ordained professional, the curiously dispassionate artist searching for a rational design in the world through his own life and the act of writing.

Three years after his year at Wesleyan he was notified by William Stevenson, president of the Aspen Institute, that he had been chosen to receive the $30,000 Aspen Award for 1968, which had previously gone to such world savants as Albert Schweitzer, Thomas Mann, and José Ortega y Gasset; and he was invited to come to Aspen in early June to accept the honor and the prize.

It was all to the good, except that the altitude of Aspen, at eight thousand feet, would make it impossible for him to risk those mountain heights because of his chronic heart and respiratory conditions. Much correspondence followed. President Stevenson hoped the award would not have to be reconsidered. Mr. Wilson was willing to accept it, but at sea level. The Aspen Institute trustees behaved considerately, and it was agreed by all that the prize would be awarded at a dinner to be held in New York at the Hotel Waldorf-Astoria on June 12, 1968. I welcomed the occasion, for it brought me together again with Edmund, and when William Stevenson asked me to make the introductory speech of the evening, I agreed. Again, as here, I sought to produce what used to be called a "character" of the subject.

There were perhaps twenty people at the dinner, presided over by Robert O. Anderson, chairman of the board of the Aspen Trustees, and donor of the prize purse. I sat in a row with Edmund next to me, Mrs. Stevenson next to him, and Roger Straus at her right. Such festivals get off to a late start after rounds of drinks. Edmund honored the tray a number of times, and when at table it came time for me to rise to my duty, he was comfortably veiled from the more unnerving aspects of the event. I could not hear what he was talking about, but Mrs. Stevenson later told me that he leaned across her to engage Roger Straus in a lively discussion of literary pornography. If anyone hoped for conventional decorum and appreciation from the guest of honor it already seemed a lost cause. But I had prepared my remarks, and when quiet fell, I entered upon them with every intention of sketching an affectionate, admiring, and sincere likeness of Edmund Wilson as a figure of dignity in our culture; but my tone was soon breached by loud comments *ad libitum* from him beside me. I began by saying to President Stevenson:

In your suggestion that I make a few remarks this evening about and in the presence of the new laureate of the Aspen Award, you lead me into certain risks. Your guest of honor is notorious for his hatred of humbug, and I imagine he would include under this heading any sort of complimentary sentiments addressed to him in public. Further, he is world-famous for his critical penetration and his lively rectitude in judgment. Who could feel comfortable offering him even the simplest professional courtesies? The terrible Samuel Johnson once put the problem this way: "The reciprocal civility of authors is one of the most risible scenes in the farce of life."

(E.W.: *a snort of amusement*)

Yet in this I detect a way out for myself. I shall speak on this occasion not as an author but as a reader—

(E.W.: *Oh, come, come!*)

and later as an associate. As a reader I claim the work of Edmund Wilson as a lifelong addiction. To a reader there is no pleasure greater than buying and reading and marking up as they appear year after year the books of an indispensable writer. It is indeed rare enough—how many authors of our own lifetime must we read book by book? Precious few. But Mr. Wilson is one of these, and any publishing season marked by a new book of his becomes memorable. My personal reading acquaintance with his work began with The Undertaker's Garland

(E.W.: *Did it really! You don't say!*)

which he produced in 1922 in collaboration with John Peale Bishop, and I moved on to all the rest. To mention only one more, Allan Nevins told me that Patriotic Gore *is the best book ever done about the Civil War—*

(E.W.: *Did he really!*)

and after I gave him a copy one summer in Santa Fe, Igor Stravinsky—who has a right to the word—praised it as a "masterpiece."

(E.W.: *M'ym, really, how extraordinary!*)

Rereading is almost a greater pleasure than the initial reading when we are concerned with such a writer as Mr. Wilson. When any new edition of his is announced, you have to have it immediately, and read it through, and make new notes in the back, and put it on the shelf alongside its earlier incarnations. My Wilson shelf must now measure well over six feet . . . first editions, hardcover reissues, revised texts, paperbacks, even, I am happy to remember, a few rarities such as japes drawn and written and privately issued by the author for holidays. The presence established through five decades of such wonderful literary fecundity became early for the private reader what it gradually and splendidly became for the world: a presence of superb honesty, magnificent skill, and incomparable breadth of thought. Living in New Mexico for many years, I never thought to meet him, for he rarely came that way—actually only once, was it?

(E.W.: *No, twice.*)

—to write about the Zuñi Shalako?—and I remained his anonymous associate in my New Mexico library. But the most odd of circumstances brought me late in life, and for the first time, to the fringe of the higher academic world, and it presently fell to me to play a part in assembling a greatly distinguished band of men and women under yearly appointment as Fellows in the Center for Advanced Studies at Wesleyan University. You can imagine how swiftly I set to work to ensnare Mr. Wilson . . . I was new at the profession of advancing studies through recruitment of the world's great, some of whom, however unjustly, were stuck with reputations for being personally formidable. But arrangements were made for an encounter with Mr. and Mrs. Wilson and a year later this constant reader became the administrative host, and, ultimately, I was made to feel, the colleague, and the friend, of tonight's guest of honor. After a year's association with him I can testify to the daily satisfaction, for all of us at the Center, to be taken from his exemplary professional style, and from the enlivening surprises of his personal warmth and humor. As a working craftsman he put in a full day every day, with what abundant results his readers soon knew. Though he always wears vast erudition most lightly, we came to know in daily personal encounters that range of his interest and authority which we had long known in his published works—taking in philosophy, politics, painting, music, theatre, social studies, and above all literature. The true humanist is always a polymath—always versatile, as he again made plain. We could feel the style of his humanity and detect in it a hint of melancholy regard upon the Horatian aspects of life—and at the same time

the countervailing warmth of his concern which he generally strove to conceal for fear of revealing a kind heart. We heard with delight that he was going to give a Punch and Judy show for his daughter's Christmas, and that some of us were to be invited.

(E.W.: *H'ym.*)

There was to be a special score for two guitars, and surely an Ur-text faultless under his scholarship. This had to be cancelled, but there were other gaieties—poker-faced marvels of prestidigitation with playing cards, a subtle program to subvert the affections of a secretarial spaniel with forbidden snacks—

(E.W.: *[laughing] I was afraid you were going to bring that up!*)

a parody correspondence initiated as by a mother rat protesting the laboratory methods of an eminent psychologist. I particularly liked one of his social improvizations: now and then late in the afternoon he would stroll down to a humble restaurant on Main Street in Middletown and preempt a banquette behind the cash register where he would invite colleagues to meet him for a drink; and this innocently crummy spot he dubbed The Ritz Bar.

(E.W.: *laughter*)

I've been trying here to pay him the modest private honors of simple association and personal discovery. The other dimension—the national, the intercultural—must surely mean more to others. So let me end with an anecdote I delight in which somehow bridges the gap between the private reader and the ultimate impersonal personage which history will make of Edmund Wilson. President John F. Kennedy appointed a committee whose members would propose to him annually a couple of dozen persons out of our two hundred millions who by their achievements deserved special recognition by the nation's highest medium of official discrimination—that is, the Presidency. Ambassador Arthur Goldberg (then Labor Secretary) helped to work out a suitable first list. By incontestable right, it included Edmund Wilson. Still when Secretary Goldberg put the list before the young President, he believed it was his duty to mention that the nominee Edmund Wilson was known to hold somewhat more than the general citizen's passionate opposition to the federal income tax policy. In fact, what might be involved here could be an incitement to popular fiscal mischief on a national scale.

(E.W.: *Yes, yes!*)

In that case, said Mr. Goldberg, who told the delightful story to Roger Straus, who told it to me, the committee believed the President should have a chance at a second choice for Mr. Wilson's place in the national honors list. President Kennedy evidently took no time at all to state his view. "The Presidential Medal of Freedom," he said, "is not a good-conduct medal—it is an award for high achievement"—

(E.W.: *That's true, true!*)

and, accordingly, Mr. Wilson's decoration was confirmed and the matter concluded. It is a conclusion with which all literate America must eagerly agree; and tonight's occasion is, to the satisfaction of us all, private and professional readers alike, one more superb recognition of Edmund Wilson's sovereign effectiveness in our national statement of mind and spirit.

President Stevenson succeeded me and in his remarks brought the heart of the occasion closer. He sketched Edmund's achievements, with the measured skill of an ex-diplomat (he had been the United States Ambassador to the Philippines). I thought Edmund stiffened in his chair, and I was sure of this when Stevenson, extracting the award check for $30,000 from his papers, said that he took very great pleasure in presenting to Mr. Wilson "the 1968 Aspen Award in the Humanities with this citation: To Edmund Wilson who, as a man of profound erudition, as a widely respected social critic, as a versatile and illuminating author, literary journalist, and prose stylist, has effectively demonstrated that for a humanist, literature is an art as well as a medium for the uplift of mankind."

Saying which, he leaned far across the table, extending the check. Edmund leaped to his feet, met the prize in mid-air, grasped it in a hawk-like swoop, and cried out, "Tax free! Tax free!" No piety lingered in the air about "the uplift of man." Yet he knew he must make some response. He brought out a script and read from it, explaining that it had been previously published. It was his affirmation, with references to Lord Macaulay and Hippolyte Taine, of their early influence on his career as a man of letters and a humanist, "which is what I have tried to be." He saw a broadening of literary studies developing in the universities, and he concluded that it was now possible "for our literate public to appreciate and understand both our own Anglo-American culture and those of the European countries in relation to one another, to arrive at a point of view from which we may be able to deal with systems of art and thought that have previously seemed inaccessible or incompatible with one another." With that, he looked about, indicating that, so far as he was concerned, the proceedings were over.

In short order he marshalled himself and Elena for departure. The after-dinner breakup with its eddies of talk as everyone was released seemed to him an unnecessary pleasantry. People closed about him with congratulations and other little claims on his personal attention.

Hating speeches and public events, he was rapidly sobering up, and he did well enough with his manners until the Stevensons came to say good night, but then his unsociable self took over—for the Stevensons brought him a copy of *The Shores of Light* and asked him to sign it. Already on his feet, he had to sit down again at the table. Stevenson handed him a pen. Edmund took it, opened the book, and asked,

"Oh, all right. What name?"—this after weeks of correspondence with William Stevenson and after just now having received from his hand a check for $30,000 ("tax free, tax free").

"Oh? —William Stevenson," muttered the ambassador in amazement.

Edmund, implacably. "How do you spell it?"

Somehow the signing got done. I offered the Wilsons a lift across town to the Princeton Club, where they were staying. It was a joyless ride through heavy rain. Silence held after that vacant aftermath that followed many a public jubilee. At the Princeton Club I saw them into the lobby and said good night. They took a few steps away, and then Edmund turned.

"Yes," he said levelly, "thanks for the eulogy."

1971

Last Days of Stravinsky

i

AFTER 1966 Igor Stravinsky's conducting engagements became less frequent, and there were reports of increasing difficulties with health. I found these disquieting. For more than a decade I had been privileged to enter into an enriching friendship with the composer, his wife, Vera, and their young companion in music and home, Robert Craft. I had met them in 1955 at Santa Fe, when they had come to oversee the production of Stravinsky's opera *The Rake's Progress*, which was the crowning event of the first season of the Santa Fe Opera. I, as a member of the opera board of directors, was asked to "take care of" the Stravinskys in as many ways as possible. It was a duty I entered into with enthusiasm born of my lifelong devotion to the Maestro for his achievements as the prime aesthetic spirit of the century. At Santa Fe they welcomed my attentions, and as their Figaro I served them with pleasure and, soon, love. In the following decade I was blessed by their continuing and unreserved friendship, and our professional concerns coincided often enough for us to meet at home and abroad. All too soon came intermittent, painful, and frightening periods of Stravinsky's hospitalization in Los Angeles, and in 1969 the household moved to New York in search of more varied medical care. They took an apartment in a hotel on Central

Park South. There I would call, or dine, and I find one notation for an evening which, despite signs of illness, I marked as "radiant."

Stravinsky was now really frail. He seemed almost to ration his utterances; but when they came they were, even concerning commonplaces, touched with his particular originality which combined a droll assumption of agreement by his listeners with a view they might never have come to for themselves. His hold on life was a marvel. Time and again he alarmed everyone by a spell of critically extreme illness—a crisis of the blood, or the circulation, or respiration—but in a few days, inquiring by long-distance telephone, I would hear that he was much improved and again at work.

But presently he must go to a New York hospital for surgery, and his discouragement was so great, it was mingled with so much angry disdain for illness and all its dreadful apparatus, that he took to muteness, and according to a tale told by Vera Zorina, he refused to speak to his nurses, only giving directions in his sickroom by imperious flicks of a finger, indicating what he wanted as though conducting.

It was all the more wonderful then, that E. J. Allen, a member of the household, was able to send me a note in June 1969, saying, "I know that you will be happy to hear that I.S. is much improved, eating now, the morale a little improved, and even working: completing the 4th fugue of four from *The Well-Tempered Clavier* (instrumentations)." Fifty-eight years earlier, from Ustilug, his Russian home, he had written to Roerich concerning their joint inspiration for *Le Sacre du printemps,* "I expect to start composing in the fall, and health permitting, I hope to finish in the spring." Health permitting! Now in 1969, possibly already mortally ill, he was, at a weight of eighty-seven pounds in his eighty-seventh year, orchestrating Bach for a little while each day. Working? "All my life." . . .

I had met Allen in Santa Fe, and it was there, too, that he had met the Stravinskys. Later, in Los Angeles, their friendship grew. Subsequently Allen had moved East from California to take a post at the Wesleyan University Library. By now he was a friend so intimate and essential to the Stravinskys that in the increasing worries and needs of the Maestro's illness he had asked for and had been granted leave by Wyman Parker, the university librarian, to stay in New York to do what he could—and it was much—for the afflicted family. The strain had been great on Madame, and Allen added in his note, "Vera, however, is suffering from a bad heart and has to remain in bed . . . Meanwhile, V. wanted you to have this—" an amusing book about the Ritz Hotel in Paris.

When she was again well enough, I was invited to call—it was December 4, 1969. I saw Madame alone for a while, and then Allen brought Stravinsky to us in his small, somehow clever-looking wheelchair. The Maestro's face was pink, he made the ride in the wheelchair resemble a child's animated excursion, and I exclaimed,

"How marvellous you look!"

"What else?" he replied with gaiety. I bent to kiss his hand, and with strength which astonished me he pulled my hand to his lips. We settled down to a conversation.

Madame said they were looking for a permanent place of their own—an apartment they could buy. She had been all over town to see various possibilities, but found them so expensive that they had decided on nothing. They liked best the idea of a place overlooking the East River.

"Eager"—so she pronounced his name—"so much liked the view from the hospital, to see the boats, and the lights of the bridges. We would like to have a place over there."

"Oh, yes," I exclaimed. "I remember the same thing from the summer when I was here in the hospital, and later in my sublet flat. It is where I would like to live if I had to live in town."

"But you have no idea," said Madame, "what they ask. We could never afford it."

"I know," I said. "I don't know how it could ever be managed."

"Pol," said Stravinsky, like one settling a problem with final practicality, "you should buy the river."

The farcical amplitude of this delighted us all. The Maestro, at our laughter, gave his effect of taking a bow. We went rambling along. He spoke of "the fragments of life," making the point that the essential matter in both living and in "making" was to "put them together." He was, of course, voicing his belief in form and design. He spoke of powers, and their use, and also said with an air of wisdom that there were other powers which could not be *used*—this

in a religious reference. I said, in a kinship with both my childhood
and his wholly simple faith beyond sophistication,

"Every time I pass the cathedral here, I go in, and light a candle,
and say a prayer for your well-being."

He thanked me silently.

All through this meeting, I was moved by the extraordinary sensi-
tiveness which Allen showed in his care for Stravinsky. He saw
signals which no one else did. He never took his eyes off Stravinsky's
face. How he knew it, I could not say, but at one moment he
understood that Stravinsky wanted to be moved from the wheelchair
to the sofa; went to him, took him up in his arms—Allen was tall and
strongly made—and resettled him on the sofa. In a few minutes, this
proved not so comfortable as Stravinsky wanted it to be, and again,
without the exchange of a word, or even a preliminary gesture visible
to me, Allen moved him to the wheelchair. There was tenderness as
well as efficiency in Allen's intuitive alertness, and it was easy to see
why he had been so fondly taken into the household. His affinity with
Russian life was great—he was studying the language, Madame said
he was making excellent progress, he had grown a Russian beard,
dark and handsomely trimmed, and, in his case as in mine, a devotion conceived in a youthhood far removed from Stravinsky was now
fulfilled in close friendship with him, his wife, and Robert Craft. As
the aged Maestro's musical and literary alter ego, the brilliant young
Craft had become a truly filial presence in the lives of both Stravinskys.

ii

With nurses both night and day, it was now not possible for Stravinsky to go out to dine as we used to do; but it was important for
Madame to have an occasional brief respite from her voluntary
confinement to the apartment, and I invited her and Craft to dine
out with me on January 19, 1970.

I came a little early to fetch them, for Craft had agreed to show
me some of the Stravinsky manuscripts—a comprehensive collection
—which were then undergoing appraisal. By now Madame had

made the hotel apartment a livable place, with some of her own paintings on the walls, and more by Léger, Tchelitchev, Bakst, and others. There were, as always, books in profusion, many in large folio size containing reproductions of works of art.

"How is he?" I asked.

The report was better again, but there had been a serious setback the previous week—"worse than at any time in the past eight months," said Craft—a thrombosis in the left ankle. But Stravinsky was already recovering from this.

"We'll see him in a moment," said Craft, and then produced some of the manuscripts, showing them to me on a low long table before a sofa. They were in themselves works of art. The chirography was extraordinary in its precision, purity, life, order upon the page, utter clarity. Each page looked as if it were designed by a master designer of typography. Their beauty as objects was allied to that of the graphic arts. They were finished scores. Their precision could not possibly be misinterpreted by later generations. I could not imagine another musical archive by such a master brought to such completeness and beauty of visual style. I turned a few pages. It was a direct encounter.

Presently Craft took me to Stravinsky, who was in his own room.

It was a small, rather narrow room, but in its formal neatness it seemed larger than it was. The light was low everywhere but in one place—that was where Stravinsky was disposed, upright, in his small wheelchair, his back to the wall, and the lamp glowing over his shoulder on the pages of a book which rested on a cushion, on a carefully folded throw, on his lap. He wore one of his cardigans. In his left hand he held a little dictionary. To his left was an ordered desk; to his right, a neat upright piano. He was in effect in a niche between the two pieces of furniture. He looked small—smaller than I had ever seen him; but his smile of welcome was full of that joke of surprise which he could always counterfeit to give a common event some extra dimension. He looked so frail that I was fearful of greeting him physically, but Craft said, "Go ahead—kiss him. He wants you to."

I leaned down and touched his cheek with my lips. He responded with a small nod. I saw that the book he was reading was Henri Troyat's biography *Pouchkine*. Merely to make sounds, I asked, "Is it a good book?"

Stravinsky replied, so softly that Craft leaned down to him and repeated the words to me: "A biography of Pushkin is no ordinary affair," and bowed in the old way of confirmation of his own statement. The dictionary he held was in French. Even in his high literacy in that language, he enjoyed meditating on even familiar words with the aid of a lexicon—a lifelong habit. This meant that he was reading slowly. Time itself was still his to command. His profile was now heroic, craggy, when seen in the scale of the diminishment of all else about him. He volunteered no remarks, but his awareness was so keen that as Craft and I talked commonplaces, he followed our words from one to the other as if watching a tennis match. He was participating in our society in silence, which rather reminded me of how autistic children enter their surroundings in full awareness while seeming not to do so. Presently Craft, preparing Stravinsky for our absence for the remainder of the evening, said in a gentle subterfuge, "We are going downstairs a little while to have a drink."

Stravinsky caught a breath in his playful manner and said with longing in his almost vanished voice, so that Craft again had to repeat for him, "I will come with you."

The pathetic impossibility of this resulted in Craft's instant decision not to leave at all. He was right: Stravinsky so plainly longed not to be abandoned. Craft said, with a fond air of daring to hope for an unexpected privilege, "If *you* will have a drink with *us*, we will stay here and have it with you."

"*Merci,*" Stravinsky indicated through a gesture.

Room service then responded to our altered plans. We ordered drinks and dinner. The waiter came, wheeled a rickety table in place, Stravinsky came in his rolling chair to the table, Craft next to him, Madame and myself facing them. A glass of watered-down Scotch was provided for Stravinsky. He made a social matter of pantomiming a toast.

What developed then was a miniature contest for life itself—for Craft, keeping up a running exhortation, like a coach putting spirit into his player, urged food upon Stravinsky, who responded like an earnest team member, so that the game took on a seriousness which stood for much more than the mere moment of its playing. It was as stark and poignant, as sweet and desperate, as the Schubert song about *Death and the Maiden,* or one of those Dürer engravings counter-posing flesh and skeleton. In loving urgency, like one who is sure he can save what may soon be lost, Craft, throughout the dinner, devoted himself wholly to the nourishment of Stravinsky. A contest in a nursery style developed—though in deadly earnest—as Craft kept saying, *"Mangez-les,"* pointing to lima beans, and assuring the Maestro that there was much protein to be had in them; and the rare, delicately cut-up beef— *"Mangez-le,"* it gives strength. Stravinsky took mouthful upon mouthful, in determined effort to win, no matter what the odds. "He is eating better than for weeks," said Craft softly in an aside to Madame and me. And then, "Drink a little Scotch," he would say in his role of coach, and the striving tiny athlete did what he was cheered on to do. In French, Craft, watching every successful bite, said that with his strength recovered (it was coming fast now, all this excellent protein), in the spring they would go to Paris, and stay at the Ritz, where, as Stravinsky must remember, the food was so good, the garden so charming, the wine so marvellous, remember the Richebourg '61, and Souvchinsky would come to call, and Boulez, and there would be those lovely long drives late in the afternoon when Paris was most beautiful . . . He took a lima bean on his own fork and posed it to Stravinsky and said, *"Mangez-la, c'est la proteine"*—both of them hungry for the same great life, and so was I.

Madame meanwhile said to me, "Bob is so sweet to him, so kind, so attentive," and then in her uncompromising realism, she added, "So unexpected, too"—for she had known for years Craft's cult of refusing to show his feeling directly to Stravinsky, or to give him any intimate attention such as he now gave with a sense of the marvel of Stravinsky's whole life, work, and presence.

"Splendid," said Craft, watching Stravinsky's unceasing movement of fork from plate to lips, "you are doing splendidly, and later we will hear some music . . ."

So it was that after dinner Stravinsky was established on a sofa, his shoeless feet in neat plain black socks resting on a cushion on the floor, while Madame and I sat together at another side of the room.

Craft, after bringing scores, set the phonograph going. He came to sit beside Stravinsky to read score with him, turning the pages, pointing out significant details in them, half conducting, indicating by finger on the page important entrances of instruments or various thematic matters.

They played the first three movements of Beethoven's string quartet, op. 125, and the last movement of the piano sonata, op. III. When I say "played," I mean that they participated; that music was never more powerfully conveyed to me than by their active musical intelligences; that Stravinsky's concentration was so complete and consuming that I felt in the presence of an act of creation. His lower lip was stuck forward, as if to inhale the music in an extra sense. His head was bent over the score, causing the few strands of hair at the base of his small powerful skull to stick out more than ever, and his breathing was shallow, rapid, regular, and expelled in gusts with, I thought, wastefully terrible force. It was another urgent—almost desperate—act of nourishment: Craft working to retain life itself in the noble musical mind with that sustenance which it still craved; that which—who knew how soon?—it would soon no longer be able to receive. I was moved almost past enduring. Madame, listening with me, knew what I felt; and though brave and real to the fullest, habitually ready to admit any truth, she now said proudly to me in defiance of truth, in her most dove-like tone, at the presence of so much realization in life, *"That is not a dying man!"*

Stravinsky and Craft were unaware of us. Madame then said, "If you want to go now, go"—this toward the end of op. III. "They will be at it for a long time."

"Shall I say good night?"

"No, just go."

I went to get my coat. She came with me. They did not notice us as we moved to the foyer. On the way I made a gesture of admiration for Bakst's drawing of her done when she was in her twenties. It showed her at her most ripe young beauty. She told me to wait a moment, went to her bedroom, and returned with a framed reproduction of the drawing, and gave it to me with a kiss.

I left in stealth and great disarray of thought and feeling; for it was the actually tremendous intensity of how Stravinsky listened to the master whom he had come to love above all others late in life, it was what came into the room through the vital concentration of Stravinsky's reception of the music which made me hear it *through him;* and since I was familiar with that music of Beethoven and ordinarily would be ready to agree with anyone about its power, it was, on this night, the longing power of Stravinsky as he listened which had exhausted me so that I could endure it no longer. It had been a contest between the certainty of death and the survival of art, neither of which could avert the particular victory of the other.

iii

On a Sunday evening—May 17, 1970—I came again for dinner. Allen was there with Madame and Craft. The table was laid, and there was a curious air of optimism which must have been called forth by the finally accepted limits of strength; for since my last visit there had been several more trying episodes with crises and periods of hospitalisation "for tests."

I had been given news from time to time, and one day in Middletown Allen brought me a copy of *Retrospectives and Conclusions,* the final volume of the five in which dialogues between Stravinsky and Craft, together with diaries by Craft, had appeared. Stravinsky and Craft had both inscribed it to me. It may be one of the last, perhaps even the very last, autograph Stravinsky ever gave. In wavering print he had written, "To Paul, with lowe, I.S.—1.30.70," and the use of the German "w" sound for the English "v" reflected his increasing tendency in those days to retreat from English and speak in German or French to everyone but Madame, to whom he now habitually spoke in Russian—"Russian, the exiled language of my heart," as he had put it earlier. Craft added his own initials.

When on that Sunday evening Stravinsky was brought to the table by a nurse, I had a shiver of recognition of how he had grown even smaller since I had seen him. His face seemed to have receded about his eyes, so that they had a newly prominent look. He was stooped as he sat. His great hands were like exposed roots in winter, all gnarl and frosty fiber. About his throat was a scarf, with its ends tucked into his cardigan. He was placed at the head of the table, still the patri-

TO PAUL

with LOWE

75. ⌐& R.C.⌐

1.30.70

arch at his own board. I was seated to his left, Madame to his right, Allen next to her, Craft next to me. A current of good feeling went from each to the other of us. It was, despite everything, a joyful condition that we were all together with Stravinsky. In one of those small silent marvels of communication of which he had always been capable, but which was now particularly extraordinary, he made us feel his own pleasure.

When drinks were before us, I saw that his was the palest ration of his favorite, for I had seen the nurse mix it, when perhaps a teaspoon of the liquor had been put in a tumbler half full of water. The doctors had forbidden liquor for him, and tonight's potion was simply a signal of festivity, like the "cambric tea" of nursery imitations of grownup tea parties.

Stravinsky looked deliberately around the table at each of us. It was in no sense a bestowal of a lingering farewell, though I for one, and possibly others, could not but think of the notion. On the contrary, his gaze was an expression of the keenest social pleasure and fondness, and when his survey ended with me at his left, he lifted his glass—weakly, at an angle, so that its contents were almost tipped out—and with beautiful formal manners, he said,

"Pol, *hier haben wir eine sehr gemütliche Gesellschaft.*"

With that he touched my glass with his, and bowed in a silent toast to us all, and took a sip. We drank with him. Food came. He ate two or three mouthfuls. Our talk rattled on in general, none of it directed with pointed consideration toward him, and he joined in none of it.

His simple presence was enough to satisfy him, and—alas—us. We were in high spirits, our give-and-take while not ignoring him did not pause from time to time to discern and attend to any needs he may have had. It was therefore to our surprise that he suddenly halted all talk by saying in a strong voice, low in pitch, while crumpling into himself as if the better to plumb his condition to its fullest,

"I am dronk."

One or two sips of water scarcely flavored with Scotch? It told us much. Allen rose at once and went to the wheelchair and turned it from the table. The nurse heard something of our reaction, came from the bedroom, and, relieving Allen at the steering knobs of the chair, wheeled Stravinsky from sight to see him into bed. I watched until his door was closed. Ah, ah—under my breath. I never saw him again.

At the table, his disappearance was granted the dignity of not being commented upon. The others were by now used to such sudden lapses of vitality. What could be done for him was being done, there, behind the closed door. Meanwhile, there he was, living, by the simple fact reassuring, and cherished in the life which continued about him.

The party resumed its conviviality. We talked of Russian writers —Madame remembered Mandelstam and the poems he had written to her long ago. Someone brought up Turgenev, which led to a discussion of the general inadequacy of translations of Russian literature. I was reading for the first time the Aylmer Maude versions of *Anna Karenina* and *War and Peace,* having previously known only the Constance Garnett translations, and I quoted the illuminating and original remark of Edmund Wilson to me: "The trouble with Constance Garnett's translations is that she makes all the Russian writers sound alike." Madame remembered a passage from a Russian writer —a word had been translated as "assiduous," and she declared that this was not the proper shade of meaning. She searched her thought for a better word, and then said, "I will find the dictionary," went and returned with one in Russian, saying, "We still have about fifty dictionaries even here," turned a few pages, and then exclaimed with satisfaction, "The proper word is 'diligent.' "

The *Gesellschaft* lingered for almost three hours, while we sat at table in the Old World fashion, drinking coffee and liqueurs in companionable comfort. It was good to see Madame so much at peace, so relieved of tension, looking so handsome and taking so much pleasure in animated conversation which relieved her for even a little while of the concern which heavied her usual days and nights. Just below our idle, spoken, convivial thoughts at the table, silently there was another—for me, for everyone there, I felt sure—of the life in the next room.

iv

In that summer—1970—I was astonished when they told me that they were taking Stravinsky abroad, to Evian, away from the hot months in New York. I could not imagine how he could endure such a commotion and effort as a flight to and from Europe. Nevertheless, they went, and evidently he stood the journey well.

I was in London in August, and saw a notable production of *Les Noces*, handsomely choreographed after Nijinska. Once again I had the sense of being beaten into awareness by the powerful rhythmic drive of the work, and every sort of atavism came to mind, hearing and seeing the ritual enacted in the peasant wedding, and I felt Stravinsky's humaneness of intuition as his ballet proclaimed its program of the mystery celebrating the coming together of two human beings in formalized love as it was consummated by marriage. How subject, I thought, mankind remains to the pathos and the power of ancient ways.

Miranda Masocco Levy was temporarily living in London, where her husband was producing films. In California she had been a close companion and neighbor of the Stravinskys. We had been friends for years in Santa Fe. I now had a lively reunion with her; our shared interest in everything concerning the Stravinskys gave us much to talk about. We fell into the habit of lunching together every Sunday. On one of these days she joined me with a fine promising rattle of her heavy gold bangles, her eyes lighted with laughter and information. She had made a point of telephoning to Madame at Evian just before lunch so she could bring me the latest news.

"Marvellous," she said in the husky, humorous voice she kept for her best stories. "Vera sounded wonderful, she sent her love."

"How is the Maestro?"

"He is not very strong, but he seems comfortable. They take drives in the country, he enjoys seeing everything, and the hotel is marvellous. But they are leaving tomorrow—no, day after tomorrow."

"Where?"

"Back to New York. Vera was glad I called. She wanted me to do something for them."

"Oh? What was it?"

"Wonderful. She said it was about the photographer."

"What photographer?"

"Please," asked Madame, "there is that photographer to come to photograph my husband. But we cannot. He is to come tomorrow. We are so busy. I am packing, packing. The airplane is to take us the next day. My husband is too tired. He should not be bothered. Why should there be photographers? Please tell him not to come."

"But who is he?" asked Miranda.

"The name I do not think of at the moment. He has an appointment for a long time. He must not come."

"Do you want me to find him and cancel the appointment?"

"Yes, please."

"Then tell me how to look for him."

"He is married to a princess in England."

"Do you mean Lord Snowdon?"

Madame, as if it were her own triumph, cried,

"That is who! Please tell him we are so busy, I do not want my husband to be bothered."

Thinking of Kensington Palace, Miranda said,

"Is he at home, now, in London?"

"No, he is in Sardinia."

"Sardinia! But where in Sardinia?"

"He is with the Aga Khan," said Madame—surely a sufficient address for anyone.

Miranda's head was now in a whirl, but she had a clear thought.

"He is a very fine photographer," she said, "an artist; and he is very sympathetic and moving in his pictures of old people. He would make some beautiful pictures of the Maestro."

"So, he should come?" asked Madame doubtfully.

"I would certainly let him come. After all, he needn't take all day."

A silent moment for thought, and then Madame said,

"Very well. He may come. Do not do anything."

"I won't," promised Miranda.

"So he is after all to take the pictures?" I said.

"Tomorrow."

"I went to visit them, you know," said Miranda, "earlier this summer. —He is so changed. I hardly dared touch him." She spoke with love, and then, in her own sense of the historical, which so often embraced the comic as well as the formidable, she said,

"Did I ever tell you about the terrible morning in Hollywood when I called him 'Pussycat'?"

"No. But you have always called him Pussycat."

"I know."

"He loved it."

"I know. But wait."

One morning in the usual routine Miranda went next door in Hollywood to see her neighbors, who were soon to move to New York. Stravinsky was not yet at work. He seemed somewhat preoccupied, if not dejected. She went to his chair, leaned over him, kissed him on his head, and said,

"Good morning, darling Pussycat."

What occurred then appalled her.

Stravinsky threw away something—his stick, or a book, or whatever—and shouted,

"I think I have lived lonk enough and worked hard enough, not without some recognized achievement, to have earned the privilege of not beink addressed as 'Pussycat'!"

Miranda said she felt herself go pale—she had seen his gusts of anger before, but never had felt one directed at herself. Shaken, she apologized. He frowned, staring ahead into his mood. He was the last one whom she ever meant to offend.

"Good heavens," I said. "What did you do then?"

"Nothing much more then, but I *tell* you, I was trembling. After that, I always called him Maestro, like everybody else."

In New York again at the end of summer, Stravinsky endured

further vagaries of health. I was in touch by telephone, and saw Madame and Craft now and then, but my duties that winter were so particularly heavy, and Madame's preoccupations and worries were so woeful, that it was not until an evening in January—Wednesday, the twentieth, 1971—that there was occasion for an evening together, though of course I could not see Stravinsky, as only the household now had access to him.

But on that evening Madame invited me to accompany her to the opening of a new production of *A Midsummer Night's Dream,* to be followed by supper. Craft and Rita Christensen, the Danish nurse who with skill was principally taking care of Stravinsky, were also with us. Weary beyond amenity, Madame nodded and slept during most of the play, despite its glaring, harsh, and stuntish production. Craft and I endured it awake, and at the end he said to me with one of his smiles of intellectual mischief, after we had shrugged over the production's style, "It is not even a very good *play.*" I agreed with him, despite passages of magic poetry in the text.

We went from the theatre to Madame's supper party at the Pavillon, where we were joined by Goddard and Brigitta Lieberson and Dominique Nabokov (her husband, Nicolas, was unwell).

Here it was most easing to see Madame rise to the atmosphere of her supper party with her fullest charm. She seated me to her right, and to my right was Vera Zorina—the stage name of Brigitta Lieberson as dancer and *diseuse.* My situation could not have been improved. Stravinsky was much in all our minds, immobilized as he was across town; and in a real sense the measure of our gaiety that evening was the measure of how our thought of him, and the memory of previous times when he was present, knitted us together in his name. We toasted him. Then Madame turned to me and said for my ear alone,

"He is not good"—meaning that he was extremely unwell. It was very much like her that even as we were gathered to enjoy a party she could recognize and speak of what was so full of unremitting ache for her. The toast reminded Lieberson and Craft of amusing anecdotes about him, and spirits rose, and presently Madame turned to me with a lustrous smile and asked,

"Did I ever tell you how I first met Stravinsky?"—I always liked her pronunciation of his name: "Stra-veen-sky."

"No, never."

"So, I will tell you." Her smile began to fill with loving recollection. She made her familiar little labial movement as if tasting her words in advance. She looked beautiful if weary that evening, but now behind the face of a lady of eighty ("I used to deny my age," she had said not long before to Zorina, "but now I am proud of it") I saw the timeless glow of a young woman's love, and she said,

"It was this way. It started this way." It was in 1921. The Diaghilev company was in the midst of ballet preparations—rehearsals, costumes, *maquettes* for scenery, endless talks about changes in script and score. "This was in Paris. One evening D'aghilev"—they always pronounced the name this way—"D'aghilev came and said we would go to dine in Montmartre. He said, I have Stra-*veen*-sky downstairs in a cab. Come. He is in very bad mood. *Be kind to him.*" Madame turned full upon me and I felt a lovely and explicit reflection of joy as she said, with a ghost of wonderfully feminine gallantry, "And I was."

Shortly before that evening, which I think of as filled with rose-colored light and warmth, Madame had at last found an apartment which was suitable in every way, and Stravinsky had bought it for her. He looked forward to having his own home again, where paintings, books, instruments, could once again be assembled about him. There was much to do. They had hoped to move before Christmas, but there were the usual delays of redecorating and equipping the place, and the weeks went by without seeing the rooms ready. But possessions and furniture were gradually being transferred from the old hotel suite to the new apartment; and Madame was at moments happy in these new preoccupations. As for her husband, he was, at eighty-nine, still putting a few notes on paper every day, according to Allen, when it suddenly became necessary for him to be taken once again to the hospital. The shock to him was great. It would be hard to think of anyone who would more fastidiously loathe the public business of stretchers, ambulances, and passages through elevators and lobbies than he. But there was again—though a diminished one—another of those extraordinary resurges of recuperative power which he had shown so often in the past many years; and when he was brought back from the hospital it was to his new home.

v

Five days later, while listening to early-morning news on television, I heard that he was dead. I then realized that for weeks—even months—I had turned on the TV with a denied sense of dread of this very news. Now here it was. I changed all my arrangements for the week. The day was April 6, 1971. I drove at once to New York and on arrival, speaking to Lillian Libman, the secretary-manager of the household, placed myself at the disposal of Madame and Craft. There was, evidently, nothing for me to do, but I wanted to be in town in case I might be of use. That evening there was to be a private Russian Orthodox prayer service and Miss Libman said that Madame asked for me to be present.

I entered a feeling of vigil. I felt absent from myself all day long. The Age of Stravinsky ended at dawn on that day. Of his nine decades of life, five had provided, for me, a nourishing union, at first far, then nearer; and in my heavied thought on that day there was yet a living edge of gratitude that my life had been touched by my encounters with his work and his presence.

I thought of Miranda in London and telephoned to her. She had heard the news, but knew of no plans; and when I offered to have flowers sent to the bier in her name, she was thankful. She would telephone to Madame. We could say little more to each other.

That evening when I came to the service being held for him I was nervous. If this was the death of a man, it was also the death of an epoch; and personal feelings were mixed in turmoil with a sense of the time now bereft of its strongest aesthetic spirit.

I came into a large square room containing perhaps thirty persons. My eye was immediately drawn to a figure sitting alone on a modest straight chair, facing a mounded hillock of flowers over a coffin. It was Madame. A black lace veil was clouded about her head. She was wanly beautiful. About her was a wide space which now and then someone crossed to speak to her. Her great eyes seemed larger than ever. Her manner was spacious and gentle. She held murmured conversations with the particular friends whom she had summoned that evening. I recognized George Balanchine, Lincoln Kirstein, Elliott Carter, among others, and of course Craft and Allen, and Miss Libman. There was a sustained hush. I saw faces marked by mystery and sorrow. Contemplating the hill of flowers, thinking of what lay beneath it, I mentally made various offices of prayer. Presently Allen came to me and asked me to cross the terrible open space separating Madame from the world.

When I came to her, she raised her cheek for me to kiss and I kissed also her hand. Her noble composure remained unbroken as she held on to my hand and spoke to me, while awaiting the entry of the bishop, his thurifers, and the chanters who would sing the service.

She said they knew all day yesterday that the end must come very soon. She said they wept all day, helpless to relieve him of his suffering. She said he had been home only five days in their new apartment, but he had been very happy, asking to be taken in his wheelchair through the rooms again and again, and he would say over and over, "It is ours, it is ours." He loved, however briefly, the look of Central Park from the windows, and as a surprise for him she had bought a bird, a canary, and wherever Stravinsky was taken in the apartment, he could hear the bird singing. It was a wonderful singer, joyous and strong in its jubilee of sound, and he listened ecstatically as long as he could. When suddenly his last crisis came, he lay in his room, his breathing was horrifying to hear—Madame as I stood holding her hand imitated how the breathing sounded and my heart beat hard for hearing it.

How can she be so strong? I kept asking myself. I feared that I must be tiring her, for so long as I would be by her side, she would for my sake continue to speak to me. I heard the echoes of that breathing, and I imagined the abstract tiny glory and sweetness of the singing bird.

After what seemed to me a shamelessly long time for me to be by her side, someone else approached, and I bent to her, and we kissed, cheek and cheek, in Russian style, and I left her as the other visitors came to whisper their words for her, and for him.

Not long afterward the small procession of religious, followed by the bishop, in his tall cylindrical headdress from which black veils fell over the back of his black robes, entered from a side room. The prayer service began. Incense from a swinging thurible billowed about the mounded flowers. The prayers began in Slavonic, now intoned, now spoken. Madame crossed herself each time the bishop did according to the liturgy. There was a group of male singers, all young, who sang the responses in magnificent tone and simplicity, with the bass voices predominating. It was a long liturgy, Byzantium audible and visible. At one moment Madame made as if to kneel but her strength for once failed her and she briefly stood instead. Craft was beside her. He was white as paper and impassive. At moments I could only half believe what was happening and why; at others I was pierced by the finality of it. At the end, when the small procession took its way out of the funeral chapel, the bishop paused to speak to Madame. When he left her, I went away myself.

The next morning at ten o'clock at the side altar of St. Theresa of Jesus at St. Patrick's Cathedral a Requiem Mass, at my request, was said for Stravinsky. Father Moher, the celebrant, agreed to say it in Latin. What had Stravinsky written so long ago? "I have always considered that a special language, and not that of current converse, was required for subjects touching on the sublime," a view consonant with my own for that, and any, sacred occasion. It was a private Mass to which I had invited those who had special relations and feelings concerning Stravinsky. Among those attending with me were John Crosby, Anne Fremantle, Robert Giroux, Charles Henderson, Thomas and Remi Messer, Charles Reilly, and Francis and Shirley (Hazzard) Steegmuller.

I remained in New York all week, until Stravinsky's public memorial service at three o'clock Friday afternoon. The actual funeral and burial would occur in Venice during the following week. On Friday, not knowing that a place had been reserved for me within the undertaker's chapel, I joined a queue of people, three abreast, which reached from Madison Avenue to Fifth Avenue. It advanced with infinite slowness. It was made up largely of young people—many of them very young, in the beards, beads, jeans, of their generation. They must truly have heard Stravinsky.

When the line turned the corner, and I reached the door, an usher was obliged to refuse admittance to me or any more other people: the rooms were crowded to the street. I went to St. Patrick's Cathedral and spent an hour in the name of the dead.

In Venice, on April 15, 1971, he was buried from the ancient church of SS Giovanni e Paolo. There Craft—summoning in his grief what strength I could not imagine—conducted Stravinsky's *Requiem Canticles*. At the same hour, in Middletown, I listened to Stravinsky's recording of the same work, and also his own performance of *The Symphony of Psalms*. *"Libera me,"* I echoed, and *"Alleluia,"* and *"Laudate Dominum."*

vi

In May, Madame and Craft returned from abroad, where, after the Venetian burial, they had sought rest first in North Africa and then in Paris. Late one afternoon shortly afterward I came to see them to ask if they would approve my plan to write a book about my lifelong response to Stravinsky. They agreed with interest and generosity. I did not stay long, but invited them to dine with me on the evening before I was to leave to go West for the summer.

It was the first time I had seen the new apartment. It was spacious and handsome. On a low bookshelf stood one of Snowdon's photographs of Stravinsky from the summer of 1970 at Evian—one of that last group ever taken of him. It shocked me. With his beret topping his costume, Stravinsky faced the camera with eyes made enormous by the further shrinkage of the flesh of his face. He held a fixed, powerful stare. The texture of his flesh was shrunken and withered like bark, or skin long submerged in water. Seeing me look at it, Madame described the session when the photographs were made.

She found Snowdon charming and considerate, but like all professionals he was thinking first of his purpose, and he had many requests and instructions for his sitter. Stravinsky sat quietly facing the camera, not answering anything Snowdon said to him. Madame told me:

"I had to stand by the camera and translate everything to my husband in Russian, and I made remarks, and gestures, to amuse him, and to bring *légèreté* into his expression. He would answer me in

Russian, and Snowdon took pictures during such moments. Finally my husband was bored, or tired, and that was all. Snowdon had dinner with us, and said to me, 'What a pity he does not know English.' "

Suddenly I heard ruffles and trills coming from a remote corridor of the New York apartment, notes which carried piercingly, rising to clear heights. It was the canary. Its tiny, detached rapture seemed to contain allusions too poignant for immediate remark.

vii

I was leaving for the West on June 10, to be gone all summer. Madame and Craft came to dine with me on the ninth in New York. Waiting for them, I was troubled to know what, or what not, to speak of concerning Stravinsky.

But I need not have worried. They arrived, sat down with me, and almost at once began to tell of events which we had not previously talked of. I felt an almost exhausting strength in their love for Stravinsky as they spoke of him, even coming to some of the most intimate and difficult details of his death and afterward.

They were still filled with the splendor and solemnity of the service in Venice, which moved from SS Giovanni e Paolo to the burial at the island cemetery of San Michele. Venice, said Craft, was chosen long ago for this event by Stravinsky himself, "because it was the Pope's parish"—Roncalli's. The world had come to pay its tribute —though, said Craft, no official notice or message of any kind was sent by the United States.

"The Mayor of Venice," he added with understated irony, "paid for the music at the funeral."

All the anonymous people of Venice hung over the bridges, filled the walks, crossed themselves as the cortège of gondolas went along the canals. The thought of John XXIII led Craft to relate how, on his last birthday, June 18, 1970, Stravinsky dressed and wore the full insignia of his Papal knighthood.

Madame said that, the day before the end, her husband kept trying to make the sign of the cross, over and over, but could only touch his brow, "Father," and his breast, "Son," but was too weak to reach his shoulders for "Holy" and "Ghost." Over and over. He looked at them, and what hurt them most was his awareness that he saw how they knew he was dying.

I remembered something Stravinsky said in his *Conversations:* "Ravel died gradually. That is the worst."

They described to me the astonishing strength of his handclasp as he reached for them. His fingers were curved into hooks to take his wife's and Craft's hands.

"He did not want to let go," said Madame.

Craft said to her now, "When he put your hand to his face he knew he was dying."

A death mask was taken. Craft said it was done without including the ears, as Beethoven's was—"That instrument of all great composers. Still, there is something noble about the mask, though the mouth is distorted."

Passing Stravinsky's room in the apartment after the return from Venice, Craft for many days could not enter it, as the death mask was there. Finally, "It had to be done," he said, and he went in to confront it.

"Have you seen it?" I asked Madame.

"No."

Craft said, "You must—you will find something true even so."

Later that evening, during our dinner after a shift of talk, and a little pause, Madame said to me,

"There is something I think about. I want to ask you. —What is the difference between belief and faith?"

It was a question large enough to take up the working hours of someone like Thomas Aquinas and it stirred me for the suggestion it made of the direction her thought was taking in that time in her life. But I must reply, and I said,

"I will take a risk in answering. I will say that belief is engendered by an intellectual faculty, while faith comes from a higher faculty—something of the whole being beyond intellectual formulation. Is this nonsense?"

Craft said, "That is a profound statement."

I thought, whatever the merit of the distinction I posed, that Madame seemed to take comfort from it.

I left the following day for the West. We exchanged a few letters during the summer. They had again gone abroad. Craft wrote to me on July 27 from the Hôtel du Palais in Biarritz, which Miranda, visiting them there later, characterized as "truly the original Steinberg drawing of the Hôtel Splendide." He was kind enough to thank me for "helping to keep Madame's spirits up. I'm afraid," he wrote, "they fell rather far in Venice, which is why we are here. *Everything* reminded her, and she began to go out to the grave all alone, without telling me, and it is quite a walk as well as a long ride on the *vaporetto*. She seemed quite calm in Rome after seeing the RAI film of the funeral—which I could not take, and simply left." They had gone to Rome to see Zorina in a performance of *Perséphone* at the Santa Cecilia with Prêtre conducting, and also to consult Giacomo Manzù about making the design and cutting it for Stravinsky's gravestone. "Then," Craft continued, "two hours later, with Manzù *chez lui*, she wanted to show her appreciation and kissed him, whereupon Manzù started to cry and told her that Stravinsky was the greatest inspiration in his life, and that he must have the gold cross of a great king. (Incidentally, the Vatican is giving the white marble.) At this point, Madame startled me by saying, 'But you know, I keep expecting him to come back.' Another indication of the terrible loneliness she feels came on the road here. Suddenly, in a restaurant, south of Aix, she began to sob, but never said a word."

viii

I think often of Stravinsky's last earthly delight—the bird Madame had waiting for him on his final return home, the bird whose song had so startled me on my first visit to that home. For him, she said, it sang and sang and gave him much joy. His own words, given in 1939, come to mind from the chapter under the heading "The Phenomenon of Music," in the *Poetics*. He spoke of "the most banal example . . . including the song of a bird. All this pleases us, diverts us, delights us. We may even say, 'What lovely music!' But all such are of course merely promises of music; it takes a human being to keep them . . ."

ix

The last scene of *Le Rossignol* might speak for anyone coming to the end of Stravinsky's life, though not of his music:

Death stands in the Emperor's bedchamber . . . Torn by his aching conscience, the dying ruler calls in vain for his musicians to make him forget. But the nightingale returns and so charms Death with its song that he agrees to allow the Emperor his life. The Emperor revives and offers his savior a place at court, but the bird refuses and returns to its woodland haunts with the promise that it will sing each evening. Now the courtiers enter, prepared to find the Emperor dead. They are astounded when he sits up in bed and bids them "Good morning!"

The nightingale, death, and the Emperor bring before us music in nature, and the mortal change of all things, and man's insistence on immortality—themes which belong within Stravinsky's vision, even as the magician's wit of the Emperor's last words. Every artist is committed in his own degree to that which never dies.